Global Feminist Ethics

feminist constructions

Series Editors: Hilde Lindemann, Sara Ruddick, and Margaret Urban Walker

Feminist Constructions publishes books that send feminist ethics in promising new directions. Continuing the work of feminist ethics critique, it emphasizes construction, aiming to build a positive body of theory that extends feminist moral understandings.

Global Feminist Ethics

Edited by
Rebecca Whisnant and
Peggy DesAutels

ROWMAN & LITTLEFIELD PUBLISHERS, INC.
Lanham Boulder New York Toronto Plymouth, UK

Rowman & Littlefield Publishers, Inc.

Published in the United States of America
by Rowman & Littlefield Publishers, Inc.
A wholly owned subsidary of The Rowman & Littlefield Publishing Group, Inc.
4501 Forbes Boulevard, Suite 200, Lanham, Maryland 20706
http://www.rowmanlittlefield.com

Estover Road, Plymouth PL6 7PY, United Kingdom

British Library Cataloguing in Publication Information Available

Library of Congress Cataloging-in-Publication Data

Global feminist ethics / edited by Rebecca Whisnant and Peggy DesAutels.
   p.   cm.—(Feminist constructions)
   Includes bibliographical references and index.
   1. Feminist ethics.   I. Whisnant, Rebecca.   II. DesAutels, Peggy.
BJ1395.G56   2008
170.82—dc22   2007034541

ISBN: 978-0-7425-5910-3 (cloth : alk. paper)
ISBN: 978-0-7425-5911-0 (pbk. : alk. paper)

♾ ™The paper used in this publication meets the minimum requirements of
American National Standard for Information Sciences—Permanence of Paper for
Printed Library Materials, ANSI/NISO Z39.48-1992.

Contents

Part 3: Persons and States

Part 4: Political and Religious Conflict

Acknowledgments

We are grateful to Hilde Lindemann, Sara Ruddick, and Margaret Urban Walker for encouraging and enabling the publication of volumes affiliated with the Association of Feminist Ethics and Social Theory (FEAST) and for including this particular volume in their Feminist Constructions Series at Rowman & Littlefield. We also thank the contributors to this volume for their insightful and thought-provoking essays that shed light on the daunting issues facing women and their communities around the world.

Introduction

Peggy DesAutels

> Now it appears, that in the original frame of our mind, our strongest
> attention is confin'd to ourselves; our next is extended to our relations
> and acquaintance; and 'tis only the weakest which reaches to strangers
> and indifferent persons.
>
> —David Hume, *A Treatise of Human Nature*, 3.2.2.8.

Much of the suffering and many of the injustices in the world are tied to
gender inequality. But it's difficult for those of us who live in developed
Western nations to determine how best to respond morally to those who
live so far away in cultures quite different from our own. Often we feel
under-informed, overwhelmed and immobilized, and we thus resort to
focusing our moral efforts on those who live closer to home. How can we
better respond to worldwide needs and inequities?

Certainly, a first step is to better inform ourselves about current injustices
worldwide, and about the understandings, structures, and practices contributing to these injustices. After becoming better informed, we can contribute
to organizations, vote for politicians, devote our efforts to causes, and even
buy from corporations that we think will best help us meet our global
moral responsibilities. If we are academically inclined, we can advance feminist ethical and social theory in ways that focus on global issues and solutions. But even feminist theorizing about global issues can be daunting.
Can Western feminists theorize approaches to global suffering and injustice
without falling prey to imperialist and essentialist ways of thinking, and
without viewing women in the developing world as passive victims in need
of saving?

Alison Jaggar has wisely warned Western feminists against naively attempting to "save" impoverished and oppressed women in other countries from their own cultural practices. She reminds us that "poor women in poor countries certainly are oppressed by local men whose power is rooted in local cultures, but they are also oppressed by global forces, including the forces of so-called development, which have reshaped local gender and class relations in varying and contradictory ways, simultaneously undermining and reinforcing them" (Jaggar 2005b, 67). She also points out, following Uma Narayan, that when we assume that the "West is best for women," we also often assume falsely that the West is somehow exempt from "cultural" explanations of its own characteristic practices that harm and victimize women and girls.

Jaggar suggests some directions for intercultural dialogues about justice for poor women in poor countries and asks us to "think more carefully about who these women are and from what or whom they need saving" (Jaggar 2005b, 71). We should raise questions about the global basic structure and about Western government policies that contribute to injustices against women. We should re-examine conceptions of sovereignty that are almost meaningless to poor countries. We should think about problems related to militarism. And we should discuss ways to compensate for past and continuing wrongs through remedial justice and reparation.

Many of the contributors to this volume pursue at least some of Jaggar's suggested themes. They certainly share with Jaggar a concern for the daunting issues facing the globe and approach these issues from a feminist perspective—that is, a perspective that values and promotes the well-being and fair treatment of women while questioning some of the most fundamental assumptions of patriarchal cultures. This perspective recognizes the ubiquity and perniciousness of patriarchy in its multitudinous forms throughout the world and attempts to identify and address at least some of its causes and effects. Just as we need to bring feminist perspectives to global issues, we need to bring global perspectives to feminist issues. Until we do, we may fail to identify very real harms being perpetrated and the roles of social and political systems and practices in contributing to these harms.

This volume contains four sections, the first of which examines some of the special moral concerns that arise from assigning distinct activities and responsibilities to women and men respectively. It is difficult to argue against the view that women and not men are the birth-givers. But it is also true that death rates tied to pregnancy and birth-giving are unacceptably high in developing countries. Are women better off giving birth in hospitals with attending physicians (often male) or in homes with attending midwives (usually female)? Which approach should be "exported" to the developing world? In the first chapter, "Exporting Childbirth," James L. Nelson questions the privileging of technological means over social means for making birth safer, and examines two distinct practices found in the Western developed world: demedicalized, home-based births with attending midwives in The Netherlands versus medicalized, hospital-based births with attending physicians in the United States. He argues that pervasive social expectations regarding women and childbirth result in forms of obstetrical practice that fail to accommodate much that many women regard as key to their experience of birth.

Childcare and domestic chores are other activities and responsibilities primarily assigned to women in Western and non-Western cultures alike. Women are expected to provide not only the unpaid labor involved in raising their own children and maintaining their own dwellings, but also, in many cases, the low-paid labor for raising the children and maintaining the homes of others. How can women working as paid domestic laborers best be protected from degradation and exploitation? Sabrina Hom, in her chapter on the morality and politics of paid housework, argues that because domestic labor can no longer be meaningfully distinguished from other forms of labor, the best way to protect paid domestic laborers is to encourage social networking and political organization. The particular political strategies used by Chicana housekeepers in the United States are offered as a possible model for other domestic laborers to follow.

In the following chapter focusing on gender identity and the ethics of care in globalized society, Virginia Held expresses optimism that progress is indeed being made toward decreasing gender inequities throughout the world, particularly those associated with sharp differentiations between "women's work" and "men's work." She argues that the ethics of care is especially well suited to guiding this progress and to resisting backlash responses against it.

Part two of this volume addresses how best to respond to certain universal human needs, such as those for food and other basic necessities. Marilyn Fischer's chapter, "Caring Globally: Jane Addams, World War One, and International Hunger," describes Addams' mobilization of American women to enter into "relations of caring" with the hungry in Europe during World War One. According to Fischer, Addams' pragmatic approach to international ethics parallels that of such contemporary care theorists as Virginia Held and Joan Tronto and can meaningfully inform contemporary efforts to extend care into the international arena. Of special relevance to global needs today are Addams' strategies for caring for those far distant, and for avoiding maternalism/paternalism and imperialism in one's caring efforts.

In "Food Fights: A Feminist Perspective," Victoria Davion points out that throughout the world, many more women than men are responsible for food production, food shopping, and food preparation. When there are food shortages, however, women and girls often eat last if at all. Thus

women have a special interest in food availability and safety. Offering a
feminist perspective on the scientific and ethical issues surrounding genetically modified food, Davion argues that fears over the safety of such foods
are justified at both local and global levels. After examining some of the
arguments used to encourage people to trust genetically modified food
"choices," she argues that such arguments assume a "model of autonomous
neoliberalism that is highly problematic from a feminist perspective."

Global poverty is certainly one of the most significant moral issues we
face. It is also morally worrisome that many more women than men appear
to be poor. But is it actually the case that women are disproportionately
poor relative to men? And if so, what is the proportion? And to what extent
are they poorer? In order to answer these important questions, Peter Higgins, Audra King, and April Shaw maintain that we first must answer the
more basic question, "What is Poverty?" They claim that many common
understandings of poverty are inadequate because the empirical data built
on those understandings fail to accurately represent who is poor, and who
is getting poorer. Rather than arguing for a conception of poverty as falling
below some standardized income level, they argue for a conception of poverty as the deprivation of certain human capabilities. On their view, a person is poor if, for any reason, she is unable to do certain things or achieve
certain ends. A person's social position relative to social relations of power
(including but not limited to those of gender) influences how effectively
she can access and use resources and thus meet her basic needs.

The third section of the book focuses on persons and states. All feminists
will easily agree that women's rights as human beings should be granted
and protected. But what conception of human rights best promotes gender
equity and combats women's oppression? Alyssa R. Bernstein examines two
influential theories of human rights: the approach taken by John Rawls in
The Law of Peoples (1999) and the capabilities approach taken by Martha
Nussbaum in *Frontiers of Justice* (2006). She argues that both of these theories are valuable and that they are more compatible with each other than
they first appear to be. As a result, both can and should be used to combat
oppression and to respect and secure women's rights.

In the next chapter, Serena Parekh draws on Hannah Arendt's theories
about statelessness and rightlessness to help explain why human rights as
traditionally construed fail to treat gender-specific harms to women as
human rights violations. She argues that, like stateless people, women are
perceived and treated according to a biological given and, consequently, are
not viewed as fully human and as able to make legitimate claims to human
rights.

Rebecca Whisnant draws on a tradition of radical feminist thinking about
women's bodily (especially sexual) sovereignty in an effort to articulate a
liberatory conception of the importance and the limits of national sover-

eignty. Using illustrations from both contemporary pornography and contemporary international relations, she argues that although the sovereignty of both bodies and nations remain vital tools for challenging patriarchy and imperialism, the sovereignty claims of nations should be regarded as having a temporary and provisional status.

The final section of the book offers feminist perspectives on how best to respond to political and religious conflict. Joan Tronto focuses on "peacekeeping," which is generally taken to involve military humanitarian interventions, but which she thinks should be more broadly and comprehensively construed. Pointing out that the idea of a "right to intervene" is increasingly being supplanted by that of a "responsibility to protect," she contends that the latter concept—especially when elaborated and informed by a feminist ethic of care—can enable more humane and effective responses to the needs of people in war-torn nations.

Bat-Ami Bar On examines the role of terror in the ethical and epistemological formation of identity. Intrigued by Hegel's suggestion of a connection between terror, freedom, and truth, she nonetheless finds both his version of this connection and those of later authors such as Fanon and Willett to be lacking in important ways. Taking care to avoid both male-identification and excessive individualism in her own thinking, she concludes that an important avenue to freedom and truth is found not necessarily in terror or violence per se, but in various manifestations of existential and embodied courage.

In the book's final chapter, Lynne S. Arnault analyzes the emotion of disgust, and the extraordinary success of the New Christian Right in using moralized disgust to promote its political agenda. That success may tempt feminists and progressives also to employ moralized disgust in the service of our global political aims. In particular, she addresses whether it would be an appropriate moral response to either the types of abuses and cruelties perpetrated at Abu Ghraib prison or the practices of genital cutting found within certain non-Western cultures. Arnault concludes, however, that because moralized disgust is inexorably linked to desires for purity, domination, and univocality, the mobilization of disgust-reactions is unsuitable for advancing liberatory causes and resisting oppression.

These authors' commitments to the well-being of women and their communities run deep and are informed by a rich variety of feminist philosophical perspectives. Global in their scope and diverse in their themes, the essays in this volume will both energize readers to address the problems and issues discussed, and arm them with some important theoretical resources for doing so.

1

WOMEN'S ACTIVITIES, RESPONSIBILITIES, AND IDENTITIES

1

Exporting Childbirth

James L. Nelson

More than half a million women die giving birth throughout the world every year. What makes a fact otherwise deeply poignant ascend to the level of tragedy is that the vast majority of these deaths result from remediable defects in social orders, rather than of failings in bodies that are beyond the state of medical art—more like deaths in a war zone, then, than deaths in an ICU.

This is shown clearly by the uneven distribution of maternal mortality throughout the world. In Eastern Africa, for example, the lifetime risk of maternal death is 500 times greater than that faced by women in some industrialized countries; 1 out of 11 women there die of pregnancy-related causes. Likewise, the vast majority of the world's four million annual neo-natal deaths occur in developing countries, as do the yearly 4 million deaths of fetuses that are beyond 22 weeks of gestational age (Bale et al., 2004).

These data are chilling, and it's natural enough that the response they prompt focuses on ways and means of enhancing the safety of birthgiving women and their children. A panel of experts brought together by the National Academy of Sciences concluded that, given the obduracy of the social, cultural, and economic context that contributes so heavily to the poverty and lack of control over their reproductive lives that especially endanger mothers and infants, the most important change was to provide every woman with the services of a "skilled professional birth attendant" proficient in basic techniques to provide a "clean and safe delivery" and able to recognize when referral to medical forms of obstetrical care is required. Second on the wish list was the availability of centers of just that kind, where women facing more challenging deliveries could be adequately supported (Bale et al., 2004).

From a feminist perspective, it may seem odd to think that the development of a medical infrastructure for birthgiving would be any less likely to collide directly with the "obduracy" of entrenched social patterns and norms in developing countries than would reforms more directly focused on alleviating women's poverty and their reproductive heteronomy (Nelson and Nelson, 1996). These countries allocate minuscule per capita amounts for health care needs, and, in many places, what government funded care had been available was severely undercut in recent decades, due in no small part to the demands of such institutions as the World Bank and the International Monetary Fund.[1] Providing professional birth attendance, backed up by obstetrical resources for difficult deliveries, may be just as daunting as, say, enhancing female literacy rates—a strong predictor of family size and birth spacing, both of which in turn correlate strongly with positive birth outcomes. Providing sufficient numbers of skilled staff, given the voraciousness of developed countries' appetites for importing workers with medical and nursing training, may be no easier than changing the legal and social climate that leads to 70,000 deaths a year from botched abortions. And so on.

Still, even if the Academy is overly insouciant about the practicability of making further professional resources available to women living in developing countries, as contrasted to increasing their authority over the conditions of their own lives, there may be some lessons to be extracted from its report for women giving birth in the developed world. It's particularly noteworthy that the experts draw no distinctions among physicians, nurses, and midwives in their recommendations. Further, they acknowledge that shifting birth to hospitals need not be regarded as a crucial component of improving obstetrical outcomes. Distinguishing between "model 2" births (home delivery with skilled attendants) and "model 3" births (delivery in a clinic or hospital with professional attendance and comprehensive essential care), they find that experience in developing countries suggests that either model "is clinically and cost-effective for uncomplicated deliveries" (Bale et al., p. 10).

The NAS panel's accommodating attitude about the level of training of the birth attendant and the site of birth is quite conspicuous, at least when contrasted with the tenor of discussions, the trend of policy, and the tenacity of practice in developed countries, where any deviation from a highly medicalized, hospital-based strategy for delivery is highly controversial. Perhaps this is due to the thought that "good enough" is acceptable for pregnant women in developing countries, who face circumstances so profoundly more challenging than their counterparts in the Global North. There is, however, reason to believe that the panel's findings replicate experience in developed areas of the world that call into question the default assumptions about safety that women there confront as they consider how they wish to give birth.

If feminists may tend to be suspicious about privileging technical over social means for making birth safer, they may also be dubious about the ways in which discourse and practice focus almost exclusively on safety. The general aim of this essay is to highlight other elements of birthgiving that women may desire in addition to safety—e.g., conditions that may contribute to making their experiences of labor and delivery as congruent as possible with a fuller range of their own values. In particular, this essay is prompted by the curious endurance of two features of obstetrical practice occurring in different areas of our distracted globe. One is the against-the-odds resilience of midwife-accompanied, demedicalized, home-based birth in The Netherlands; the other is the dogged resistance to midwife-accompanied, home-based or otherwise demedicalized birth in the United States. In both these countries, giving birth is reasonably safe (although caveats concerning economic status need to be filed in the U.S.). Nonetheless, safety remains such an important concern that, even when risk increments are marginal, in both the U.S. and The Netherlands (albeit in different ways) it threatens to dominate every other value.

If the contrast between the situations facing women in The Netherlands and women in the U.S. contains a lesson for women in developing areas of the globe, it may be that the NAS panel is, as it turns out, not making any kind of *simple* mistake in singling out increased professional and medical resources as the likeliest way to ameliorate the situation in Eastern Africa and elsewhere. Even where available resources are enormously greater, socially entrenched patterns of expectations regarding women and childbirth result in forms of obstetrical practice that fail to accommodate much that many women regard as key to their experience of birth, and, as I hope to show in what follows, tightly regulate even what possibilities many women are able to imagine in this context. If it could be determined how to disrupt such patterns and regulations effectively, the developed world might have something of real value to export.

BIRTH IN THE DEVELOPED WORLD: VARIATION AND THEME

When a Dutch woman becomes pregnant, she faces a situation that is effectively unparalleled anywhere else in the world. She may choose to be accompanied through gestation and delivery by either her *huisart* (primary care doctor) or a *vroedvrow* (midwife); barring unusual circumstances, she is unlikely to be referred to an obstetric specialist (*gynecoloog*). The woman may then elect to give birth at home, or during a short hospital stay (*polikli-niek*); the choice of either location, with either type of first-line care provider, will be seen as fully responsible and financial considerations will not bar her from these choices.

Pregnant women in the U.S., on the other hand, typically find themselves under the care of a physician, and quite often an OB/GYN specialist at that—if, of course, they have decent health care insurance. If American women want a midwife to attend their birth—and still more, if they want to have their babies at home rather than in the hospital—they will act against medical advice and social norms, and will sometimes find that there are even more substantial obstacles to be overcome as well.

This sketch of childbearing practices might suggest a kind of logical exclusion, as though the range of options to which the Dutch tenaciously cling, and the stubborn hospital-OB/GYN defaults of American birthgiving exhaust the possible, or at least practicable options for contemporary birth in the developed world; one could easily anticipate that their respective assessments will be just as bivalent ("Dutch resilience good, American resistance bad."). Descriptively, such an impression should be easy to shed: for example, while the prevalence of home birth is distinctive to The Netherlands, midwives are very much more involved in institution-based births in, say, Scandanavian countries, than they are in the U.S. What might take a bit more showing is that a straightforward endorsement of Dutch practice is also too simple. I will take that task on, arguing for alertness to the ways in which *both* models constrain the agency of pregnant women.

As it turns out, however, the normative criticism will pivot on the observation that the assumed mutual exclusion of the models actually turns out to be a difficult thought to get free of; the alternatives for women need to be more richly and expansively imagined. Social scientists—including those whose work I will draw on extensively here—tend not to be altogether sanguine about the effectiveness of individual choice, and its consort, imagination, and they point to constraints on systematic change that may seem deflating for feminists. Part of my task will be to suggest that within social scientific analysis of both global and local phenomena itself can be found the stimulus to imagine new and improved possibilities, as well as the rough contours of practical strategies for achieving institutional change.

THE RATIONAL IS THE DOMESTIC: DUTCH BIRTHGIVING

The resilience of Dutch home birth is curious because of the strength and character of the currents it bucks: The Netherlands stands quite alone among all the other nations of the European Union, North America, and the developed states of the world generally, in providing women a readily available, socially supported choice about whether they will deliver at home or in the hospital. In this, it resists both the contrary consensus of international practice and the authority of international medical judgment.

By far the most thorough and accessible account of the Dutch situation for Anglophone audiences (and quite possibly the best *san phrase*) is Raymond De Vries's *A Pleasing Birth* (2004). He reports that about half of Dutch pregnant women currently elect to be accompanied by midwives rather than physicians during gestation, and that about 30 percent of births in The Netherlands take place at home (where midwives provide assistance about two-thirds of the time). The European country with the next highest percentage of home births is the U.K., at about 2 percent; in the U.S., less than one percent of deliveries occurs at home.

To convey just how unusual all this is, however, De Vries takes readers beyond the numbers. As a start, he emphasizes how strikingly standardized medical care is in its general outlines throughout the developed world. While there are some interesting country-to-country variations, advanced specialty care in particular is virtually indistinguishable (language apart) from New York to Amsterdam to Tokyo. As a social scientist, De Vries is particularly struck by The Netherlands' violation of a well corroborated sociological generalization: that strong professions dictate to weaker professions. (Consider the very powerful role doctors have had in influencing how nurses do their jobs, for example.) The distinctively Dutch pattern of childbirth, then, resists both powerful homogenizing forces that seem resident in medical care itself, as well as otherwise well-confirmed generalizations that sociologists rely on to illuminate other inter-professional relationships (De Vries 2004, 8ff).

IF IT'S MORE EXPENSIVE, IT MUST BE BETTER: BORN IN THE U.S.A.

The continuing hostility of American obstetrics to home birth is something of a curiosity as well. U.S. practice seems unmoved by two redoubtable forces, often thought antagonistic, but in the present instance, pulling in harness. One force is quality: in the U.S., as elsewhere, safety and effectiveness are celebrated: reliable, low-mortality, low-morbidity interventions are just what's wanted. The other force is efficiency: the costs of contemporary medicine, particularly in the U.S., press health care institutions to pare expenses to the bone, or as close to it as they can get, and it seems flatly irrational—to give the status quo the benefit of every doubt—to expend large amounts of money for vanishingly small gains.

Yet obstetrical practice in the U.S. seems remarkably insensitive to both the quality and the cost of care, at least as these considerations bear on where women have babies, and who attends them. While these data are not altogether unchallenged, the information available strongly supports the view that midwife-accompanied, home-based birth is as safe for women and infants as physician-managed, hospital-based birth, *if not safer*. It is certainly substantially cheaper.[2] Nor is it likely that home birth is rare simply because the vast majority of American women happen to have free and informed preferences for the institutional over the domestic when it comes to having their babies. Home birth simply isn't on the standard range of options with which women in the U.S. are presented, and when the topic is broached, the response tends to be discouraging, if the American College of Gynecologists and Obstetricians's (ACOG) active opposition is indicative.[3]

Further, there are also good grounds to believe that those relatively few American women who, without necessarily aspiring to give birth at home, want to ramp down the involvement of medicine in their deliveries, have often been frustrated in their efforts to do so. When such women try to tailor their birthgiving to suit their own values—educating themselves about relative risk data, seeking out (apparently) sympathetic medical providers, and making many other careful arrangements to achieve a "natural" (i.e., demedicalized) birth—something about obstetrical care in the U.S. tends to subvert their chances of getting what they want.

Elizabeth Bogdan-Lovis has provided a striking account of this phenomenon from an anthropological perspective (Bogdan-Lovis 1996–97 and 1995; see also the discussion of her results in Nelson 2001). Her work details the experiences of several American women, all highly committed to the idea that "birth works," very keen to experience birth free of needless or harmful medical interventions, and well supported by friends, partners and professionals. Repeatedly, she found not only that these women's carefully laid plans were overturned, but that they also came away from the experience believing that what had gone "wrong" was something about the particularities of their own labor and delivery. They took themselves to have autonomously authorized all the departures from their plans because it had turned out to be reasonable at the time to do so, each concluding that they were the rare exception that proves the "birth works" rule (Bogdan-Lovis 1995).

On Bogdan-Lovis's analysis, what they had actually encountered were not unanticipated, late-arriving medical problems in how their deliveries progressed, but rather default practices, values, and attitudes too deeply engrained into the organizational structures in which they gave birth to be unseated by their own autonomous agency, even when supported by such tools of liberal feminism as consciousness-raising, "consumer education," a rise in the rate of female physicians involved in births, interpersonal agreements and sympathy, personal choice, and rational persuasion. For example, a physician might step in on the grounds that labor was progressing "too slowly," without anyone being aware that this apparently authoritative judgment reflected not good evidence but merely sedimented obstetrical convention (Bogdan-Lovis, 1996–97, 61 and *passim*).

THE GLOBAL AND THE LOCAL

For different reasons, then, it's odd that Dutch home birth endures despite being so exceptional vis-à-vis the rest of the developed world and otherwise so sociologically anomalous, and that U.S. medicalized birth is so resistant to the mutually reinforcing values of quality care and cost containment, to say nothing of the reflective, well-informed, and vigorously pursued choices of some of its constituents. But another dimension of what's so strange about these two situations becomes clearer by noting a feature they have in common.

De Vries makes a very plausible case that practice patterns in The Netherlands can be attributed to the Dutch "national culture." In a careful deployment of this idea, he relates historical and current patterns of self-understanding, popular attitudes, and civic practices that are largely specific to The Netherlands to the active support available for this odd way of giving birth. American obstetrics might best be accounted for by a similar invocation of "culture" (that accommodating concept) particularly if we understand it to include behavior-shaping forces that go beyond the symbolic, the discursive, and the explicitly reasoned, to the material and the structural. Bogdan-Lovis certainly relies on notions like this to account in particular for the resistance to specific requests for demedicalized birth (as well as for the failure of ethical or ideological critique alone reliably to change the situation). It's reasonable to believe, then, that explanation of U.S. practice hinges on peculiarities of "American medical culture," in which economic incentives and concerns about legal liability, as well as daily habits and attitudes about patients, play important roles in shaping how doctors practice in this particularly entrepreneurial and litigious society.

In both the U.S. and The Netherlands, there are customary ways of acting and evaluating, standing dispositions, default assumptions, background practices, and ranges of options that have come to strike people as natural and right (as well as those that seem beyond the pale), all of which can be localized to their specific contexts, and which provide part of the explanation for the persistence of accepted practice. It's worth underscoring that, at least from the perspective of social scientific analysis, these practices are not well understood as functions of individual choices. They neither exist because of, nor can they be effectively challenged or changed by, individual women's reproductive decisions; rather, they create the context in which options are presented and outcomes occur. De Vries approvingly quotes Peter Berger to the effect that *we desire the very things that society limits us to* (De Vries 2004, 19). Bogdan-Lovis, writing that our choices bear "the mark of multiple subjective and—most often—invisible influences including socialization, technology, power and authority" (1996–97, 68), connects liberal feminism's failure to alter in any substantial way the technocratic character of birth in the U.S. to its mistaken assumption that "if one could only substitute female control for male control and educated, consumer-dictated choices for blind trust, then available health care choices would be woman-centered and thus better: better for women exerting their individual and educated will in choosing sympathetic birth attendants while simultaneously accepting only minimum technological, surgical, and pharmacological intervention to effect a desired outcome" (1996–97, 75).

It isn't necessary, however, to believe in the sovereign effectiveness of individual choice to see in the obduracy of those local cultures a final curiosity shared by these markedly different patterns of practice. By (virtually) all accounts, we live in a time of *accelerated globalization.* What is often taken to be distinctive and even partly definitional of globalization's contemporary phase is the permeability of local mores and practices, the world's movement toward a homogenized culture (the "McDonaldization" of the everywhere), or, perhaps more plausibly, toward a kind of hybridization of cultures—a "global mélange," as Jan Nederveen Pieterse has called it (Pieterse 2004)—in which social relations, forms of cultural expression, modes of economic intercourse, and resources for (and results of) self-understanding, all tend to mingle.[4] Against the move toward mélange, how comes it that The Netherlands' local culture manages to retain sufficient integrity to support a highly distinctive form of practice in the face of an overwhelming international consensus that births belong in hospitals? Given America's sponge-like absorbency of attractive features from other world locations, how can we make sense of the resistance of American medical culture to obstetrical practices which could improve outcomes and slash costs—a resistance that actively subverts autonomous and canny women who energetically seek out just this kind of birthing experience? What's keeping the "tariff barriers" against a global trade in obstetrical practice so high here, and operating in both directions?

OBSTETRICS AS A CULTURED SCIENCE

One tempting possibility is that obstetrics is somehow particularly sensitive to local culture. This is the explanation that De Vries favors. Obstetrics, as he notes, differs in many ways from other medical specialties, but perhaps its signal distinguishing feature is that its "patients" are typically perfectly healthy.[5] The processes that, qua science, obstetrics investigates, and that, qua practice, it tries to facilitate, are normal physiological functions. De Vries sees this fundamental aspect of obstetrics as connected, by some not altogether clearly described mechanism, with a constellation of culturally mediated attitudes about, among other things, society, family, the future, and women, such that variations in those attitudes substantially alter what differently placed observers take obstetrics to be, what they tend to accept as good evidence for an obstetrical claim, what are entrenched as unassailable obstetrical givens, why they are so unassailable, and so forth.

Also involved in this constellation of cultural associations are the assumptions about the "natural" way of giving birth that tend to be held by women and other members of society. Some will regard having babies in hospitals as if it were as normal as breathing, finding reassurance in the presence of expensive machines that go "ping"; some will regard hospitals as harsh, alienating environments, no place to bring a child into the world. Accordingly, having babies at home will seem to some—say, to many women in the U.S., and certainly to ACOG—a risky, irresponsible, rather primitive thing to do, insofar as they think of it at all. Others—say, many women in The Netherlands, and the Dutch government—will see home as the best, most welcoming place to start or extend one's family. These attitudes will sometimes be pre-reflective and evidence-resistant, or at least have a depth and tenacity that cannot be attributed altogether to what, upon reflection, good data support.

It may be worth pushing a bit on the thought that it's the nonpathological character of most births that makes obstetrics particularly prone to capture by local culture. Why would that feature, striking as it is, make a health care practice more susceptible to the individuating influence of local social understandings and activities, and less disciplined by the generalizing force of scientifically informed international standards? Perhaps the connection is just that illness, disability, trauma, and death tend to focus the mind on a small range of values—on what actually works to avoid death, ease suffering, cure disease, and extend ability.[6] In obstetrics, precisely because things will usually go just fine anyway, there is more room for the nonpragmatic. Different values, differently active in different local cultures, will influence both practice and the understanding of practice, and thus help account for both "Dutch exceptionalism" and "American irrationality," as well as for certain distinctive features of obstetrical science that De Vries identifies, such as the tendency to take professional disagreements personally, and the difficulty of publishing iconoclastic results in mainstream journals (cf. De Vries 2004, ch. 6).

This is not to say that the persistence of home-based birth in The Netherlands is simply a feature of a set of cultural attitudes that converge automatically on a broad and deep consensus that having babies at home is perfectly natural and reasonable. It is also a function, at least in part, of explicit policy measures, including a lengthy history of making economic advantages available to midwives that are denied to the other class of primary obstetrical service providers, the *huisarten*.[7] Such policies are themselves, of course, cultural phenomena, but the fact that intentionally engineered incentives have played a role in the persistence of home birth suggests (although it does not, of course, demonstrate) that the practice's viability would not be ensured by simple reliance on women's choosing home birth spontaneously—or even as "spontaneously" as might be possible given a culture that generally supports this option.

Further, the appeal to a supposed special cultural malleability of obstetrics might overstate both the distinctiveness of obstetrics and the routine character of birthgiving. Primary care in general spends a great deal of its time and effort on attending to the well, the worried well, and those whose problems would get better if left to themselves. It's worth noting too that while pregnancy is not an illness, and giving birth is a natural thing to do, as natural things go, it is fairly fraught. One wonders whether many people would be quite so casual about air travel if the mortality rate for flying approximated that of having a baby. Another avenue for explaining the distinctive features of these obstetrical practices is by seeing them as local variations on a widely shared and socially profound theme. On grounds familiar to feminist analysis, it would seem reasonable to suspect that explanations for particular obstetrical practices will have a good deal to do with the complex, conflicting, and often destructive attitudes concerning women in general and pregnancy in particular prevalent across cultures and times.

REGULATING WOMEN AS A GLOBAL PROJECT

If Andrew Marvel had written, "The womb's a fine and private place," he would have been mistaken. Fine it may well be, but, as many observers have noted, it is hardly private. Social commonplaces ranging from the tendency of passing strangers to touch pregnant women's bellies, to signs in bars warning women against drinking if they might be pregnant, to the enormous popularity of such draconian conduct books as *What to Expect When You're Expecting*, all testify to a socially prevalent and historically tenacious sense that reproduction is public business and that how women conduct their pregnancy is a matter appropriate for public scrutiny and regulation via public norms. Pregnant women are, the thought seems to go, unruly individuals doing work of social importance, and they need lots of direction from social authorities if they are going to do it right.[8] The precise form that direction takes may well reflect features of local culture. Yet the master theme of control of women is, if not precisely globalized in the sense of being an idea that has moved from a local origin to form part of a general mélange, globally ubiquitous due to mechanisms of patriarchy that may be even more fundamental than migration.

These two heuristic perspectives—obstetrics as a uniquely culture-sensitive science, and control of women as a transcultural force—are not logically exclusive, but they do present the persistence of obstetrics's parochial flavor in different ways, and as such they spark different morals. If we take the extreme cultural sensitivity of obstetrics to be doing the basic explanatory work here, then there seems nothing in the way of extracting the following kind of lesson: *while women generally are limited in the settings and circumstances of birthgiving they can elect or perhaps even readily envisage, some women (i.e., those living in The Netherlands) enjoy an unusually wide and valuable set of choices about childbearing as a result of fairly specific features of their nation's history, cultural practices, and government policies.* Further, according to this view, the value of these options isn't simply quantitative, not simply a matter of more options concerning with whom and where to give birth. The choices that many women make are arguably valuable in more substantive ways: for example, home birth, and demedicalized, midwife-accompanied birth in general, lead to a markedly lower incidence of Cesarean sections. (The Dutch rate is roughly half of that in the U.S.)[9] Moreover, exercising control over the setting of birth may enrich many women's sense of being at the center of their experience, of *performing* rather than undergoing birth, and that too may be very important to many birthgivers.

On this story, the implications for feminist bioethics and politics seem tolerably clear. Dutch obstetrical practice should look as attractive as, say, the Canadian universal coverage, single-payer health insurance system, and its importation should be advocated and otherwise worked for. De Vries, for example, seems to have this general attitude toward Dutch practice; while he is certainly aware that local ideas about women are important parts of what accounts for the particular character of Dutch obstetrics, he doesn't seem inclined to see those attitudes themselves as incorporating ideas about and practices concerning women that are neither local nor innocuous.[10]

This alternative explanation, which draws on the notion that different obstetrical practices reflect a broadly shared social interest in controlling how women conduct the reproductive parts of their lives, is grimmer: *women everywhere are confronted with a socially sanctioned, artificially limited set of choices about childbirth, whose scope reflects interests other than their own.* On this view, Dutch practice does not represent even a rough realization of a feminist paradise for parturition. It's better seen as a variation on a theme, more benign than U.S. practice no doubt, but still a reflection of cultural attitudes and practices that slight the importance of women, the respect-worthiness of their agency, and their unique contributions to the common weal.

LEAVING HOME

A stronger case for this less laudatory interpretation of the Dutch situation would draw on more than just the general misogynistic tenor of social insti-tutions. A more focused critique of birthing practices would fit this bill, and while it may be asking too much to demand that it explain just why local specifics have taken the form they have, it needs to be able to construe those practices plausibly as constraints.

The distinction between "medicalized" and "demedicalized" birth is an attractive place to start our imagination working: anything that's presented so starkly is at least prima facie suspicious. Women have plenty of reason to avoid medicalized birth: medical interventions can add danger, discom-fort, and depersonalization to their labor and delivery. Yet many women might have other interests as well: reducing labor pains, for example, and timing delivery to fit best into ongoing, complicated lives. Demedicalized or "natural" birth, including, perhaps paradigmatically, home birth, is vir-tually defined, at least in part, by women's willingness to forgo these inter-ests, and there are ideological pressures operating that try to undermine the notion that women could have any real or defensible stake in them.

Epidurals, for instance, are not going to be available outside the hospital in The Netherlands (or anywhere else, presumably). If you want to be sure to have that resource available to help with your labor if you think you might need it, you have effectively opted for an in-hospital birth.

The timing of childbirth is also of crucial importance to many women now, particularly given the scope of responsibilities that they so often undertake. These responsibilities sometimes prompt an interest in inducing labor, or possibly even in elective Cesarean operations. There's nothing innocent about these pressures, of course—in part, they reflect the stub-bornly male-oriented character of out-of-home work life, to which some women are now admitted, but on terms that often disallow, or at best are grudging about, accommodating women's difference. In part, they reflect the lack of social or familial support for domestic responsibilities that con-tinue to fall disproportionately upon women. But these pressures ought not to be dismissed as though a woman's interest in timing her delivery is frivo-lous, representing the desires of someone too immature or otherwise ill judging to realize what her primary motivation and goal as a birthgiver needs to be.

Recent reportage about the rise in cesarean section rates in the U.S.—a rise that takes the country continually further away from both national and W.H.O. norms for the optimal rate—has been attended by headshaking over what is called the "convenience factor." A recent National Library of Medicine web publication announcing that C-section incidence had reached record highs, expressed disapproval of women scheduling C-sections in order to fit the birthgiver's other demands, or even of women having elective induction of labor, which also increases the chances of delivery via C-section. (HealthDay 2006). Yet, in addition to the fact that no actual data about the incidence of elective cesareans were provided (nor any discussion of, for instance, many obstetricians' insurance-driven reluctance to participate in vaginal birth after cesarean delivery), the facile disapproval of women choosing to influence the timing of their deliveries reflects a dismissive attitude toward women as people.[11]

Like a woman's desire for labor with pain reduction technologies at hand, her desire for timed delivery guarantees a hospitalized, highly medicalized childbirth, at least under current conditions. But why assume that those conditions are immutable? Is it flatly impossible to reduce the number of C-sections that women *don't* want and that don't offer benefits to them and their babies, while allowing them to time their birthgiving if they want to, all in a setting that more fully accommodates what is distinctive and valuable about the experience of giving birth? Why *can't* midwife-accompanied birth, even if conducted in the home, include the possibility of advanced forms of pain control?[12] Why, for that matter, haven't science and medicine developed better forms of rendering birthpains more manageable for more women no matter where they deliver?[13] (Here, we may detect an instance of the effect of culture on other sciences.) Why can't delivery in hospital be made more "homey," safer, more open to familial involvement as desired, and a good deal less medically intrusive?

If timing deliveries and pain control are valid considerations for women making reproductive decisions, simply importing a Dutch style of birthing, even were that possible, won't accommodate them. No one, of course, enjoys unlimited options. But the significance of birth as a social phenomenon, its ineliminably sexed character, the need to repudiate a legacy of social control over women, and the specific disadvantages and dangers presented to women by standard birthing practices in *both* the U.S. and The Netherlands, all argue that a casual attitude about restrictions in this sphere is misplaced. On this reading of the matter, feminist practice would, presumably, aim to make a greater range of better choices more readily available to women *in The Netherlands,* as well as in the rest of the world.

There *may,* of course, be good reasons for thinking that the limitations in birthing women's choices are intractable—that birth is going to be either "medicated" or "meaningful," and the best that can be hoped is that women get to choose which. History, however, suggests otherwise—suggests in fact that not only the going options, but even the imagination necessary to construct notional alternatives, have been constrained by prevalent practices, social structures, and cultural attitudes. This point resonates with the skepticism about individual imagination that seems implicit in the De Vries and Bogdan-Lovis critiques of choice—we "choose" among options that given social practices present to us, a thought that carries with it the suggestion that we aren't particularly good at coming up with alternatives on our own.

If we have interest in making those alternatives more than simply notional, we confront another problem. De Vries insists that reform must be culturally informed (2004, 237–45). Effective systemic change means cultural change, and cultural change requires that a reformer's goals and methods draw on values and practices already circulating within the culture to be changed. Given the obduracy of American birthing practices, reform requires attention to complex and sometimes inconsistently expressed values concerning pain, the natural, technological rationality, and money, as well as attention to successful models elsewhere.

This seems to me quite unexceptionable as far as it goes—as a general idea, it indicates a plausible path toward effective change. Yet if we add to the list of culturally effective values that need to be accounted for, the conviction that women's reproductive actions are open to public monitoring and control, the situation takes on a different and more worrisome cast.

In sum, then, what critical analysis and action appear to face are two serious barriers: skepticism about critical imagination and choice, and skepticism about implementing reforms that can be justified dialectically, but that have at best a very vexed relationship to values and practices powerful in mainstream culture. But if the results of social scientific analysis caution us about the limits of individual choice and imagination, they also provide social resources that individuals can use for expanding those limits. For example, a resource for critical and constructive thought may be found in an application of Pieterse's "mélange" trope: *birthing practices should in principle be open to the same kind of hybridization as are other cultural formations and practices.*

I turn to the hybridization notion here purposefully. De Vries argues—plausibly, as I think—that study of the relationship between health policy and national culture indicates that reform must be sensitive to pertinent dimensions of how life is actually lived in the specific location that reform targets;[14] this point seems altogether consistent with Bogdan-Lovis's instance on attention to the power latent in institutional structures. While these observations need to be taken to heart, it's also important to cultivate a sense of the increasing permeability of the various membranes of history and practice that bound national culture. Hybridity, as a process and in effect, is becoming more and more what it has long been—a part of national cultures. This is, of course, not an altogether benign phenomenon. Insofar, however, as the interpenetration of cultures doesn't merely happen willy-nilly to people and their societies, but also offers new notional and material possibilities for critical imagination and progressive practice, it ought to be recruited to renew obstetrical imagination.

It is clear from De Vries's account that the rest of the world already exerts influence on Dutch practice. Although still immense by international standards, the percentage of women in The Netherlands who deliver babies at home is as low as it has ever been recorded, and there is no shortage of domestic critics who seem troubled by what they see as the embarrassing "backwardness" of Dutch obstetrics. These critics are concerned, among other things, to demonstrate that babies born in the hospital enjoy subtler advantages over their home-delivered counterparts than those that have been traditionally tracked in studies designed to compare the safety of the different birth venues. Such efforts repeatedly come to nothing—initially reported variations vanish when data or methods are more critically scrutinized (see De Vries 2004, chapter six *passim*). Yet some gynecologists continue to mount pressure in The Netherlands for repeated demonstrations of the safety of home birth, with the subtext clearly being an interest in somehow finding legitimization for the view that "birth is normal only in retrospect" (the going professional perspective internationally) and hence for marginalizing out-of-hospital deliveries. Important counterpressure comes from a government concerned that more hospital-based births means more health care expense with no improvement in health outcomes.

In the U.S., in contrast, what pressure there is to legitimate and encourage home birth is faint (although something approaching the reverse is the case in the U.K. and Canada, where there are government-sponsored, Dutch-inspired initiatives to make home birth more possible and more popular). Yet even in the U.S., there is a continuing chorus of criticism about birth's overmedicalization—for example, with respect to the routine use of advanced fetal monitoring techniques, whose only impact on birth seems to be to raise the rate of C-section deliveries. There is, for example, a nationally endorsed goal of reducing the cesarean rate to around 15 percent of deliveries by 2010.[15]

The question is how whatever movements may be going on in global birthing practices can be influenced by feminist reflection and action, and, in particular, how resistance to the processes of change as described and explained by social scientists can be taken up into feminist criticism and institution building.

One possibility is suggested by the insight that one ought not to expect a demedicalized experience when one goes into the house of medicine. Bogdan-Lovis has argued that if American women want "natural" births, they will need to seek them at home or in birthing clinics where their attendants should be midwives. Her advice coheres with the lessons bioethicists have drawn from data concerning the "other end" of life: if you want a demedicalized death, don't go to the hospital, get hospice care (Nelson 2001).

The hospice model indeed might stand as the feature of local culture upon which new possibilities for birth in the U.S. might come to seem attractive and feasible. While the majority of deaths in America still take place in hospitals, the National Center for Health Statistics (2004) reported that 105,000 Americans were receiving hospice care in 2000, almost all of whom were beneficiaries of a Medicare program that supports palliative care for people diagnosed with terminal illness; apart from the personal and familial benefits available from "nonmedicalized" deaths, there are also cost savings involved, making support of hospice excellent public policy and the current program a well-entrenched feature of contemporary end of life care in the U.S—despite its inconsistency with cultural values enshrining technology, optimism, and the authority of physicians. Analogous benefits and values might also be provided with respect to birth, including the notion that "nonmedicalized" does not necessarily imply that serious efforts at pain control are not possible.

Further, the economic savings caused by shifting birth progressively to nonmedical contexts, whether homes or birthing centers, might be transmitted to women in the form of a free or greatly subsidized birth experience. Alternately, some of the savings might be devoted to an importation of what does appear to be a pretty straight-up praiseworthy and distinctive feature of the Dutch culture of birth: the *krammverzorgenden*, or postpartum caregivers, who offer a range of important teaching and domestic services to all recent mothers for a period after birth.

A movement toward mélange, then, might occur *within* a national culture as well as between cultures, so that obstetric care might borrow from palliative care, and perhaps from other specialties as well. American medicine seems to have little trouble in hybridizing home spaces with medical technology in cases of chronic illness, disabilities, or even PVS (see Arras 1995). If anything in the ideology of "natural" childbirth is blocking such a range of possibilities for pregnant women, it may be past time to subject such features to critical examination, and consider whether women-centered, domestically located births could go on with some birth technologies present.

HYBRIDIZING CHILDBIRTH

As De Vries sees it, changes in health care policy and practice must emerge from a basis that makes sense in terms of the values and meanings resident in the local culture. If home birth is to become a real option for women outside The Netherlands—and if birthing in general is to incorporate a greater range of possibilities, reflecting the diversity among women's lives and understandings, for women everywhere—then attention will have to be paid to elements of local culture as well as to what the best normative arguments support. Part of that attention will need to be a developing practical knowledge of how to achieve systematic reform by taking advantage of characteristics in the system itself, and in the wider, but still local culture in which it is embedded.

For feminists, this insight extends both a promise and a challenge. It may be heartening to think that accelerated globalization might be to some extent shaped, and even guided, by features of the local—that it is not inevitable, say, that women in The Netherlands will come to lose the options they now enjoy simply because the rest of the world has such an enormous momentum operating in the contrary direction. It may at the same time be discouraging to wonder how a critical and imaginatively expansive sensibility can be incorporated into that process of resistance and shaping in a creditable way.

The wider world presents American women with possibilities of birthing their children that are decidedly superior to what is generally on offer here. What prevents their adoption is not simply—or simple—sexist venality. There are features of culture that make specific practices endure and flourish, not all of which are easily portable, and not all of which are even desirable. Import strategies will need to find analogs in American culture that will support the same, or functionally equivalent, practices.

But perhaps even more importantly, it needs to be kept firmly in mind that the superior options are not necessarily prepackaged, to be accepted or rejected *in toto*. Dutch practice should spur a re-imagination of what birthing might be like—in The Netherlands as well as in the U.S., in the developed world and beyond it—were cultural values, social practices and individual choices to take women and their interests more seriously.[16]

NOTES

1. On the impact of World Bank and IMF policies on socially supported health care in developing countries, see Callahan and Wasunna (2005).

2. See Johnson and Davis (2005), a study of 5418 home births in the U.S. and Canada, which reported an intrapartum and neonatal mortality rate of 1.7 per 1000—quite similar to rates reported in hospitals. The rates of medical intervention (e.g., epidurals, episiotomies, forceps deliveries, vacuum extraction) were markedly lower. The cesarean section rate was 3.7 percent. In a 1998 National Center for Health Statistics study reported by De Vries (2004, 14), it was found that midwives had significantly better results than physicians, e.g., a 19 percent lower infant mor-

tality rate and a 33 percent lower neonatal mortality rate. For data on costs, see Anderson and Anderson (1999). They found that the costs of an uncomplicated vaginal birth in a hospital are triple those in a home setting.

3. Johnson and Davis (2005) report that ACOG's opposition was expressed in *Frequently Asked Questions About Having a Baby in the 21st Century*, a web-based publication they accessed on 3 April 2005 (http://www.acog.org/from_home/publica tions/press_releases/nr12-12-01-4.cf m). As of October 16, 2006, that document was no longer posted on the ACOG website. Perhaps this is related to a more systemic gap in informed consent discussions in U.S. health care: the advantages and disadvantages of different places for the provision of various kinds of health care simply don't form a part of standard discussions of virtually any kind of intervention.

4. An anecdote to distinguish Pieterse's position: although you can find a McDonald's in Moscow, you will not find the food fast, the service efficient, or the choices familiar (2004, 50).

5. As De Vries notes, this may also be true of pediatrics (2004, 15).

6. I don't mean to suggest that other medical specialties are immune to the influence of other values, of course: "small area variations," the tendency of doctors with economic interests in screening technologies to refer patients for screening at a higher rate than doctors without such interests, etc., etc., all remind us that physicians of all stripes are human beings.

7. See De Vries's discussion of the history and controversy attending the now ended *primaat* policy, which effectively compelled women to use midwives rather than *huisarts* in any area in which midwives were available (2004, 53–55, and *passim*).

8. See Kukla (2005) for a powerful development of this thought, which she traces, in Europe and its heirs, importantly to the Enlightenment, and specifically to Rousseau.

9. De Vries (2004) reports that in 2002, the cesarean rate in The Netherlands was 13.7 percent. In the U.S in 2002, by contrast, over 26 percent of deliveries involved cesarean section. According to the National Center for Health Statistics, in 2004, 29.1 percent of deliveries were via cesarean. See "C-Section Rate at All-Time High in U.S." http://www.nlm.nih..gov/medlineplus/news/fullstory_37513.html (Accessed October 18, 2006.)

10. In the discussion of Dutch critical responses to home birth cited in note 9, De Vries confesses himself "surprised" that feminists might be concerned about whether the pain involved in natural childbirth is objectionable, prompting me to wonder whether the thought that gives rise to the surprise might be something like "What *do* women want, anyway?"

11. A task force convened by the National Institutes of Health to study elective C-sections concluded that the increase in patient requests does not account for the pronounced increases in cesarean deliveries since the mid 1990s. See Laino (2006). It may be worth asking whether women face more opposition in electing demedicalized birth than elective C-sections. For a discussion of the ethical issues involved from the American College of Obstetrics and Gynecology, see "Surgery and Patient Choice," in ACOG (2004). See also De Vries (2004b).

12. A question Dutch feminists have in fact raised. See De Vries's discussion in chapter seven of (2004), where he writes "It is not feasible to administer epidurals at home" (215). Presumably, this means "not feasible given the acceptance of certain constraints on what's available at home as 'natural'." Certainly other advanced medical resources are being progressively installed in homes—see Arras (1995) for treatment of the issue.

13. See Caton (1999), but more importantly, Bogdan-Lovis's review (2001).

14. Another example of his approach is provided by a letter to the *New York Times*, in which he argues that calling for a Canadian-style, monopsonistic health care system in the U.S. fatally neglects the power of the "lobbyists who work on behalf of our $2 trillion-a-year health care industry," who will not allow "the wholesale dismantling of our insurance system" (De Vries 2006).

15. Healthy People (2010).

16. I'm grateful to Hilde Lindemann for her philosophical and editorial observations about this paper.

2

Housekeepers and Nannies in the Homework Economy

On the Morality and Politics of Paid Housework

Sabrina Hom

Many feminists condemn paid domestic labor as necessarily unjust—specifically, as conducive to the degradation and exploitation of individual domestic workers and to the oppression of domestic workers as a group. Thus, they suggest that paid domestic labor be replaced by or assimilated to labor in the public sphere. In this paper, I will address four characteristics of domestic labor which underlie such concerns: domestic labor's ostensibly natural character, its isolation, its resistance to regulation and formalization, and the intimacy of the relationship between domestic employer and employee. After Haraway, I will argue that these characteristics, all inimical to workers' interests, increasingly characterize labor outside as well as inside the home; their prevalence, which amounts to the "feminization" of labor, is a signature of the globalized economy. The collision of the public and private in what Haraway terms the "homework economy" means, firstly, that domestic labor cannot be fully differentiated, morally or politically, from other forms of labor. Secondly, it means that feminists can no longer hope to address the problems of paid domestic labor by moving women's labor from the private to the public sphere; the feminization of labor complicates efforts to produce more just working conditions in public labor much as it does in private. In the final section of this paper, I will explore the political organizations of Chicana housekeepers in the United States as an example of a political strategy appropriate to workers' predicament in the global economy.

THE MORALITY OF PAID LABOR
IN THE PRIVATE SPHERE

I will define domestic labor as work performed within private homes that is dedicated to maintaining life, health, and standards of cleanliness for oneself and others, such as cooking, cleaning, tidying, laundry, and minding children and other dependents. For the purposes of this paper, I will discuss care work and other sorts of housework together as domestic labor. There are quite distinct issues regarding the ethical value and the ethical difficulties of care work that I will not treat in this paper; here I am concerned with care workers only insofar as they are paid laborers within others' homes. More specifically, I am interested in domestic labor that is sold on the market. In the following four sections, I address several aspects of such labor that have led some to see it as inherently more oppressive than labor outside the home.

Natural and Gendered Labor

> Personality factors are paramount in a baby-sitting situation. I mean, Nilda happens also to love to clean. The personality to me is everything, and Nilda is a good cleaner and she has that personality where she doesn't rest. (Tara, employer, American) (Hondagneu-Sotelo 2001, 68)

Domestic labor is generally unpaid and performed by women, who are often described as naturally predisposed to caring, cleaning, and cooking. When domestic labor *is* bought and sold in the marketplace, it is almost always performed by lower-class women of color and immigrants—persons who are multiply vulnerable (on the bases of class, gender, race, and/or ethnicity) to being represented as a naturally inferior servant class. Domestic labor is cast as unskilled labor and remunerated as such, which reinforces a degrading conception of the worker's expertise as a characteristic natural to her kind.

Others are less likely to recognize the validity of domestic workers' demands due to the naturalized status of their labor. When women do work, such as childcare, which is considered both natural for them (as women) and of great affective (if not economic) value to the employer, it is often surprising to the employer that the employee is not compensated for her low wages by the "natural" pleasure of the job. Demands for wages, raises, or other workers' benefits for women's "natural" labor will, in this context, appear perverse, greedy, or simply unreasonable. Thus, domestic employees are ill-placed to articulate themselves as economic agents or to successfully demand improvements in their working conditions, because their status and the conditions of their labor are seen as naturally ordained.

The "natural" identification of women, particularly women of color and immigrants, with housecleaning and care work perpetuates sexist and racist stereotypes that limit opportunities for women of color while devaluing them as laborers and as caregivers. The employers of immigrant and women of color domestic workers may "hope to import the benefits of Third World 'family values'" (Hochschild 2002, 23) in the form of third-world women's loving and maternal nature; often employers consider the care of their children to be a "natural" and therefore unpaid extension of housekeeping labor.

Workers in the public sphere, on the other hand, are more easily able to distinguish their identity from their labor, casting their work as a commodity sold on the market rather than a "natural" activity, and their expertise as a valuable and cultivated skill.

Isolation

> Sunday is the day all the Filipinos meet and they have basket-ball, they eat Filipino food and it's so nice, it's all I ask, once a month. Saturday and Sunday at the basket-ball court. I am very, very lonely because I live far from Athens, and I want to have Sunday off and my employer just said, "we'll see." . . . Because they're out on the boat at the weekend and the house is lonely so I am in the house and maybe somebody will break in or something like that, so I just have to be there and it's so quiet. And all the time I'm thinking, "Oh now they're in the basket-ball, they're talking," and I have to put on the television or the radio, because it's quite as if I'm going mad. (Remedios, housekeeper, Filipina, working in Athens) (Anderson 2000, 42)

Domestic workers typically work alone, often in white, upper- or middle-class neighborhoods, always within private homes. The domestic employee's isolation from others of her class and gender makes it difficult to create ties with other workers in similar situations and to work collectively for improvements. Without contact with other workers, many domestic employees remain ignorant of their rights and of the shared issues of social justice that inhere in their private grievances. Despite their common interests, workers will easily be turned against each other if they lack the means to organize: for instance, a resistant domestic employee will easily be replaced by another who is willing to accept her low wages and poor working conditions.

The most isolated and vulnerable domestics are those who live with their employers. The fact that the live-in domestic employee both works and lives in the employer's usually white, upper- or middle-class neighborhood means that she is cut off from almost all contact with other members of her class, ethnicity, and race, and, in some cases, from others who can speak her language. A live-in domestic employee may be further isolated by extremely long working hours, controlling employers, and lack of public transit. If she has a family of her own, her contact with them is limited and often mediated by the employer. As the above quote shows, domestic isolation can itself be profoundly harmful; furthermore, the conditions of live-in domestic employment separate the worker from support systems that help domestic workers to resist and escape unacceptable working conditions.

Labor in the public sphere has traditionally depended on the coordination and proximity of workers whose interests coincide; this provides workers with the means to organize and make credible demands of the employer.

Informal Labor: Privacy and Invisibility in the Liberal State

> Until I had my permit, I was working illegally. This made me afraid every day. I knew I was illegal and if there was something I didn't like at home or at work, I couldn't say anything, because my employer could say, "Okay, you go. It's finished. No contract." (Miriam Elvir, housekeeper, Salvadorean, working in Canada) (Bakan and Stasiulis 1997, 150)

Liberal ideology conceives of the home as the householder's benevolent dictatorship, where the allegedly unitary interests of household members provide guarantees against exploitation and abuse. Paid domestic labor often resembles the work people do for their own families more closely than it does public labor, in that it is lacking formal labor agreements, explicit limits on hours or duties, guaranteed benefits or government oversight. Interventions into the household are considered an invasion of privacy justifiable only under extraordinary circumstances. As the private location of domestic labor exaggerates the rights of the employer as householder, it is inimical both to the assertion of the employee's rights and to the state's right to regulate labor relations.

The domestic employee's workspace is also someone's private space, so the protections and benefits available to other workers are often denied to domestic workers (Hondagneu-Sotelo 2001, 213; Bakan and Stasiulis 1997, 121); in many states care workers and live-in domestic employees are specifically excluded from laws that limit the workweek, set a minimum wage, and provide for overtime pay. These state interventions, standard for public-sphere labor, are considered to be unjustifiable invasions into domestic privacy when applied to the upper- and middle-class homes of domestic employers. The American and Canadian immigration processes for domestics sponsored by their employers demand that the employee work for and live with the employer consistently, but do not regulate the employees' hours, working conditions, or access to social security or other benefits (Bakan and Stasiulis 1997, 123); thus the only state intervention into domestic employment serves to reinforce the householders' sovereignty over the employee rather than the workers' rights.

The privacy of domestic labor also leaves domestic workers, particularly live-in workers, vulnerable to physical, verbal and sexual abuse (Hochschild 2002, 142; Bakan and Stasiulis 1997, 5). Such workers may have no friends and no witnesses, and lack the social status to make credible claims against the employer; furthermore, many immigrant domestic workers are dependent upon their employers not only for wages but for shelter and immigration status.

Domestic labor traditionally lacks a formal employment contract. The informal quality of working contracts in the field of paid domestic labor, and the privacy of working conditions, make those labor regulations that do apply to domestic employees extremely hard to enforce. Lacking formal contracts, regulations, and unions, domestic employees are often not paid overtime or social security, provided with paid vacations or sick leave, or accorded unemployment insurance or health insurance (Hondagneu-Sotelo 2001, 241). As part of an informal and non-contractual segment of the economy, domestic workers also lack job security and a defined "job description" to delimit their duties. Domestic employees report that their hours often stretch long past the prescribed maximum; that their duties are constantly expanding, sometimes as a prerogative of employers who seem to resent any breaks taken by the employee (Anderson 2000, 41); and that their employment can be suspended or terminated at the employer's whim. The liberal ideology of household privacy leaves domestic employees extremely vulnerable to abuse and ill-equipped to make demands of the employer.

Intimacy

> If you are so fortunate as to find a maid you love with your whole heart, you might try binding her to you by having a child or two born in her tenure. Not high wages or Christmas gifts of blue-chip stock or every weekend off will prove so much a lure as children to whom she has grown attached. (McGinley 1963, 64)

Domestic labor takes place at the site of familial intimacy, where love and care are expected and self-interest is stigmatized. Affective relationships often arise between employer and employee, carer and charge. Domestic employees and employers often describe their relationship in filial terms; employers are "like a mother" to employees, while care workers "mother" their charges (Rollins 1985, 173ff). As Anderson points out,

> for the employer there are clear advantages to the obfuscation of the employment relationship, since it seriously weakens the employee's negotiating position in terms of wages and conditions—any attempt to improve these are an insult to the "family" and evidence of the worker's moneygrubbing attitude. (Anderson 2000, 123)

Furthermore, the fiction of filial relations can be deeply degrading, as when employees are treated with the infantilizing and dictatorial attitude of "maternalism" (Rollins 1985, 173; Anderson 2000, 144). Maternalistic employers believe that they are rescuing their unfortunate employees from poverty and ignorance; they care for their "childlike" employees with love, guidance, and gifts as much as or more than with wages and benefits. Maternalism obscures workers' position as economic agents and independent adults, casting them instead as dependent children.

Intimacy can serve to keep workers working, and working harder than they otherwise would, under adverse conditions. When the workplace mimics the family, leaving is not as simple as quitting; it may be charged with guilt, worry and loss. A factory or office worker risks economic hardship when she strikes or quits; a domestic employee who is intimate with her charges and employers also risks the loss of valued relationships. A domestic employee may also fear that she will not enjoy such affectionate relations with new employers; thus, as Anderson observes, she "will often consider a lower-paying job if she feels happier with the family" (2000, 123). Particularly in the case of care work, shirking—the deliberate avoidance of excessive or underpaid labor and claiming of unofficial break time—can cause distress or harm to charges; striking, for the same reason, is morally problematic. Many of the means by which workers in the public sphere pursue their interests are complicated, for domestic workers, by such affective and moral considerations.

The proximal intimacy of domestic work, even in the absence of a bond of affection or care, can be degrading and abusive. In the intimacy of the home, many employers seek deferent as opposed to reciprocal social relations with their domestic employees (Rollins 1985, 157). Many ignore their domestic employees altogether, literally enacting the traditional invisibility of domestic labor and its practitioners. Domestic workers, under the close supervision of their employers, are often treated as appendages to their employers' will, expected to adhere to the employer's values and preferences as to how to clean the floors or raise the children (Rollins 1985, 104; Hondagneu-Sotelo 2001, 153). Employees, particularly live-ins, are typically denied privacy (as with the infamous nanny-cam) and autonomy (as they are expected to obey employers' limits on behavior, lifestyle, even diet) (Romero 1992, 117; Hondagneu-Sotelo 2001, 33). Even acts that employers may represent as kindnesses, such as the giving of gifts, are often degrading and exploitative; gifts of unwanted leftovers and ragged clothing reinforce an employee's subordination, and such gifts often serve to pre-empt or avert employees' demands, as when Christmas gifts are given in lieu of the more lucrative annual raises common to public laborers (Romero 1992, 109; Rollins 1985, 189). Such degradation reinforces the worker's "natural" identification with her subordinate job.

Relations between domestic employer and employee, whether warm and familial or chilly and distant, easily become degrading or exploitative. Even employers who honestly hope to act in their employee's best interest often act harmfully, particularly under the influence of maternalistic rescue fantasies. The relation between employer and employee, then, seems to be one of all but irredeemable oppression and injustice.

Although few would argue that public labor is, necessarily and in each instance, more just or advantageous than domestic labor, some do believe that public labor is structurally more conducive to resistance, organization, and labor-friendly regulation than is domestic labor. Public labor has an established means of organization and a record of past victories. Domestic labor lacks such a history and infrastructure, as well as the proximal solidarity on which labor organizations are traditionally built. Furthermore, paid domestic labor is structurally conducive to degradation and exploitation, and it does not confer the usual economic, political and social benefits of public labor. Domestic isolation denies the worker the means to develop collective strategies to improve labor conditions; domestic employees are isolated from other women like themselves and are seemingly unable to find the grounds for solidarity with their employers. Public labor, then, offers at least the possibility of resisting oppression and demanding justice, while the distinctively oppressive character of domestic labor consists largely in its structural resistance to such actions.

These structural characteristics of paid domestic labor have led some feminists to label it as in itself morally problematic. The moral status of paid domestic labor is of special interest to feminists because women's success in paid labor outside of the home is often facilitated by women who are hired to perform the work of housewives and mothers within their homes.[1] Some argue that, by displacing degrading and oppressive household labor onto less privileged women and entering into the unequal and often exploitative relation of domestic employer and employee, women who hire domestic employees participate in an "intrinsically unjust practice" (Tronto 2002, 41).

FEMINIST SOLUTIONS TO THE
PROBLEM OF DOMESTIC LABOR

Cleaning, laundering, food preparation, and care work are necessary forms of labor, and some people—especially the disabled and those responsible for small children—require outside assistance to reconcile the necessary domestic labor with public-sphere participation. Under current conditions, paid domestic labor is an important source of such assistance. Many critics of domestic labor relations have looked hopefully toward the intervention of public labor practices into the home. Such a move takes the laborer out of the isolation and intimacy of the employer's home or provides her with a team of colleagues with whom she can organize; it places her work under the auspices of labor regulations and provides her with the stability of an employment contract, unemployment insurance, etc.; and it transforms her from an invisible servant into a worker analogous to other blue-collar workers. This move depends on the assumption that public labor does not share with domestic labor the oppressive characteristics listed above.

Feminists have differed widely, however, on the extent to which it is possible or beneficial to bring paid domestic labor into line with public labor practices.

Abolishing Housework

Davis advocates a socialization of domestic functions such as childcare and housework, to the extent that we might say housework is obsolete because the private, domestic sphere itself has been absorbed into the public. With Firestone, she hopes that, once society has an interest in greater efficiency in domestic labor, machines will take over much of it (Davis 1998, 193; Firestone 1980, 158–59). The labor that remains is done collectively and is recognized as labor, allowing the laborer solidarity with others and resisting domestic labor's traditional naturalization and invisibility.

Transforming Paid Domestic Labor

Tronto gestures to formalized and public care arrangements like daycare centers as the more just alternative to in-home arrangements, presumably because the workers involved have the benefits and protections that accrue to public-sphere laborers and because their labor is collective and publicly recognized (2002, 43). Similarly, some critics of the maid's or housekeeper's situation look hopefully toward the increasing formalization and commercialization of the housework industry represented by the rise of housecleaning agencies, in which teams of workers are dispatched by managers to the homes of several clients per day; such labor conditions are all but indistinguishable from those of many other blue-collar workers (Meagher 2002, 56). Domestic employees are less enthusiastic about this solution, since it introduces expensive middlemen, enforces taxation, and excludes (in theory) undocumented workers.

Between Worlds

Romero has described as a positive trend the "modernization" of domestic work by her Chicana subjects (1988; 1992, 147ff). In the process of modernization, workers aim to preserve the flexibility and unregulated nature of their work while creating innovative means of organizing and improving labor conditions. Romero's "modernized" domestic laborers, while benefiting from the incursion of public-labor norms and practices into domestic service, unmistakably straddle the line between public and private labor. This sort of fundamentally ambiguous model is not only empirically more beneficial to domestic employees than the others (Romero 1992, 143), but I will argue it is also the only model, of those cited, which offers an effective means to resist the predicament of domestic workers and other workers in the homework economy.

HOUSEKEEPERS AND OTHER WORKERS IN HARAWAY'S "HOMEWORK ECONOMY"

To draw a clear line between domestic labor and private labor overlooks the ways in which the working conditions and moral problems of domestic and public-sphere labor are increasingly converging. As a result, we risk offering "solutions" to the problems of domestic laborers that, in practice, only shunt them into public-sphere labor which will reproduce the oppressive characteristics of labor in the home. Following Haraway, I argue that the means of domination that have so effectively brought about the isolation, exploitation, and vulnerability of the housewife are increasingly deployed against workers in the public sphere.

Haraway's brief analysis of what she terms the homework economy (2004, 25) offers a valuable corrective to some of the feminist approaches to housework outlined above. The homework economy is a capitalist strategy that tightens control of labor and enhances profits through tactics of isolation, dispersal, destabilization and naturalization:

> Work is being redefined as both literally female and feminized, whether performed by men or women. To be feminized means to be made extremely vulnerable; to be able to be disassembled, reassembled, exploited as a reserve labor force; seen less as workers than as servers; subjected to time arrange-

ments on and off the paid job that make a mockery of a limited workday; leading an existence that always borders on being obscene, out of place, reducible to sex. (Haraway 2004, 26)

This feminization propagates the dangers and promises of domestic labor throughout the economy through a "restructuring of work that broadly has the characteristics formerly ascribed to female jobs, jobs literally done only by women" (Haraway 2004, 25).

The homework strategy works by blurring the distinction between the public and private spheres. I will argue that, globally, public workplaces increasingly mimic the isolation, intimacy, invisibility, and "natural" appearance of domestic labor. This feminization of labor is accomplished by using technologies and geographies of globalization to reproduce the oppressive conditions of domestic labor for non-domestic workers. Through the following examples—some drawn from Haraway and others, some my own—I will clarify the nature of the homework economy and demonstrate its effectiveness as a strategy to control and exploit workers.

"Natural" and Global Labor

Haraway observes that the categories of "natural" labor are becoming more specific and more global; images like that of the "nimble little fingers of 'Oriental' women" manufacturing microelectronics reveal supposedly "natural" work in the homework economy as an amalgam of race, gender, ethnicity, technology, global economics and politics (Haraway 2004, 12). That workers in the developing world are conceived as selling personhood as opposed to labor can be seen in businesses as different as manufacturing—wherein countries can attract business by touting "national characteristics" like east Asia's allegedly diligent and obedient workforce—to tourism, where colorful "native" cultures and warm personalities become commodities.

In the service sector, naturalized affective commodities such as the cheerful attention of the stewardess or the friendly, American-accented concern of the Filipina tech-support operator are a significant "natural resource." Hochschild has documented the way in which affective "products" such as airline stewardesses' sincere smiles and the customers' sense of contentment are extracted, commodified and sold. The young women recruited as stewardesses are represented by their employer (both in marketing and in recruiting and training materials) as naturally embodying the characteristic charm and warmth of the American south (1983, 92, 97). As they are seen as producers of services rather than goods and, worse, of mere *feelings*, the stewardesses' labor is devalued and naturalized, their affective agency appropriated: despite the intense training that stewardesses undergo, the work of cultivating and maintaining a cheerful demeanor is cast as part of their naturally "sunny personalities." Such labor verges on the same sort of naturalized invisibility as that of the domestic worker.

Isolation, Communications Technology, and Global Dispersal

Contemporary workers can often be isolated from one another both spatially and temporally with no sacrifice of productivity. Through new technologies of communication, transportation, and surveillance, the capitalist can extract labor from workers who are abroad, in their own homes, in taxicabs and airports. Employees may work most closely with coworkers with whom they communicate only through more or less closely monitored work email. Inch-scale communication devices, advances in home computing, and high-speed, high-quality internet connections mean that many office workers are expected, overtly or covertly, to work during their "off" hours, communicating with clients or doing work for which they have no time during the regular workday. Flex-time and job-share policies allow laborers to work together without temporal coordination; while these policies can be beneficial to workers, they also afford companies a group of employees who are not in the workplace at the same time long enough to organize.

The "feminization" of labor works against the stability of traditionally unionized jobs by creating working conditions in which the tenure of the employee is by definition precarious and temporary. Factory workers in the developing world, freelancers, temps, and contract employees all may find themselves with different employers and different coworkers from week to week, and their jobs might disappear at any moment due to slight economic fluctuations or obscure offenses against management. In such an unstable and polymorphous workplace, worker solidarity and organized resistance are discouraged.

Many workplaces are constructed such that workers do not share the same economic and political interests, while the means of production is organized such that workers with similar interests may be in different countries and have different employers. In a single workplace, workers may be employed by a given corporation, by temp agencies, and by outside contractors responsible for anything from tech support to housekeeping; at the same time, a single product—for example, a computer—might be designed by a company in the U.S., produced in component form in several different countries in Southeast Asia, and assembled in Mexico by employees who work for the factories, not for the computer company. These complicated and polymorphous labor relations destabilize the process of production, making large-scale employee organization very difficult. Under these conditions, extra labor is extorted without overtime pay, while potentially "dangerous" collectives in the workplace are dispersed physically and medi-ated by capital-controlled communication networks.

Informality, Invisibility, and the Global Workforce

Sassen points out that there is "a gathering trend toward the informaliza-tion of an expanding range of activities, as low-profit employers attempt to escape the costs and constraints of the formal economy's regulatory appara-tus" (Sassen 2002, 258). The homework economy disperses workers physi-cally, profiting from labor done in their own homes, in factories and businesses concealed in private homes, and in distant countries: this dis-persal makes regulation problematic both practically and legally (as regula-tion would have to invade homes and other nations). "Outsourcing" labor to the global south is a common strategy to avoid regulations regarding workers' safety, benefits, and rights. Furthermore, workers in the develop-ing world are generally invisible to first-world consumers, which compli-cates attempts to form coalitions between workers and consumers.

When jobs cannot be exported, workers can be imported; undocumented transnational migrants from the global south are actively recruited for jobs in wealthier nations because, unable to avail themselves of governmentally enforced labor protections, they must accept below-standard wages and working conditions. Contemporary corporations also avoid labor regula-tions by hiring un-benefited, unprotected "temporary" workers in the long term and by outsourcing labor-intensive work to shadow corporations that take on the risks of exploiting labor. On a global level, gainful employment, whether domestic or not, increasingly means invisible, informal and unreg-ulated labor.

Intimacy

When dispersing and destabilizing the workforce is not cost-effective, companies can nonetheless discourage workers from developing solidarity or demanding better conditions by creating a milieu of domestic intimacy in the workplace. Since, in the quasi-familial workplace, upper manage-ment is cast as benevolent and paternal, workers are discouraged from articulating their interests in opposition to those of the employer; as in the case of the domestic worker, to do so can appear ungrateful and disloyal. Hochschild has documented the efficacy with which the pseudonymous corporation she studied in *The Time Bind* inspired a sense of filial affection and obligation in its workers; many of the employees interviewed got sig-nificant emotional support from their coworkers and, while most rarely saw their extended families, they regularly socialized with their coworkers at the corporation's so-called family reunions (1997, 36, 42, 167). Such structures recreate the ties of intimacy found between family members in the workplace, using this intimacy to gain in terms of worker productivity and loyalty; one doesn't, after all, quit one's family.

The homework economy, then, creates a dangerous and lonely situation for workers throughout the global economy, one prone to abuses and structured in ways that make collective resistance very difficult. This strategy depends on the "feminization" of labor, in which work throughout the economy comes to resemble women's domestic labor.

THINKING OPPOSITIONAL STRATEGIES

Moral condemnations of paid domestic labor, and political strategies to assimilate domestic labor to public labor, depend on the belief that public labor provides better conditions for workers, or at least the possibility of improving conditions through collective action. Haraway notes that the homework economy resists traditional labor-organization strategies, which depend on working conditions—particularly, the existence of large and homogeneous collections of workers—which are no longer prevalent. Haraway writes that "our dominations don't work by medicalization and normalization anymore; they work by networking, communications redesign, stress management" (2004, 11); thus, traditional labor strategies, which rely on collectives bound by the extreme temporal, spatial, political and economic normalization of the shop floor, are no longer suited to the homework economy.

The "feminization" of labor demands that we imagine ways to dignify and organize labor that, even if public and commercial, does not create homogeneous collectives of workers. Organizing efforts in the homework economy will require the formation of "elective affinities" and unexpected coalitions. As described by Haraway, these coalitions are not based on natural resemblances or perfect coincidences of interest; instead, they are "monstrous and illegitimate" (2004, 13), dangerous chimeras pieced together of parts with no natural affinity. Such unities are never wholly innocent, Haraway contends: the affinity groups she has in mind, enabled as they are by connections produced in the morally questionable networks of the global economy, are the "illegitimate offspring of militarism and patriarchal capitalism" (2004, 10). Nonetheless, she argues, they have the potential to subvert and appropriate for oppositional purposes the very connectivity of the homework economy.

In the remainder of the paper I will consider, as an illustration of Haraway's model, the attempts of some Chicana housekeepers and nannies to "modernize" their labor conditions through social networks[2]—coalitions of employees, located outside of the workplace, that seek improved working conditions. These networks are just the sort of non-innocent coalitions that Haraway sees as appropriate to organizing in the homework economy; by examining them, I hope to clarify both the potential and the dangers of such coalitions.

Collectivization

Examples of social networks are found among both the housekeepers studied by Mary Romero and those studied by Pierrette Hondagneu-Sotelo. Both studies focus on Chicana women working in the western United States, the majority of whom are first-generation immigrants. The house-keepers work alone, in their employers' homes in upper- and middle-class, predominantly white neighborhoods, for as many as fifteen different employers each week. Despite their isolation while actually working, these workers form strong social networks among neighbors, relatives, and more distant acquaintances. The networks assist job-seekers and transmit information about workers' rights and standard wages, alleviating the exploitative potential of isolated domestic labor and helping to standardize unregulated working conditions. The women trade tips on asking for raises, avoiding employers' unreasonable requests, and expressing reasonable and clear standards and limits for their work to their employers. Social networks thus help to combat the oppressive effects of domestic isolation.

These networks are largely made possible by the move from live-in to day work; the women generally network at family, religious, and social events, or in places like neighborhood medical clinics and busses where women might encounter others who share their class, ethnicity, etc. Such networks are formed outside of the workplace, on the basis of the women's common experiences, language, and faith; and also from the ghettoization and isolation of people of color, the poor, and immigrant populations, which often brings domestic workers into close proximity in their private lives.

These networks are by no means innocent or unambiguously morally admirable. They are shaped by the exigencies of the global economy that brought Hondagneu-Sotelo's subjects to Los Angeles; by the discrimination, linguistic disadvantages, and poverty that pressed these women into domestic work and into the generally poor, segregated neighborhoods where they network; and by the insular tendencies of these women to gather along ethnic and racial lines. The network that Hondagneu-Sotelo studied is described as exclusive, making it very difficult for new people to enter the profession, and there is no mention of the inclusion of members of other racial or immigrant groups. Perhaps most disturbing are the sub-contractor relationships bred between established housekeepers and other women, usually new immigrants, who "apprentice" to them, learning the job and possibly finding clients of their own while working alongside the veteran housekeepers—generally for no, or almost no, pay. Hondagneu-Sotelo describes these negative aspects of the networks as predictable outgrowths of the housekeepers' situation, which is in some ways inimical to solidarity: "job work characteristics prompt domestic workers to alternately share mutually beneficial information, and to compete with one another in an individualistic manner" (1988, 62). While the networks of domestics have grave dangers and pitfalls, stemming from their illegitimate origins in global capitalism, they also have the potential to oppose the degradation and exploitation of domestic workers.

Professionalization

> They [the employer's children] started to introduce me to their friends as their maid. "This is our maid, Angela." I would say "I'm not your maid. I've come to clean your house and a maid is someone who takes care of you and lives here or comes in everyday and I come once a week and it is to take care of what you have messed up. I'm not your maid, I'm your housekeeper." (Mrs. Fernandez, Chicana, working in Los Angeles) (Romero 1992, 155)

The domestic employees' networks and unions place a special emphasis on the professionalization of their work. Subjects in both studies insist on being called "housekeepers" instead of "maids," a term which to them evokes unskilled and servile labor. The women wish to present themselves, instead, as skilled professionals who offer their expert housekeeping services on a contractual basis, and they may admonish their employers to address them as such. Similarly, the domestic workers seek to carefully define and delimit their services to employers and to discourage employers from attempting to supervise and manage their work practices. More formal networks like the Long Island housekeepers' collective *Unity* arrange training for new domestic workers so that they can gain more respected and skilled positions (Cornell 2002). By emphasizing the skilled nature of domestic work, workers disrupt their "natural" identification with such work, asserting themselves as economic agents who sell valuable services.

The women of *Unity* refuse to do any childcare work, and Hondagneu-Sotelo's and Romero's subjects also avoid such positions. Such resistance disarticulates and denaturalizes domestic work, challenging the natural unity of care and housework. Such disruption is particularly important and subversive for women of color and immigrant women, who are especially vulnerable to exploitation as "natural resources" and who have a great deal to gain, in wages, working conditions, and social status, from challenging their "natural" identification with maternal and domestic labor.

Improvement without Formalization

Domestic workers' networks aim to resist abuse and exploitation, to regularize duties and wages, and to provide job security without relying on formalizing their work—that is to say, without ceding their autonomy to the management of housecleaning agencies or exposing themselves to state and Federal regulation. Formalized work is rejected because it is disadvantageous to illegal immigrants and to those who work "under the table" to preserve means-tested benefits; because the long and inflexible hours of formal work interfere with familial caring duties; because working for housecleaning agencies introduces an expensive middleman; and because the interviewees' informal, and often unreported and untaxed, domestic-work wages compared favorably to the wages and benefits offered by the formal jobs they had held in the United States[3] (most frequently, in low-paid factory jobs) (Romero 1992, 143). Domestic workers' networks oppose the formalization of for-profit agencies and tend to be ambivalent toward state intervention, and they campaign for laws that would assert and protect workers' rights without increasing direct regulation or surveillance of workers.[4]

Social networks help live-in domestics to find day work and all workers to find more or better employers. This reduces workers' isolation and vulnerability to individual employers and moves them toward the most advantageous form of work, in which live-out workers service several employers. By taking on many employers and helping each other to find jobs in times of need, workers minimize their dependence on any particular employer, freeing themselves, in some cases, to demand more pay and more respect. The Long Island domestic workers' cooperative *Unity* matches workers with "dignified" domestic jobs (Cornell 2002, 96). *Unity* also keeps a list of bad employers—those who pay too little, demand too much, or otherwise abuse workers—for the use of job-seekers.

Intimacy and Solidarity

> I don't ask for raises anymore. I have one woman who kind of sets the pace and she's given me a raise almost every year and then she hints around to some of the other ones that she knows I work for and then they all bring it up to her standards. (Mrs. Salazar, Chicana, Los Angeles) (Romero 1992, 160)

As contract workers with many employers, often one or more for each day of the week, workers are not subjected to the sort of intimacy that, as documented above, is so conducive to exploitation. Most of Romero and Hondagneu-Sotelo's subjects have families of their own and all prefer live-out work; having her own home and family helps the worker to resist the fiction that she is an inferior member of the employer's family. Most of the workers interviewed show a marked preference for working employers (as opposed to housewives) who are not present when the work is performed and who tend to be "grateful" rather than meddlesome (Romero 1992, 153); removing the homeowner from the workplace reduces the potential for degradation and exploitation.

While the majority of domestic workers prefer not to have an intimate and everyday relation with their employers, they benefit from enlightened and concerned employers. Romero observes the importance, to the modernization of domestic labor, not only of networks between employees but also of those between employers. Both Hondagneu-Sotelo and Romero report that employers sometimes help domestic workers to find more and better employment, referring their employees to women in their own social networks. Romero finds that some employers transmit knowledge of appropriate working conditions and wages to prospective employers in their network. Furthermore, she observes that

> employers' involvement in modernizing the occupation may not be limited to exposing new employers to contemporary expectations. Two domestics reported that employers . . . applied pressure on other employers to upgrade working conditions. Both domestics worked for employers who set standards of fairness and urged their friends and neighbors to conform—for instance, by complying with federal regulations by filing income tax and social security forms and by giving annual raises. (Romero 1988, 331)

Employers have the ability and, in a few cases, the willingness to help improve domestic workers' conditions by treating their employees justly and applying pressure to others in their social networks to do the same. Furthermore, closeness between employer and employee can help domestic workers to gain better pay, job security, and the flexibility to modernize her labor and fit it to her needs (Dill 1994, 85).

The affinity between the domestic employer and employee can only be an unstable and dangerous one. Such relationships, born in the intimacy of the private home, are always situated in the power imbalance created by the householders' domestic sovereignty, class, and social position. The potential for degradation and exploitation in such relationships has been well established, and is no less present when the employer hopes to act in the employee's best interest. Employer-employee intimacy and coalition can only succeed in the domestic sphere if the parties, and particularly the employers, avoid the dangers of maternalism; the employer must conceive of the worker as an independent adult involved in what is, at least in part, an economic relationship. Employers who wish to avoid unjust or oppressive behavior must be very careful to avoid fantasies of filiality or rescue as they embrace the goals of the "modernization" of domestic labor.

Despite their differences, however, the employer and the domestic worker share some grounds for coalition. Most domestic workers are hired by women, usually married women. The women hiring domestic workers share with their employees the distinctively female burden of domestic duties; while they have the resources to hire other women to do much of this labor, they are nonetheless ultimately responsible for it in their families, and as such they take on the hiring and supervision of nannies and housekeepers. The relation between employers and their housekeepers and nannies, as a point where the partial and complex resemblance between women as domestic workers is made manifest across class barriers, is a potential point of coalition. As Romero observes,

> Domestic service is a unique social setting in which to explore relationships between women. Rarely in our society do women (or men) from different social-economic, racial, and ethnic backgrounds interact in an informal or intimate setting. The employer's home, in which domestics and employers interact, brings several important factors to bear simultaneously; shared gender, interracial and interclass oppression, and location within women's primarily unrecognized workplace—the household . . . In their own homes middle-class white women make decisions that transform sisterhood into a means either to extract emotional and physical labor or, conversely, to improve working conditions and to increase pay and benefits for women of color employed to do their housework. (1992, 120)

Domestic laborers, then, are able to form coalitions both with other domestics and with their employers despite many divergences in their interests. The intersection of domestic workers and employers, on the contested ground of the nursery or the kitchen, is a fine example of Haraway's non-innocent and dangerous affinities, here based on the ambiguous resemblances between women who live out a gendered relation to housework and care work despite their vastly different social positions.

Domestic employment is structurally conducive to the oppression, abuse and exploitation of workers. However, we should neither condemn nor aspire to abolish all forms of paid labor in the home. Assimilating domestic labor to public labor cannot alleviate its moral problems, because its oppressive characteristics are increasingly mimicked in public labor. In the global economy, workers consistently find their skills reduced to a "natural" (often also national or ethnic) characteristic; workers, particularly transnational migrants, are increasingly invisible and unregulated; technological advances and global expansion isolate and disperse workers; and the semblance of domestic intimacy proliferates in the workplace.

Feminized labor, inside and outside the home, resists traditional political strategies to improve labor conditions, but it holds the potential for improvement by unconventional means. We can look to domestic workers' strategies to improve their working conditions as one model for resisting more broadly the unjust and oppressive tendencies of the homework economy. Workers in both the public and private sphere can make use of oppositional strategies borrowed from domestic employees' networks: building solidarity outside as well as inside the workplace; demanding recognition of their work as skilled rather than "natural" labor; seeking more effective labor protections while avoiding formalization; avoiding forms of workplace intimacy that degrade the worker and obscure her proper interests; and building coalitions on the basis of unexpected and imperfect affinities between very different groups.

NOTES

1. Not only middle- and upper-class women in more developed countries, but also their immigrant domestic employees, may benefit economically from the ability to displace household labor onto less privileged women. Pei-Chia Lan (2003) has documented the frequently ambivalent identity of immigrant domestic employees in Taiwan, who often hire domestic employees to care for their homes and families while they work abroad.

2. These social networks are only one example of the sort of coalitions that might be used to resist the pernicious effects of economic globalization. In addition to social networks, networks enabled by contemporary communications technologies are a potent means of resisting the international dispersal of labor in the global economy.

3. It might be argued that it would be best for workers if all labor came to resemble public labor as it was prior to the "homework economy"—labor that was formalized and regulated. While the organizational tactics of social networks could perhaps be used to pursue such an end, the domestic workers' rationales for preserving the informality of their labor show that such a strategy is not best suited to the interests of all workers.

4. For example, see the "Domestic Workers' Bill of Rights" (A2804) put forward in New York State, which would compel employers and employment agencies to provide workers with written accounts of their rights.

3

Gender Identity and the Ethics of Care in Globalized Society[1]

Virginia Held

WOMEN AND EQUALITY

It is plausible to start with an assumption that—slowly and unsteadily, with periods of sometimes violent backlash—women will progress toward greater equality, and that other groups whose gender identities differ from the one that has been dominant will gradually do so also. As these previously subordinated groups advance, there will be strong opposition, but how and when such opposition will temporarily prevail is probably not predictable.

In the United States, the rise of Ronald Reagan's conservatism, and then of the influence of religious fundamentalism in the administration of George W. Bush, depended on many factors other than the progress of women and gay people toward equality, although the latter was certainly an important factor and reactions to it certainly have brought about setbacks in that progress. The global rise of Islamic fundamentalism is certainly fueled in part by antipathy toward the progress elsewhere first of those not male and then of those not heterosexual. And yet the advancement continues, even in religiously conservative Islamic societies, with progress thwarted at times but moving forward at other times and places. I regret to say that many policies of the U.S., U.K., and Israel are, in my view, hindering rather than assisting this development through misguided attempts to use military force to impose their will on the Islamic world, but one can hope that these policies will change as the degree to which they are counterproductive becomes increasingly evident. And in the U.S., even as the Bush administration puts obstacles in the way of women's most basic reproductive rights and presses for firm prohibitions on gay marriage, women continue to make some progress toward economic equality, women hold some visible and powerful positions in governmental and academic institutions, and lesbians and gays are more often favorably presented in the media.

With progress toward equality, the sharp differentiations between the social roles of women and men will markedly decrease. At a global level, of which a global audience is increasingly aware, women will more often than in the past be leaders and managers and professionals along with men, and will more often do adequately paid work. And gay people, who have long occupied such positions, will occupy them more openly. Although trends toward the global feminization of poverty and toward the exploitation of female domestic and sexual workers from the global South by those in the global North work against equality for many women (see, e.g., Jaggar 2005a), these trends may gradually be offset by the necessity of increased male participation in the work of care giving. Such work cannot be dispensed with, since, in order to have new generations of people, it is utterly necessary. And as men are pressed to do caring work by women, who demand men's participation as they themselves increasingly do other work as well as caring work, men will come to value care in ways they often have not. They will identify more as fathers who do fathering labor, not just as men who "father" children in the sense of impregnating women. Already, there are increasing demands for restructuring work to be more hospitable to family life.

Gender identities built on associations with social roles rigidly separated into "women's work" and "men's work" will thus decrease. On a parallel path, as tolerance grows concerning sexual orientation, and as awareness increases concerning the vagueness and variability of the distinction between the biologically male and the biologically female, gender identities based on physiology will also soften.

This paper will argue that the newly developed moral theory known as the ethics of care is well suited to reflect and guide these progressive trends, and to resist traditional opposition to them and to the newer backlashes they may provoke. I will start by considering how "gender identity" is best interpreted and understood. I will then give a brief overview of the ethics of care, and argue that it is more promising for dealing with the issues involved in gender identity than are the standard, dominant moral theories of recent decades. The ethics of care appreciates the diverse gender identities of persons, and promotes their equality in appropriate ways.

GENDER AND SEX

Feminists have for some time been theorizing the categories of men, women, sex, and gender, asking about the possibilities for self-transformation. Tamsin Lorraine examines the formation of gender identities from a perspective based on feminism and continental philosophy. She writes, "Gender identity is one way of representing ourselves. By labeling myself a 'man' or a 'woman' I am also conjuring up a range of possibilities presented to me in my culture and language" (Lorraine 1990, 17). "I can create a gendered self within conventional bounds," she continues, "or I can push beyond them, adding to my culture or language new possibilities of what a man or woman could be" (17). Cressida Heyes writes along similar lines that "feminists are not only interested in establishing who to count as 'women' with regard to some already foundational definition, but also in troubling and transforming the definition itself. . . . We need to ask what makes it possible to change one's identity—and not just incrementally within a defined category (e.g., as by becoming a more assertive woman through consciousness raising), but also more drastically . . . asking what makes a particular facet of identity into something the individual *can* transform?" (Heyes 2006, 266).

Many feminists have explored what they have come to call a conception of the self as relational. According to Lorraine, "human identity is a product of a social and communal enterprise—no single individual can form and maintain an identity without the help and support of the others around her" (1990, 202). Similarly, in examining the process of remaking a self in the aftermath of trauma, Susan Brison finds that this remaking depends crucially on a person's relations with others (Brison 1997). It thus seems likely that gender identity, like other aspects of identity such as whether we are able to act autonomously (Meyers 1994), deeply involves our relations with other persons. As Lorraine concludes, "Once we start seeing how various kinds of selves constitute one another in a community of interlocking human relations, we can better understand . . . the way current gender categories work in preserving both masculine and feminine selves; then we could envision a transformation of gender categories." (1990, 202).

Amid such change, a large factor in gender identity will undoubtedly remain: only women will give birth, at least for the foreseeable future. But much less of women's and men's identities will be tied to this fact. It will increasingly be recognized that gender identity is much less a given than has been thought, and that it need not and should not determine the shape of persons' lives except as they develop their own gender identities and decide in relations with others how to organize their lives around them.

One important thread in feminist thinking about the aspects of gender identity that are subject to change and those that are not has been feminists' extensive debate about a possible distinction between gender and sex. It has been suggested that "gender" refers to socially constructed roles for men or women, roles which could be changed, while "sex" refers to an underlying biological reality distinguishing males and females (Money and Ehrhardt 1972, Rubin 1975).[2] The distinction has more recently been challenged, however, by those who emphasize the extent to which theorizing about biological categories is also socially or culturally constructed, often imposing a rigid male/female dichotomy on a more ambiguous reality (Ortner and Whitehead 1981, Butler 1990, Fausto-Sterling 2000). On this view, there is no biological "given" about sex differences, or about bodies generally; how we think about them and how we act with respect to them are greatly influenced by our cultures and societies.[3]

Nancy Hartsock points out that the distinction between "sex" and "gender" played a useful role in the development of feminist thinking: "the development of the distinction between sex and gender was an important step forward for feminist theory," she writes, "since it helped move the debate away from the 'natural differences' between men and women" (Hartsock 2006, 182). These so-called natural differences had been taken to require that women confine themselves to roles such as wife and mother, caring for their families while men ran the world beyond the household. Hartsock thinks the time has come to move beyond the sex/gender distinction. Although I largely agree that we should not rigidly fix the meanings of these terms in the ways earlier suggested in the debate, I do not think we should too easily assert that everything is socially constructed. Understanding the cultural shaping of bodies and their attributes is important, but we still need to be able to discuss their biological aspects. Efforts to soften the rigidities of traditional gender dichotomies by emphasizing how much about them depends on our ways of interpreting them should not undermine efforts to understand what scientific inquiry can reveal.

In a sense, we should agree that the world as we can know it is constructed by language. Even the most material realities are only real to us if we notice them, name them, try to explain them, and so on. But then an important question arises: what is the difference between the realities that would be as they are even in the absence of human thought about them and influences on them, like molecules and galaxies, and the realities that are highly influenced by the human constructions of history, society, culture, and intentional action, like literature and government? Granted, the line between these two kinds of realities is not sharp, but it is possible and often important to be able to note clear cases at either end of a continuum. Chimpanzees would behave more or less as they do in the absence of human society. If humans had not developed the languages and reasoning capacities they have, it would still be the case that no men can give birth to children, and that many women can. That men cannot themselves give birth may well be the deepest source of men's desires to control women, in that by doing so they also control their own capacity to reproduce. This hypothesis would help explain the anxiety about gender identity that affects men much more strongly than women.

I believe that the biological fact that only women can create new human beings is significant. To say that this aspect of human reality is socially or culturally constructed can be misleading. What clearly is socially or culturally constructed is what human beings make of this biological fact, such as holding that women are unsuited for social leadership because they give birth. Aristotle thought that the function of man was to reason, that the function of woman was to reproduce, and that the social destinies of women should be determined by this difference (Mahowald, 1994). This kind of view has had an extraordinarily wide and deep influence. The social pressure that almost compels women to be mothers, and to feel deficient if they cannot or do not want to be mothers, is also a result of how cultures interpret female biology rather than of the biology itself. But this does not mean that the biological facts of reproduction, or of brain function, are unimportant. And the fact that the lines between male and female bodies are much less clear than the norms of compulsory heterosexuality have tried to make them (Butler 1990) does not imply that there are no clear cases of biological maleness and femaleness.

Some recent critiques of the sex/gender distinction emerge from a postmodernist perspective that rejects the idea of an autonomous self, or of a subject beyond what is produced by social relations of power. Postmodernists also often reject the possibility of justifying norms and concepts beyond those established by the social and cultural relations within which persons have been constituted. I share some of the worries expressed by Seyla Benhabib, who thinks that the strong theses of postmodernism can undercut feminist critique: "How is the project of women's emancipation even thinkable," she asks, "without regulative principles of agency, autonomy, and selfhood?" To Benhabib, if we have no discourse of justification, social criticism becomes impossible and one can only describe "regimes of discourse and power as they succeed each other" (Benhabib 1995, 25). On the other hand, one can appreciate Judith Butler's suggestion that any given conceptual or normative scheme must remain open both to an examination of the power relations that have led to its acceptance, and to appropriate reformulation based on such examination. "The critique of the subject," she writes, "is not a negation or repudiation of the subject, but, rather, a way of interrogating its construction as a pregiven or foundationalist premise" (Butler 1995, 42). Perhaps we can agree that, although the facts of biology as well as the norms of social organization and individual action all require inter-

pretation, the ways these interpretations should proceed are often significantly different.[4]

What we make of men's and women's different biological traits and
capacities is what has been important for gender identity. It has led in the
past (and in many parts of the world it still leads) to the extremely oppressive confinement of women to the roles associated with reproduction, from
the nurturing of infants through the care and education of children, and by
extension to the care of the old and the ill, and finally to the care of men.
It has led, also, to the invisibility, exclusion, pain, and often persecution of
gay, lesbian, bisexual, and transgendered persons.

When we realize the extent to which the associations and exclusions of
gender are the products of social and cultural construction, we can free ourselves from the oppressive features of traditional thinking about gender
identities. To start with, "reproduction" is an unfortunate term for all but
the most purely biological aspects of giving birth. It suggests that all activities involved in bringing up children and in the caring labor of households
is mere repetition, as if human reproduction were like the reproduction of
nonhuman animals. This standard picture of "reproduction" has accompanied the idea that only men, in the public sphere, work to transform their
environment and create what is historically and intellectually new. The
reality is that the care, upbringing, and education of children are potentially
among the most creative and historically transformative activities in which
human beings engage, for they create new *persons*.[5] Both women and men
should engage in this kind of work, as well as in the full range of other
kinds of work, so that gender identity is not a determinant of occupation,
and occupations are not structured by gender.

Identities are constructed, and construct themselves, in the midst of
social conditions. As Nancy Hartsock summarizes this process, offering a
view with which almost all feminists would agree, "My body certainly carries the marks of, and is in many important ways created by, the social and
power relations within which my subjectivity constitutes itself and is constituted" (Hartsock 2006, 182). At the same time, we can resist the established social order and bring about changes in it. Once we understand that
we are embodied subjectivities, shaped within networks of social relations,
our identities emerge as a combination of influences acting on us and of
resistances and initiatives which we marshall (Hartsock 2006).

Feminists have also discussed the ways in which violence contributes to
shaping identities, as some persons understand themselves to have identities especially vulnerable to violence (Mason 2002, *Hypatia* 2006). Some
feminists focus especially on domestic violence and other violence against
women, and others on how male gender identity seems connected with the
willingness to use violence (Harris and King 1989, Held 1993, Chapter 7).
Whether brain function or other biological or evolutionary factors predis-

pose men toward aggression, or women toward nurturing, is still uncertain. We should keep an open mind on such issues while maintaining skepticism regarding overly simple biological explanations (Fausto-Sterling 2000). What is important, and what does not depend on the outcome of such investigations, is that we commit ourselves to respecting persons as equals, and to seeking social goals that can be morally justified. Respecting persons requires not coercing them into gender roles that violate their equal worth. Seeking the good of society, and increasingly of humanity on a global scale, requires curbing tendencies toward aggression, enhancing tendencies toward nurturance, and adopting policies that contribute to these processes.

Many feminist theorists have concluded that when we appropriately value the caring activities to which women have historically been largely confined, and when we appropriately recognize the values involved in those activities, we need to construct a new moral outlook or theory. The ethics of care is a leading candidate for such theory. Increasingly, men as well as women, whatever their sexual orientation, will engage in caring activities, thus gaining the appropriate experience to appreciate this new outlook—one which provides moral guidance not only for the "private" caring activities neglected by dominant moral theories, but also for activities outside the household.

GENDERED BODIES

As gender identity becomes less tied to traditionally constraining social roles and divisions of labor, and as it also becomes increasingly loosened from anatomy, what will be the source of gender identity? Although it is theoretically possible that gender identity will wither away as relatively unimportant, there are few signs of this happening. One reason for this may be that in combating patriarchy and compulsory heterosexuality, subordinated gender identities may be emphasized as they are revalued and asserted in the face of denigration. And sometimes gender identities are emphasized in a mood of parody and playfulness, to bring about awareness of stereotypes and reconsideration of what behavior is or is not acceptable.

Another important factor in the continuing cultural strength of gender identity may be that bodies have increasingly become sites not only of self-expression, but also of commercial exploitation. Adornment, playful manipulation, and various forms of training of bodies have burgeoned in ways that often heighten gender identity. Some of these developments are harmless or occasionally even healthful. But alongside this trend is the increase in the aggressive use of bodies, and in the manipulation of people's feelings about their bodies, for commercial gain. Cosmetics, clothes, fashions that heighten gender identity or play with it for profit, plastic surgery to change appearances and prolong a youthful look, and ever more elaborate makeovers offer constant opportunities for commercial exploitation— opportunities that are being seized by corporate interests.

The use of sexuality to promote and sell commodities expands daily, and ever more activities and ways of being are being pulled into the market. Pregnancy and other aspects of reproduction (for instance, egg "donation") are often seen as marketable services, a trend also reflected in commercial childcare, healthcare, education, and "privatized" security and military forces. The effects of the increasing marketization of everyday life are greatly magnified by the expansion and reach of media images and forms of entertainment. With sexualized bodies offering yet another site for economic exploitation, gender identity seems likely to be increasingly a product of commercial manipulation—a trend magnified, of course, by economic globalization.

The extent to which gender identity and its expressions in sexuality and behavior are being driven by economic interests diminishes the opportunities for such identities and expressions to be freely chosen and humanly satisfying. At the same time, political opposition to freely chosen gender expression is strong. As early as 1983, two scholars noted that

> the dominant power to define and regulate sexuality has been shifting toward . . . large-scale social and economic forces, the most salient of which is perhaps the state. States now organize many of the reproductive relations that were once embedded in smaller-scale contexts. . . . Today, abortion, sterilization abuse, sex education, homosexual rights, and welfare and family policies are explosive political issues in the United States and much of Western Europe. For as states claim a greater and greater interest in the structuring of sexuality, sexual struggles increasingly become part of public, consciously defined politics. (Ross and Rapp 1997, 164)

The intervening decades have only made these observations more compelling. And as liberalized attitudes are spread by global culture, reactionary pressures in traditional societies often turn ugly and sometimes violent.

Since constructions of sexuality and gender can be used for political and economic gain, it is probably too much to hope that they will not continue to be so used, though resistance could temper the effects. Economic and political forces will often stifle the free development and expression of gender identity. But control of sexuality is another form of the opposition that is to be expected as part of the process of freeing gender identity from traditional constraints. As with opening to women occupations from which they have been excluded, opening the free and responsible expression of sexuality and gender identity to those previously highly constrained (such as lesbian, gay, bisexual, and transgendered people) will have many setbacks but will probably proceed. In the long run, occupational equality and free expression of sexuality will grow regardless of how gender identity develops. As this process unfolds, the ethics of care can provide helpful guidance.

THE ETHICS OF CARE

Now developed far beyond its earliest formulations in the work of Sara Ruddick, Carol Gilligan, and Nel Noddings, the ethics of care is a distinct moral theory or normative approach, one relevant to global and political issues as well as to the personal relations that can most clearly exemplify care.[6] It is not merely a concern that can be added onto or included within the most influential moral theories, as some of those theories' advocates have suggested. Examining its central ideas and characteristics demonstrates that the ethics of care is a promising alternative to more familiar moral theories.

In this context, "care" refers both to certain practices and to certain values by which to evaluate those practices. Taking care of children, or of those who are dependent in other ways or who have unusual needs, involves work; that work should be done with appropriate motives and should meet appropriate standards. Thus the ethics of care examines the values implicit even in existing practices of care, unjustly structured as those practices usually are, while also providing guidelines for improving caring practices and extending their characteristic values into other areas. Care ethics includes concern for transforming the structures within which practices of care take place so that they are no longer oppressive, as well as recommendations for reflecting and enacting the values of care in political institutions and relations between cultures.

Where other moral theories such as Kantian morality and utilitarianism demand impartiality above all, the ethics of care emphasizes the moral importance of our ties to our families and other groups. Such ties are a major evaluative focus of care ethics, which differs from virtue ethics in its focus on caring relations rather than on the virtues of individuals. The caring person not only has the right motives or dispositions, but also participates adeptly in activities of care and in cultivating caring relations. Thus the ethics of care focuses on the cluster of values involved in fostering and maintaining caring relations—values such as trust, empathy, sensitivity, mutual consideration, solidarity, and responsiveness to need. Relatedly, rather than focusing only on the dictates of reason, the ethics of care appreciates both the importance of the emotions in discerning what morality requires and the importance to moral life of cultivating caring emotions.

Although it has developed out of feminist thinking, the ethics of care is an approach to morality that can have universal appeal, as it rests not on divisive religious traditions but on the experiences every person has had of being cared for, and on the experiences many persons have of caring for others. No child would survive without extensive care, and most persons need additional care for some periods of their lives. The idea that care is only for children and the ill or disabled, and is thus not relevant to political and social life, reveals the power of the libertarian myth of self-sufficiency that pervades so much Anglo-American thought. Not only have those who imagine themselves self-sufficient already benefited as children from enormous amounts of unacknowledged care, they are still dependent on webs of social relations that enable them to earn their income, invest their money, and hold onto their property. Without such webs, their property would be looted, their money worthless, and their jobs nonexistent.

Everyone needs the care and concern for others that foster their willingness to participate in such webs of social relations. Everyone benefits from the valuing of care that supports public concern for healthcare, education, and childcare. The values of care can thus guide improving public policies as well as supporting respect for individual rights. After all, recognizing certain rights as important presupposes that persons are sufficiently interconnected through caring relations to care whether rights are respected. Overall, the ethics of care provides vital resources for understanding community and shared identity, and it can suggest what a caring society might be like.

Historically, care, women, and the household have been devalued and not thought relevant to morality, in contrast to men's activities in public life. Kantian moral theory and utilitarianism differ significantly from each other, but both are theories of justice that are thought suitable for public life insofar as they emphasize impartiality, rationality, equality, and universal principles.

Although care is often contrasted with justice, feminist philosophers developing the ethics of care have explored how care and justice might be meshed into a satisfactory comprehensive moral theory. One approach is to conceptualize caring between fellow human beings as the wider network of relations within which we can agree to treat persons *as if* they were liberal individuals for the limited purposes of legal and political interactions guided by justice (Held 2006). Without implying that the discourse of rights is dispensable, the ethics of care does impose limits on the reach of law and legalistic thinking, suggesting that the model of morality based on impartial justice and liberal individualism is useful only for limited legal and political contexts, rather than for the whole of morality as has been supposed.

The ethics of care has deep implications for political and social issues. Consider, for instance, the question of whether corporate and market-based approaches to a range of activities should be expanded through privatiza tion and commercialization. The ethics of care is more promising than the dominant moral theories for dealing with this question, since it makes clear why non-market values should have priority in such activities as childcare, healthcare, education, and the arts. The ethics of care can provide strong arguments for limiting markets, and for freeing cultural expression from commercial domination—arguments that are much-needed in the context of accelerating privatization and economic globalization.

CARE AND GENDER IDENTITY

How would the ethics of care approach gender identity? Would it offer better moral guidelines than more established moral theories for constructing and responding to people's gender identities?

Accommodation to the identities of women, as they change and develop in the direction of greater equality, is greatly aided by recognizing the value of caring labor and emphasizing the values of care. Women can be formally accorded equal rights, but even when such rights are interpreted in reasonable ways and enforced (as they too often are not), many women will be unable to make use of them if their attempts to do so are met with such hostility and resistance that the burden becomes too great. This hostility can be personal, as when husbands and potential husbands oppose women's aspirations, or social, as when social and economic supports for women's progress are inadequate. Such resistance can and should be challenged as a failure to support caring relations as well as the development of women as individuals.

Progress for women requires fundamental social restructuring based on a suitable valuing of caring labor and of caring relations. When there is a lack of appreciation for the caring labor women provide in addition to any paid work they may do, women face large obstacles to achieving equality. The ethics of care never loses sight of the labor involved in childcare, health care, caring for the elderly, and many other pursuits. The central values of care ethics can also inform our response to the enormous global problem of violence against women, reminding us that an adequate response must include not only punishing offenders, but also caring for victims and, especially, promoting the kind of care and education of children that will reduce such violence in the future. In general, social policies should encourage the caring relations that sustain persons, both those of family and personal friendship and the broader civic friendship that supports healthy societies. Caring relations between citizens are fostered by policies that recognize persons' interdependence and the responsibility that society should take for the well-being of all its members.

Instead of rigid attitudes demanding heterosexuality, the ethics of care encourages appreciation of the caring relations that tie persons to each other, whatever their affective inclinations. Among the most important factors in fostering acceptance of homosexuality in U.S. society has been that, as gays and lesbians have become increasingly open, more people have realized that they have gay relatives and acquaintances whom they care about. If such people are at all caring, they do not want their gay children, other relatives, or friends to suffer needless pain. They should not want anyone to suffer needless pain, of course, but they may be relatively indifferent toward gay strangers, thinking their pain unfortunate but necessary to maintain standards of heterosexuality. The pain of one's own child or friend, however, is likely to be weighed differently. For a justice-based moral theory, this difference is an unfortunate fact of psychology that should not be taken as morally significant. The ethics of care, in contrast, acknowledges the difference as significant, while also encouraging people to move from empathizing with the pain of those close to us to empathizing also with those more distant. In this way, although the greater openness of gays and lesbians provokes inevitable backlash, the ethics of care can promote and accelerate the trend toward acceptance.[7]

In fact, the ethics of care may be especially helpful in dealing with the backlash provoked by women's progress and by the increasing acceptance of diverse gender identities. To counter the hostility, its sources need to be understood. For instance, it is important to understand the threatened sense of masculinity felt by young men with few social and economic prospects; care as well as firmness or punitive legal measures may be needed in efforts to deflect these young men's rage that so often leads to violence. An example of this caring approach is the Scandinavian group EXIT, which helps young men caught up in neo-Nazi and skinhead organizations to leave them and reclaim their lives. Sponsored by the Swedish government, EXIT has expanded into Norway and Denmark. The young men that EXIT helps have a strong sense of masculine entitlement, yet feel humiliated and powerless due to downsizing and outsourcing; many work only sporadically and are filled with hatred for immigrants. They typically feel emasculated, too, by the changing status of women, and they join neo-Nazi groups as a masculinizing project. Often they have been bullied. EXIT provides safe houses and support for them to move on (Kimmel 2006).

Defending the rights of gays, lesbians, bisexuals, and transgendered persons to nondiscriminatory treatment is certainly important. While such rights can be based on the abstract principles of justice and equality offered by dominant moral theories, the willingness actually to respect such rights depends on the deeper acceptance that is fostered by caring relations; their mere rational acknowledgment can be of very limited use. Virtue theory can provide useful supplementary understandings; however, which virtues to acknowledge and how they should be interpreted are highly contested.

In particular, virtue theory itself may not make clear why we should accept a plurality of gender identities rather than the standard bifurcation. And in its focus on the dispositions of individuals, virtue theory may miss the central importance of caring *relations*. The ethics of care, in contrast, can assert persuasively the values of caring relations, whatever the gender identities of the persons involved.

Consider gay marriage. Should it be defended based on arguments for all persons' rights to enter into this institution? Questions about which rights all persons have, beyond the very most basic, are often bitterly contested and are not clearly answered by dominant theories of rights. Thus, rights-based arguments concerning gay marriage can become a replay of the Hart/Devlin debate in England concerning the legal status of homosexual acts (Hart 1966). Those persuaded that (as Lord Devlin argued) permitting homosexual acts would undermine society hold that no right to engage in such acts should be legally recognized. For the most part, in contemporary liberal democracies, those agreeing with H.L.A. Hart that, in the absence of harm, law should not enforce morality as such have won this argument: even those who believe that homosexual acts are immoral often agree that the law should not prohibit them. But in the U.S. debate concerning gay marriage, far more people lean toward a position analogous to Devlin's, that because in their view gay marriage undermines the family and, through it, society itself, gay marriage should remain legally prohibited.

To a Kantian, rights should be respected regardless of whether doing so contributes to the general welfare, and this is a strength of the theory. But whether, on this theory, gays have rights to enter into the legal institution of marriage may be unclear. Since marriage is publicly recognized, the right to marry, unlike the right to engage in private homosexual acts, would not flow from the right to privacy. A Kantian would hold that, just as it is not a violation of Kantian respect for persons that those who lack the financial resources cannot own houses, so it is not a violation that same-sex partners fail to qualify for marriage.

A more promising and persuasive approach is to argue that caring relations have value, and that permitting and even fostering them is of value to persons and societies. Marriage represents a deep caring relation between persons and should be open to nonheterosexuals as well as to heterosexuals. One can argue that marriage as presently constituted is such a flawed institution that lesbians and gays should reject it (Card 1996a), but as long as marriage is an important part of the basic structure of societies, gays and lesbians should be able to participate in it if they wish to. Excluding them from the institution of marriage is unjust, as one can try to use dominant moral theories to argue, but perhaps even more importantly, the values of caring relations should be cultivated. Similar arguments extend to adoption, parental rights, and the other ways in which society now structures its "private sphere" to favor heterosexuals (Calhoun 1994). That children do well in families with gay parents should be made widely known. That permitting gay marriage will be good for society as well as for gays may sound like a utilitarian argument, but the argument I have in mind appeals not to individual preferences or utility maximization, but rather to the values of care. It would thus avoid the pitfalls of a utilitarian calculation that, in a society with many homophobic people, might turn out to permit restricting marriage in ways such people would favor.

Concerning gender identity of any kind, the ethics of care understands that pleasure that does not cause harm is of value. Hence sexual pleasure can be a highly important good, as well as an important support for caring relations. The aspects of gender identity that contribute to sexual pleasure, and to its pleasurable anticipation, can also be goods. The playfulness and openness possible in deep caring relations have value, and they may take sexual forms. Gender identity magnified by distinctive dress and decoration is not inherently harmful, though such uncomfortable and confining clothing as the Islamic chador and even headscarf should not be required, only permitted as an expression of affiliation. By the same token, Western standards of appearance that demand many hours of attention to hair, skin, and form, and that waste significant economic resources that could be better spent, should certainly be subjected to critique by the ethics of care. Caring persons will promote the appreciation of multiple gender identities and the avoidance of punitive policing.

On the other hand, the ethics of care values sensitivity and consideration for those who are offended by oversexualized displays. To object to gays who "flaunt" their sexuality while accepting heterosexuals' flaunting of theirs is unfair discrimination, and even a caring person need not respect the feelings of the merely prejudiced (though prudence may counsel awareness of those feelings). With regard to those who are made uncomfortable by any highly sexual displays, however, care would recommend sensitivity and respect for privacy, though one might continue to try to persuade such persons that their discomfort is misplaced if one believes it to be so.

Finally, concerning the commercial exploitation of bodies and sexuality that has reached such new heights in recent years, the ethics of care, unlike dominant moral theories, can offer clear grounds for critique. Kantian ethics requires that persons not be used only as means, and that the rights of all persons be respected. But whether markets should expand to handle more and more human activities or be restricted to only certain activities is unclear on such a theory. As long as the rights of all are respected, Kantian theory does not indicate, for instance, whether persons should be cared for by doctors and in hospitals that operate according to market norms that prioritize commercial gain, or by those who give priority to the value of health over market gain. And while utilitarianism can recommend what is conducive to the general happiness, if the preferences of persons have been formed to favor market arrangements for given activities, utilitarianism has difficulty asserting other values in their place. The ethics of care, in contrast, can show how markets should be limited and how non-market values should have priority in such activities as childcare, health care, education, and the production of culture (for further discussion, see Held 2006, Chapter 7). It can show, too, that the values in free but considerate expressions of sexuality and gender identity, and in caring relations, should have priority over market values in the uses made of our bodies.

Finally, media culture is among the most important forces shaping contemporary society, both locally and globally. It is most unfortunate that it is, in the U.S., governed almost entirely by the norms of the market rather than by those of free expression, aesthetic merit, and moral admirability. That even the news and other sources of information on which citizens must rely are similarly beholden to the demands of the market is a threat to democracy and political responsibility. In place of a media structured for greed and personal gain, the ethics of care provides the basis for an alternative structure as well as for the media's treatment of gender identity, along with other issues, to be consistent with the values of caring relations.

There is no doubt that issues of gender identity and of gender equality will remain contentious in an increasingly globalized world. I have argued here that the ethics of care, with its valuing of caring relations, offers the best guidance available for those seeking to deal responsibly with the conflicts and possibilities involved.

NOTES

1. This paper was originally written for a conference on "Gender Identity in a Globalized Society" that was organized by the Social Trends Institute and held in Barcelona, Spain, October 13–14, 2006. I am very grateful to the editors of this volume for helpful suggestions on that earlier version of the paper.

2. For discussion, see Fausto-Sterling (2000).

3. For an illuminating discussion of the development of sexual and gender identities and a critique of Judith Butler's account, see Ferguson (2005).

4. For further discussion, see Held (2002).

5. For further discussion, see Held (1993).

6. This section is based in part on my book *The Ethics of Care: Personal, Political, and Global* (2006).

7. I do not mean that the goals of lesbians and gays should be mere acceptance or assimilation into the social institutions of a heterosexist society, any more than the goals of women as women should be mere integration into the structures of sexist society. Nor do I mean to suggest that the goals of nonheterosexuals are the same as those of feminists. See, e.g., Calhoun (1994) and the discussion of this and Calhoun's other articles in *Hypatia*'s "Author Meets Critics Panel" (Cuomo 1998).

2

ADDRESSING HUNGER
AND POVERTY

4

Caring Globally

Jane Addams, World War One, and International Hunger

Marilyn Fischer

Several feminist philosophers, including Virginia Held, Joan Tronto, and Fiona Robinson, see the need for, and the potential of, care ethics for achieving far-reaching political and even global transformation. Tronto recommends that care be used as "a basis for political change" and a "strategy for organizing" (Tronto 1993, 175). Held advocates that "the ethics of care should transform international politics and relations between states as well as within them" (Held 2006, 161). During and immediately after World War One, Jane Addams attempted to do just that. She sought to bring perspectives and moral sensibilities that have since been theorized in the ethics of care to bear on concrete, international problems. She worked with the U.S. Food Administration to meet the needs of Europeans who faced malnutrition and starvation because of the war and advocated that the League of Nations adopt as its first and foundational task feeding all those made hungry by the war. In her work on behalf of these organizations, Addams presented a theoretical framework of global ethics that connected women's care-giving activities with structuring international institutions principally in response to basic human needs.

After briefly describing current views on care's potential for international ethics, I will describe how Addams tried to place American women in relations of caring connection with the hungry in Europe. I will then show how she used the proposed League of Nations as a focal point for an international ethic based on meeting human needs. I will conclude by projecting how Addams would respond to contemporary concerns about extending care into the international arena, specifically concerns about how to care for those far distant, and about how to avoid maternalism/paternalism or imperialism in one's efforts to care. To avoid anachronism, I do not claim that Addams's theory was an ethics of care. Her conceptual framework relied upon outdated conceptual apparatus, particularly nineteenth century theories of evolutionary anthropology and psychology. However, Addams's patterns of thought are strikingly similar to those used by contemporary care theorists, and her responses to their concerns may be helpful today.

CARE'S POTENTIAL FOR POLITICAL AND GLOBAL TRANSFORMATION

Tronto and Held claim that care is a political concept, one that is useful beyond the personal or familial levels of relation. Tronto writes that through exercising the practice of care, with its components of attentiveness, responsibility, competence, and responsiveness, people develop the skills and capacities they need to function as democratic citizens (Tronto 1993, 167–68, 161–62).[1] Held argues that care is more embracive than concepts of justice or rights, and takes priority over justice and rights both in the family and in the social and political realms. Caring relations create and sustain the degrees of trust and social cohesion that are prerequisite to respecting rights and working out issues of justice (Held 2006, 135–36).

As a political concept, care can function as a useful lens for analysis and critique. It can point out the limitations of liberal theory, revealing how liberalism's emphasis on autonomy and rational agreement masks the amount of care-giving and interdependence upon which autonomy rests (Tronto 1993, 162–63). Instead of focusing exclusively on the procedural and contractual dimensions of politics and the market, a care perspective asks how well political and economic institutions foster cooperative and consensual working relations and serve basic human needs for health care, education, and so on (Held 2006, 159–68).

Held and Robinson claim that a care ethic is relevant in analyzing international relations. A care perspective focuses attention on the inadequacies of the Hobbesian conception of an anarchic collection of sovereign nation-states, accompanied by unbounded global market relations (Held 2006, 154; Robinson 1999, 55–56, 81–82). Held envisions that if practices of care were improved and extended globally, the military-industrial complex and the market driven excesses of globalization could be restrained. A care analysis would make explicit the masculinist cast to these practices, in which women's and children's safety and well-being are disproportionately disadvantaged (Held 2006, 159–67). Robinson advocates a "critical ethics of care" for examining international relations, one that views the world in terms of the moral relationships in which people are engaged and the institutional structures in which those relationships are enacted. A care perspective assesses those relationships and structures in terms of how well they meet needs, facilitate and sustain care, and prevent conflict and injustice from arising (Robinson 1999, 2, 110, 29–32).

A care perspective places relationships, rather than the autonomous individual of liberal theory, at the center of analysis. To capture the dynamics of relationships, a care perspective is particularly attentive to context, noting concrete interactions among persons within the environments in which they function. Narratives, with their ability to show the interplay between intellect, emotion, and action, are particularly appropriate for describing these contextual features. In what follows I will tell the story of how Addams used moral sensibilities and methods of analysis that today's care ethicists employ to create cross-national ties of understanding and affection, and to advocate for an international order founded on meeting human needs.[2]

WEAVING WEBS OF CONNECTION: ADDAMS AND THE U.S. FOOD ADMINISTRATION

The Great War began in Europe in August 1914 when the Central Powers of Germany and Austria-Hungary aligned against the Triple Entente of Great Britain, France, and Russia. The United States remained neutral until April 1917. Once the U.S. entered the war, Addams worked under the auspices of the U.S. Food Administration, directed by Herbert Hoover, to ameliorate disruptions of the food supply caused by war. Hoover, having made his fortune as an international mining engineer, was in London when the war began. At close range he watched Germany march across Belgium, disrupting its fields and cutting its supply lines for importing food. By October Belgium's prospects were bleak; Hoover was told that Brussels had only four days' supply of flour left. Using an engineer's efficiency at problem solving and dedicated to public service, he quickly organized the Commission for Relief in Belgium, and found cash, grain, meat supplies, and ways of delivering food to hungry people throughout Belgium and German-occupied Northern France (Smith 1984, 78, 81–82). His biographer, George H. Nash, gives this assessment: "For the next 2$\frac{1}{2}$ years Hoover's London-based organization, in collaboration with the Belgians' own Comité National, acquired, transported, and distributed over 2,500,000 tons of foodstuffs to more than 9,000,000 helpless people in Belgium and German-occupied northern France. An emergency relief effort directed by an American engineer evolved into a gigantic humanitarian undertaking without precedent in history" (Nash 1996, 4).

When the U.S. entered the war in April 1917, the food needs in Europe continued, while the food supply in the U.S. was itself unstable. The 1916 harvest had been weak, food supplies were tight, and prices rose very rapidly. Women marched and protested; food riots broke out in northeastern cities (Nash 1996, 9). President Wilson appointed Hoover to head the U.S. Food Administration, with the authority to regulate all aspects of food production, distribution, and pricing. Using a blend of regulatory control and calls for voluntary cooperation, Hoover set out to meet his objectives of delivering enormous quantities of food to the Allied populations in Europe, while keeping food supplies and prices at home within reasonable limits (Nash 1996, 25, 31).

Under his slogan, "Food Will Win the War," Hoover sought to persuade the American public to conserve food in every possible way. Hoover knew that women were crucial to the war effort, as they prepared most of the food for America's 22 million households. To him, women were "a great army drafted by conscience into what is now the most urgent activity of the war" (Nash 1996, 153). He enlisted public relation firms, news organizations, teachers, ministers, children's clubs, restaurants, and schools in the effort. This voluntary cooperation, he believed, was more American, more democratic, more efficient and effective, than Europe's formal programs of food rationing (Nash 1996, 153–58, 18–19).

Before the war, Addams had been widely admired for her work with immigrants at the Hull House settlement in Chicago, for her efforts on behalf of women's suffrage, and for her many books and articles. After the U.S. entered the war in April 1917, however, Addams's opposition to the war quickly made her a *persona non grata*. Most of her family and the majority of Hull House residents supported the war (Linn 1935/2000, 332); fellow pragmatists such as Dewey and Mead did as well (Dewey 1917, 267; Mead 1917). Civil liberties were suppressed, greatly restricting what Addams and her fellow pacifists could say. Newspaper accounts eliding "pacifist" with "traitor" and "pro-German" were ubiquitous (Addams 1922/ 2002, 43). Addams herself was placed under surveillance by the Department of Justice (Davis 1973/2000, 247). Addams opposed war, arguing that hostility and violence are destructive to mutual tolerance, understanding and willingness to cooperate, without which democracy is impossible. To Wilson's claim that he was making the world safe for democracy, Addams responded, "Was not war in the interest of democracy for the salvation of civilization a contradiction of terms, whoever said it or however often it was repeated?" (Addams 1922/2002, 82).[3]

Addams knew Hoover from his work in Belgium; their paths had overlapped in 1915 when Addams was in Europe for the meeting of the International Congress of Women at the Hague. Addams welcomed Hoover's invitation to work on behalf of the Food Administration (Linn 1935/2000, 330). This gave Addams the "anodyne of work" she had been craving, thinking that "here was a line of activity into which we might throw ourselves with enthusiasm" (Addams 1922/2002, 43, 44). She particularly enjoyed speaking to members of the country's extensive network of women's clubs, saying that such work was "both an outlet and a comfort to me" (Addams 1917e).[4]

In her speeches to these clubwomen, Addams fulfilled her responsibilities to the Food Administration. She outlined the dimensions of the food crisis, giving many details of crop failures in France and Italy, of famine in Russia (Addams 1918a, 1659–60). She encouraged her audience members to plant backyard gardens, to cut back on fats, sugar, wheat, and red meat, substituting perishables for foods that could be shipped (Addams 1917d, 1596). She gave specific advice: "One potato used universally instead of a slice of bread is many million bushels of wheat a year. A universal corn muffin at breakfast instead of a piece of toast is so many million bushels more" (Addams 1917c, 1574).

However, in other ways, Addams's speeches did not conform to Food Administration expectations. Taking hold of Hoover's statement that "the situation is more than war, it is a problem of humanity," Addams placed her emphasis entirely on addressing the "problem of humanity," without mentioning the partisan task of winning the war (Addams 1917d,1587). Absent from her speeches were popular Food Administration slogans such as "Sow the Seeds of Victory," "Every Garden a Munitions Plant" and "Food is Ammunition: Don't Waste It."[5]

Addams's reasoning patterns in these speeches will feel familiar to readers of feminist ethics today, although some of the specific content is outdated. For Addams, the purpose of these speeches was to help clubwomen and their families find the "motive power" to make extensive changes in their habits of food preparation and consumption (Addams 1918a, 1670). Robinson shows a similar appreciation for motives when she writes, "From the perspective of an ethics of care, it is our personal and social relations—our feelings of connection and responsibility—which motivate us to focus our attention and respond morally to the suffering of others" (Robinson 1999, 157). Addams wanted the audience members to construct such feelings of connection and responsibility, hoping they would "so enlarge their conception of duty that the consciousness of the world's needs for food should become the actual impulse of their daily activities" (Addams 1922/ 2002, 47).

Enlarging their conception of duty would require a synthesis of intellect, emotion, and action. Addams told her audiences, "A great world purpose cannot be achieved without our participation founded upon an intelligent understanding—and upon the widest sympathy. At the same time the demand can be met only if it is attached to our domestic routine, its very success depending upon a conscious change and modification of our daily habits" (Addams 1918a, 1665). Care ethicists today could identify elements in this statement with the practice of care. With sympathetic attentiveness and an intelligent understanding of the needs to be addressed, one takes responsibility by structuring one's activities in response to these needs (Held 2006, 39, 119; Tronto 1993, 102–5).

Addams tried to place her audience members in what Robinson terms a "relational ontology—that is, from the position of a self delineated through connection" (Robinson 1999, 39). Held describes this as seeing persons "enmeshed in relations with others" (Held 2006, 156). The challenge for Addams was enormous: to help audience members see themselves "enmeshed in relations" with people who lived thousands of miles away, and whom they had never seen. This sense of relationship would need to be strong and deep enough for the women and their families willingly to alter their food habits and the family dynamics associated with food, for the undetermined duration of the war, and beyond. The need for food was a powerful theme with which to make these connections. Tronto writes about care as "a universal aspect of life," noting how women throughout history have been associated with care (Tronto 1993, 110, 113). The need for food has been a constant, universal need throughout history and across all cultures. It has also been historically associated with women, defining their relations with and responsibilities to family and social group.

Today's theorists stress context and narrative as appropriate methodologies for care ethics (Held 2006, 157; Walker 1998, 109–15). Addams created narratives about the need for food through the very specific context of the clubwomen's activities. She described the audience members as women "who are accustomed to look at questions from the larger horizon," drawing on the clubwomen's penchant for study groups (Addams 1917c, 1575).[6] Addams told an audience, "And because thousands of women made a sustained effort to comprehend the world in which we live, it may now be possible to summon to the aid of the clubwomen everywhere an understanding of woman's traditional relation to food, of her old obligation to nurture the world" (Addams 1918a, 1666). That is, by connecting what the women were being asked to do for the hungry in Europe with "woman's traditional relation to food" as described in literature with which they were familiar, Addams hoped that the women would be able to see themselves as partners in a much larger drama.

Drawing on myth and anthropological theories of the day, Addams wove webs of connection temporally back to the Neolithic era, and spatially across continents. Addams took her audience back to hunter-gatherer days, telling them, "Students of primitive society believe that women were the first agriculturists and were for a long time the only inventors and developers of its processes" (Addams 1918a, 1667).[7] In this narrative, Addams presented women's traditional activities regarding food as activities of nurture, as taking responsibility for the needs of their families and tribe. Addams's narrative stressed the political and economic dimensions of nurture, with women as strong agents of change. When the women could not carry out their care-giving responsibilities under hunter-gatherer patterns of food procurement, they insisted that their tribes adopt settled habitats and agricultural patterns that were adequate for carrying out their responsibilities to feed. Addams also added a mythic and religious dimension to this account. Noting that myths present a people's morality in narrative form and that their basic truths are often later confirmed by science, Addams reminded her audiences of Demeter, the Corn Mother, the Rice Mother, and other female deities of food found in myths from all over the world (Addams 1918a, 1666).[8]

To us today it seems a long distance from Neolithic women to the clubwomen Addams was addressing. She bridged this distance by talking about recent immigrants to the U.S. and peasants from around the world, telling her audience, "Those of us who have lived among immigrants realize that there is highly developed among them a certain reverence for food. Food is the precious stuff which men live by, that which is obtained only after long and toilsome labor." She spoke of having seen peasant women all over Europe, in Palestine, and in Egypt, working the fields, carrying water, and grinding grain (Addams 1917d, 1600, 1605). She mentioned Russian peasant soldiers, eager to leave the field of battle and perform "bread labor," working the land to feed their families.[9] Her immigrant neighbors and these peasants were living connections to the ancient deities of Corn and Rice, embodied in myth.

In moving seamlessly from Neolithic women to immigrants and peasants of her day, Addams was calling upon her own and the clubwomen's familiarity with how anthropologists wrote at that time. Their reasoning seems dizzy to us today, but the convention was to use the practices of existing nonindustrialized cultures, which they called "primitive" and "uncivilized," as evidence for the practices of Neolithic cultures.[10] It is true that these theories embodied racist and cultural stereotypes and were often used to reinforce western imperialism. However, Addams gives these theories an interesting twist. Rather than presenting immigrants and peasants as the "other," Addams in effect framed the clubwomen as the "other," and their activities as the exception rather than as standard practice. It was only because industrial methods were used in U.S. agriculture that the women had leisure to form such clubs. It was only because of their exceptional circumstance that the past seemed so past to them, rather than being in vivid connection with the present (Addams 1917d, 1605).

Addams also connected the Neolithic past to the present through her appeal to "primitive instincts." Theorists at that time often referred to a variety of instincts, acquired in early stages of human evolution, to explain human behavior. War was a demonstration of the instinct of pugnacity, or the fighting instinct, allied with a host of other instincts. The question under debate was whether and how these instincts leading to war could be controlled, redirected, or subordinated to the social instincts.[11] Using this logic, Addams appealed to the clubwomen's instincts to feed the helpless, which she claimed were a million years older than the instinct to fight in war. She asked, "Could not the earlier instinct and training in connection with food be aroused and would it be strong enough to overwhelm and quench the later tendency to war?" (Addams 1922/2002, 44).[12]

In these speeches Addams appealed to sensibilities and methodologies utilized by care ethicists today. She showed sensitivity to context by drawing on the clubwomen's ongoing study and activism. She used narrative, incorporating information about food needs in Europe with anthropological and psychological theories of the time. She hoped this would prepare the clubwomen intellectually and emotionally to enmesh themselves within webs of connection, leading to humanitarian activism that was international in scope.

A NEW INTERNATIONAL ORDER BASED ON AN INTERNATIONAL ETHIC OF NURTURE

In her speeches on behalf of the Food Administration, Addams identified the efforts underway to feed the hungry in the Allied nations as "a new internationalism" and "a new international ethic" (Addams 1918a, 1670; 1922/2002, 49). Her advocacy for the Food Administration and for the proposed League of Nations was essentially an argument for placing an international ethic of nurture at the heart of the international order.

During the war Americans widely believed that the international order needed to be reconstituted. President Wilson justified both the United States' initial neutrality, and its subsequent participation in the war, in terms of his ability to influence the reconstruction of the international order after the war ended (Knock 1992, 34, 96, 118, 121; Addams 1922/ 2002, 38). People along the entire political spectrum agreed that the old international order was bankrupt, although they disagreed about what form a new order should take (Knock 1992, Chapter 4).

To Addams, the need for a new international order, structured by an international, humanitarian ethic, was apparent; the war itself was a devastating demonstration of that. In a May 1917 speech, given shortly after the U.S. entered the war, Addams said, "May we not say in all sincerity that for thirty-three months Europe has been earnestly striving to obtain through patriotic wars, that which can finally be secured only through international organization? Millions of men, loyal to one international alliance, are gallantly fighting millions of men loyal to another international alliance, because of Europe's inability to make an alliance including them all" (Addams 1917a, 160).

Much like Held and Robinson, Addams associated flaws in the old international order with classical liberalism, which she termed "the eighteenth century conception."[13] That international order was essentially a Hobbesian state of nature among nation-states that claimed exclusive rights of sovereignty. Addams argued against that order on grounds that it was "maladjusted" to meeting the most pressing needs of the time. Addams often used the notion of "adjustment" in identifying moral and social concerns that needed to be addressed. In her 1902 book, *Democracy and Social Ethics*, her basic argument was that a morality based on individual virtues, and governance based on protecting individual rights, were maladjusted to meeting the needs of a highly interdependent, urbanized, industrialized society. Analogously, the international order as constituted before the war was maladjusted to addressing the central issues of the day. These issues were international in character, having social and economic, as well as political dimensions that crossed national lines (Addams 1919b, 1859–66).

Addams made this claim in her many speeches on behalf of the proposed League of Nations. One example she frequently used to illustrate the failures of the old international order was the political response to repeated cholera epidemics in Europe from 1851 onward. Political representatives, she claimed, "got so mixed up in questions of national prestige, of national honor, of not giving over to some other nations their national prerogatives that after they had met for months, they disbanded and did nothing whatever about quarantining cholera." Only after meeting six times in forty years could they arrive at a minimal and largely ineffective agreement. Meanwhile, international medical associations found some ways to work around this political impasse, but the eighteenth century conception of sovereignty hindered efforts toward effective, international public health measures (Addams 1919b, 1855–56).

Furthermore, living and working with immigrants, and with families of mixed national citizenship, enabled Addams to offer more intimate illustrations of how maladjusted the old international order was. She told audiences about a widow in Illinois who could get a state pension for her U.S.-born 3-year-old son, while she could not get a pension for her 5-year-old who was born in Italy.[14] He "needed exactly the same thing his brother needed, but was not getting it because we are still going along in this old Eighteenth Century nationalism" (Addams 1919c, 0011). This example illustrates how even national policies based on humanitarian motives did not map onto the needs of actual, existing families. Only international coordination and cooperation, transcending particular nationalisms, could deal adequately with these needs.

In the liberal conception, peaceful relations between nations are essentially commercial ones, based on national self-interest. According to Addams, these commercial relations were also maladjusted to meeting human needs. Addams noted, "In international affairs the nations have still dealt almost exclusively with political and commercial affairs considered as matters of "rights," consequently they have never been humanized in their relations to each other" (Addams 1918a, 1669). Even food, essential for human survival, was treated as a purely commercial commodity, and exchanged only when profitable. This commercial basis for relations among independent, sovereign states, Addams called "that aspect of national life which is least human and least spiritual" (Addams 1918b, 176). In a similar vein, Held points out how the market system is at times inimical to care. Noting the pernicious effects of increasing commercialization on health care, education, and other care-giving functions, Held argues that fostering caring relations should be the guide for assessing where limits on markets should be drawn (Held 2006, Chapter 7).

The end of the war was a historic pivot point, a brief window of opportunity for making Addams's proposed new international ethic truly international by extending the feeding programs to include the Central Powers. All across Europe, a desperate need for food aid would continue after the Armistice until crops could be planted and harvested, and transportation and distribution networks reestablished. Hoover returned to Europe and, as Director-General of Relief for the Allied and Associated Powers and Chair of the American Relief Administration, organized food delivery to people in over twenty nations, many of which had barely functioning governments (Nash 2003, 52–53).[15] Hoover, Addams, and others were horrified when the victorious allies stated their intention to keep the naval blockade against Germany in place after the armistice was signed on November 11, 1918, and not to lift it until Germany agreed to the terms of the peace treaty (Nash 1996, 494).[16]

Traveling with the Friends Service Committee in summer 1919, Addams was one of the first Americans to enter Germany after the war (Hamilton 1943/1985, 243). After seeing listless, skeletal children in cities all across Germany, Addams and her traveling companion, Dr. Alice Hamilton, wrote, "What they are facing is the shipwreck of a nation and they realize that if help does not come quickly and abundantly this generation in Germany is largely doomed to early death or a handicapped life" (Addams and Hamilton 1919, 210). Addams noted that without adequate nutrition, German citizens would be incapable of exercising the democratic rights and responsibilities that the Allied victors were demanding of them (Addams 1919c, 0014). This was a concrete manifestation of Held's insight that having needs for care met is prerequisite to exercising the responsibilities of citizenship and addressing issues of rights and justice (Held 2006, 135–36).

Addams recommended that the fundamental, organizing function of the new League of Nations should be feeding all those made hungry by the war, thereby placing an international, humanitarian ethic at the League's very center. Just as the members of the women's clubs needed a motive with which to stretch their sense of obligation, so Addams asks, "Must not the League evoke a human motive transcending and yet embracing all particularist nationalisms, before it can function with validity?" (Addams 1922/2002, 115). The League needed a motive strong enough to make the trajectory of cooperation, already established among the Allies and enacted in their food programs, fully international by extending it to include the hungry among their former enemies. Only in this way could the new international order overcome the hypernationalism that led to the destructiveness of war (Addams 1922/2002, 98). Just as Addams asked the clubwomen to bring their obligation to family into adjustment with meeting food needs in Europe, so she asked that national loyalties be adjusted in response to international, humanitarian needs.

Seen from the viewpoint of changing the international order from one based on liberalism to one based on a humanitarian ethic, Addams's proposal may seem revolutionary and perhaps idealistic. Addams did not see it this way. She claimed she was not giving an idealistic call for peace and harmony among nations. Her proposal, she claimed was based on "actual achievements" rather than being "a counsel of perfection" ("Addams 1918b, 180). Addams identified herself as a sociologist; much of her theorizing took the form of identifying emerging patterns in the social and political landscape. Thus, her ethical arguments often took the form of identifying which emerging patterns, if encouraged and reinforced, could lead to social justice and international cooperation and well-being. In keeping with her theme of adjustment, Addams pointed out that many of the humanitarian motives and practices needed for a new international order were already in place. Extending these to include former enemies was more a matter of continued adjustment than of radical change (Addams 1919a, 1836–38).

Addams located the Allied food programs within several of these emerging patterns. She considered the progressive social reform legislation enacted in the United States, Germany, Great Britain, and other counties as evidence that within individual nations, nurture of life and obligations of care-taking were coming to be seen as legitimate governmental functions. The process was gradual, but signaled a fundamental change in the nature of government itself, i.e., nurture was gradually replacing military control and protection of property rights as the state's primary responsibility. Although the circumstances were tragic, the war was the historical occasion through which a parallel development was emerging among nations (Addams 1918a, 1669). Addams noted that of the world's forty-eight nations, thirty-four Allied and neutral nations had already institutionalized structures, organized expressly to meet humanitarian needs, replacing "commercial motives" with humanitarian ones (Addams 1919a, 1834; 1919b, 1857). She pointed to the maps in Hoover's Paris office that located existing food supplies and ships as concrete indications of this (Addams 1922/2002, 95).

Also, those women and families who had participated in the U.S. Food Administration program during the war had already stretched their intellects and sympathy and adjusted their daily routines to provide for the hungry in Europe (Addams 1919a, 1834). In a speech on behalf of the League of Nations, Addams told the audience that through this effort, "Thousands of men, women and children not only entered European life through a sense of participation in a great cause; they entered it through an enlargement of their sympathies, through a stretching out of their imagination, so that they knew not only with their means ["minds" was most likely meant here—ed.], but they knew with their deepest sympathetic understanding that those people were dependent upon them, and dependent upon them almost hourly" (Addams 1919c, 0013).

Addams projected a hope that if food needs were addressed through the League of Nations irrespective of national borders, participants would continue to develop the sympathy and the skills at cooperative action and organization with which to address other international issues and concerns. She wrote, "Could [the League] have considered this multitude of starving children as its concrete problem, feeding them might have been the quickest way to restore the divided European nations to human and kindly relationship. . . . Might not the very recognition of a human obligation irrespective of national boundaries form the natural beginning of better international relationships?" (Addams 1922/2002, 98). If nations could cooperate on providing food, these acts might restore them "to human and kindly relationship." This would strengthen the attitudes and habits of international cooperation needed for dealing with other pressing issues of the day (Addams 1918a, 1670). Here Addams indicated that she, like Held, believed that attending to nurture and care creates a basis of social trust and cooperation upon which just decisions can be made.

As the League began to function, Addams was disheartened when she saw that the League's "first work involves the guaranteeing of a purely political peace and a dependence upon the old political motives" (Addams 1920, 217). She described the League's first representatives as "fumbling awkwardly at a new task for which their previous training in international relations had absolutely unfitted them" (Addams 1922/2002, 114). Unlike the clubwomen, these representatives had not stretched and synthesized their intellects, emotions, and actions, and so they failed to bring local, national, and international obligations into adjustment.

RESPONDING TO CONCERNS ABOUT CARE ETHICS: CARING AT A DISTANCE AND AVOIDING IMPERIALISM

In much of the literature on care ethics, intimate settings form the paradigm for caring relations (Tronto 1993, 109; Held 2006, 32–33). Tronto worries about extending care to more distant arenas (Tronto 1993, 170). Held writes that it is possible to form caring relations with far-distant others, but does not elaborate on how to do this (Held 2006, 157). Addams did not offer arguments about whether or to what extent people in privileged positions had obligations toward needy, distant others, a question much debated by liberal theorists today.[17] Instead, she offered narratives to help people make conceptual or paradigm shifts, so as to locate themselves within webs of connection in which their responsibility and motivation for care would become obvious. We have already discussed how Addams used narratives about women's traditional relation to food and about primitive instincts to enable the clubwomen to understand and feel themselves connected with the hungry in Europe. Here are two additional narratives that Addams offered to diminish distance and enmesh people in caring relations.

The first narrative, sketched explicitly for the U.S. context, asked Americans to question the assumption that "distant others" are distant at all. Given the intense anti-immigrant rhetoric of the day and expressions of hostility given sanction by the war, it was an astonishing counter-narrative to the standard tales of American exceptionalism.[18] In her May 1917 speech for the City Club of Chicago, Addams made her point, as she so often did, by telling stories of her immigrant neighbors. Neighbors with relatives in European countries on both sides of the war, she pointed out, worried about their loved ones' suffering and deprivation. For those Americans who came from Germany and other nations of the Central Powers, the war was "exquisite torture." These neighbors' experiences with the war, Addams recounted, gave poignancy to "the cosmopolitanism which is the essence of (America's) spirit" (Addams 1917a, 158, 160). According to Addams, to be an American is to be connected by ties of history, blood, and labor to all the nations of the earth. Americans are members of a nation whose history is a story of migration, including involuntary migrations from Africa as well as Native Americans' forced internal migrations. When Americans understand and feel themselves so connected, for them there are no distant peoples. Americans cannot understand who they are without seeing themselves as enmeshed in relations that stretch across the globe. When Americans go to war, they go to war against themselves.

In the second narrative, Addams described how distance could be overcome through fostering an "international mind." Her use of the term gave a twist to its usual associations at that time. Nicholas Murray Butler, longtime president of Columbia University and of the Carnegie Endowment for International Peace, gave the phrase its prominence. In *The International Mind* Butler set forth his vision of a peaceful world of independent nations, linked through an international judiciary that derived its principles from natural, international law. Only those rare persons with this judicial temperament, Butler thought, had international minds (Butler 1912/1972, 73, 102; Herman 1969, Chapter 2). Butler's image of internationally minded persons is not far removed from that of many liberal cosmopolitans today. Robinson identifies these cosmopolitans as holding a Kantian-based ethic in which persons are viewed as abstract and autonomous, and as having a sense of duty guided by impartial and universal ethical principles (Robinson 1999, 54, 70).

Addams used the term "international mind" more widely to refer to many diverse groups of people, only some of whom might qualify under Butler's definition. For example, she included research scientists whose international connections were based on a shared dedication to the methods and findings of science, irrespective of national boundaries (Addams 1915, 91). Among the internationally minded Addams also included migrant farm workers who formed international connections as they traveled with the harvest, picking the crops from the southern to the northern halves of the western hemisphere. For Addams, an international mind was not achieved through intellectual abstraction, via respect for natural law or for the inherent dignity of all rational beings. Addams would agree with Robinson's criticism of liberal cosmopolitans insofar as they "ignore both the *particularity* and *connectedness* of persons" (Robinson 1999, 54). For Addams, people developed international minds in versions that reflected their own particular histories, through the connections they made with particular others. There are many paths through which understanding, affection, and ties of affiliation come to cross local and national boundaries.

Addams did not reject nationalism per se. She valued the love of country, as adjusted to one's plurality of affiliations. In her Presidential Address to the Women's International League for Peace and Freedom's 1924 Congress, Addams said, "In offering you this welcome I am speaking in a dual capacity as it were. First, as your international officer and servant, and second, as an American citizen. To my mind these dual roles do not conflict. I am not of those who believe that devotion to international aims interferes with love of country, any more than devotion to family detracts from good citizenship; rather as Mazzini pointed out, the duties of family, nation, and humanity are but concentric circles" (Addams 1924, 259). Holding onto what Robinson calls "a complex world composed of overlapping networks of personal and social relations" (Robinson 1999, 55), Addams maintained that becoming internationally minded included bringing one's plurality of affiliations and responsibilities into adjustment.

Thus, Addams's response to concerns about how to extend care to distant others employs the moral sensitivities and methods that care ethicists recommend. She closes distances through narratives that attend to persons' concrete contexts, forming webs of connection that cross political boundaries.

Interventions in the name of care or benevolence are not necessarily benign but can carry imperialistic overtones. Tronto worries about paternalism/maternalism that might accompany efforts to extend care beyond the intimate and local (Tronto 1993, 170). Held and Jaggar note imperialistic tendencies in both liberal feminist and radical feminist writings (Held 2006, 164; Jaggar 2005a, 185–86). Held states, "the ethics of care . . . must be attuned to the dangers of neocolonial insensitivities" (Held 2006, 165). Jaggar warns feminists in the global North against criticizing practices that oppress women in the global South without also attending to how structural features that carry this oppression are often strengthened by a history of western political and economic imperialism (Jaggar 2005a, 189–95).

Addams had expressed opposition to imperialism since 1899. During the Spanish American War she opposed not only the United States' territorial land-grabs, but also its commercial and economic imperialism (Addams 1899, 1900). Much as she supported President Wilson for maintaining U.S. neutrality during the early years of World War I, she condemned his imperialistic interventions in the Caribbean, Central America, and Mexico (Addams 1922/2002, Chapter 3).[19] Addams would agree with Jaggar that "social criticism should be immersed rather than detached and immanent rather than transcendent" and that people of privilege need to be self-reflective and aware of the power they bring to cross-national relationships (Jaggar 2005a, 189, 194). She would appreciate Held's insight that "Those from the global North need to listen and understand, as in friendship, rather than bestow limited benevolence" (Held 2006, 167). Where Addams is helpful, though sobering, is in her accounts of the process through which well-intentioned persons of privilege could reach the point Held and Jaggar recommend. Rather than asking, "How can people of privilege avoid imperialistic insensitivity?" Addams would reframe the question: "Through what processes can people of privilege mitigate these tendencies that are deeply inscribed in themselves?"

I will point to two discussions in which Addams described these processes. Both discussions illustrate how our perceptions and moral sensibilities are shaped and limited by the contexts in which we live, and indicate
that we change these sensibilities through action and through enlarging our
realms of experience. Addams wrote, "We are under a moral obligation in
choosing our experiences, since the result of those experiences must ultimately determine our understanding of life" (Addams 1902/2002, 8). As
we encounter new contexts of experience, we bring our limitations into
these encounters. Inevitably, we will blunder and offend, but given good-
will, attentiveness, and persistence, change is possible.

The first and more extended discussion is in Addams's chapter on the
charity visitor, a young, educated, well-meaning social worker, who visits
an Italian immigrant washerwoman to teach her and her family the virtues
that will lead to middle-class success (Addams 1902/2002, Chapter 2).
Through many perplexing encounters the young woman comes to recognize that her own values and perspectives are parochial, while the washerwoman's values are sensible adaptations to the problems posed by living
in urban poverty. Because she is attentive, open, and reflective, the charity
visitor mitigates her parochialism to some extent, though it is left ambiguous at the end of the chapter just how successful she has been.

A second, though less developed discussion comes from Addams's
speech at the National Conference on Foreign Relations in May 1917. She
pointed out how rubber workers in the Congo and diamond miners in
South Africa were exploited ruthlessly by the colonial powers, and advocated establishing an international commission that would give these workers protection. She asked, "What would be more natural than to begin the
new international morality, so sorely needed, with that simple impulse to
protect the weak?" (Addams 1917b, 166, 167) Here Addams appealed to
pity and benevolence as motives for intervention, motives that are often
accompanied by imperialistic tendencies. But her next move is instructive.
She went on to identify "three great human instincts or tendencies, exhib-
ited in striking degree by laborers . . . which I believe will in the long run
result in finer conceptions of internationalism." These were bread labor, the
instinct for workmanship, and a reverence for food, all well-known and
admired virtues at the time.[20] We can read Addams here as making the
point that though intervention may begin with pity, the privileged can
come to see that the recipients themselves have resources to offer. Toward
the end of the speech Addams observed, "Such a conception of international relationship may be sound not only because it is founded upon genuine experience, but because it reaches down into the wisdom of the
humble" (Addams 1917b, 167, 169). Even if one starts with pity, one's
relations can be transformed through attentive engagement toward equality
and reciprocity.

However, even if one's relations with others are transformed, this is not sufficient in itself to determine outcomes. Care ethicists recommend responsiveness to context in carrying out the practices of care. Addams knew from experience that contexts are ambiguous; one cannot anticipate, much less control, all the variables. This awareness underlies many of Addams's stories. A pacifist, she chose to run Hull House as a democracy. The Hull House residents, exercising democratic decision-making, chose to locate a draft office there. Addams recounts one draftee's bitterness as he said to her, "I really have you to thank if I am sent over to Europe to fight. I went into the citizenship class in the first place because you asked me to. If I hadn't my papers now I would be exempted" (Addams 1922/2002, 68). Addams was clear-headed about how irony and tragedy can accompany the most well-intentioned, well-planned, humanitarian practices.

Implicit in much of Addams's writings is the belief that all we can do is the best we can with what we have, and then treat gently and with tolerance those well-meaning people who see things differently. If this statement feels too sober, we can pair it with her statement of hope, uttered on a dark day shortly after the U.S. entered the war: "We realize that it is only the ardent spirits, the lovers of mankind, who will be able to break down the suspicion and lack of understanding which has so long stood in the way of the necessary changes upon which international good order depends" (Addams 1917a, 163). Addams deeply believed that humanitarian nurturance belongs at the heart of the international order, and she was willing to face ambiguity and failure to work toward that vision.

NOTES

1. Tronto writes that care is not the only political ideal; it needs to work in tandem with concepts of rights and justice, concern for due process, and so on (Tronto 1993, 161, 167, 169).

2. Addams used the term "international" where we today would use "transnational" or "cross-national" to describe relations among persons and groups that cross or transcend national boundaries. John Dewey captures this dimension of her thought in his foreword to the 1945 edition of *Peace and Bread in War Time*: "The process of organization upon which Miss Addams would have us depend is one which cuts *across* nationalistic lines. Moreover, instead of setting up a super-state, it also cuts *under* those lines" (Dewey 1945, 152). Addams also used "international" to refer to relations among nation-states. I will follow her pattern and use "international" for both meanings. The context should make clear which one is intended.

3. For discussions of Addams's pacifism see "Jane Addams's Pragmatist Pacifism" (Fischer 2000), and the editors' introductions to Thoemmes Press's four-volume set of Addams's peace writings (Fischer 2003a, 2003b; Whipps 2003a, 2003b).

4. For a history of Women's Clubs in the United States, see Anne Firor Scott, *Natural Allies: Women's Associations in Women's History* (Scott 1991).

5. Many internet sites and archives have images of Food Administration posters. See, for example, http://www.archives.gov/education/lessons/sow-seeds/ and http://library.fandm.edu/archives/spcoll/wwiartists.html.

6. For a history of women's clubs that focused on study, see Theodora Penny Martin, *The Sound of Our Own Voices: Women's Study Clubs 1860–1910* (Martin 1987).

7. Otis Tufton Mason makes this argument in *Woman's Share in Primitive Culture*. See Chapter 2, "The Food Bringer" (Mason 1898). Frazer also makes this point in *The Golden Bough*. See Chapter 17, "Woman's Part in Primitive Agriculture" (Frazer 1890/1991, 411–16).

8. See Frazer (1890/1991, 417–34).

9. See Addams's extensive discussion of bread labor in *Peace and Bread in Time of War* (1922/2002, Chapter 5), "A Speculation on Bread Labor and War Slogans."

10. In *Primitive Culture*, Tyler writes, "This hypothetical primitive condition corresponds in a considerable degree to that of modern savage tribes" (Tyler 1871/1958, 21). In *Ancient Society*, Morgan developed a highly detailed sequence of stages of social development from savage to barbarian to civilized. His evidence was based on his field research with Native American tribes (Morgan 1877/1963).

11. The following journal articles make this argument: George Malcolm Stratton, "The Docility of the Fighter" (1916); D.E. Phillips, "The Psychology of War" (1916); and Mary Whiton Calkins, "Militant Pacifism" (1917).

12. Spencer hypothesized that the earliest humans had instincts to aid the helpless and to care for their offspring (Spencer 1896, Vol. 1, Part 1, 6–7, 66–67). Nicolai, in *The Biology of War*, wrote, "Universal brotherhood among men is older and more primitive than all combat, which was not introduced among men until later" (Nicolai 1918, 15). Nasmyth, in *Social Progress and the Darwinian Theory*, writes that war was a relatively recent anthropological development (Nasmyth 1916/1973, 168).

13. Addams frequently criticized liberal theory. In *Newer Ideals of Peace*, for example, Addams scorned the enlightenment's autonomous, independent, self-interested man of nature, who "never existed save in the brain of the doctrinaire" Addams (1907/2003, 34).

14. For an introduction and collection of primary documents on widows' pensions, see Kleinberg, "How Did the Debate about Widows' Pensions Shape Relief Programs for Single Mothers, 1900–1940?" (Kleinberg 2005).

15. The need was enormous. In Austria, 96% of the children were suffering from malnutrition. It is estimated that Hoover and his organizations fed more than 83 million people between 1914 and 1923 (Nash 2003, 53–54).

16. A resolution to lift the blockade was passed unanimously at the May 1919 Congress of the Women's International League for Peace and Freedom in Zurich, of which Addams was president (Addams 1922/2002, 91–92). Many Americans, both public officials and citizens, were strongly opposed to feeding the enemy. A *Washington Post* editorial read, "Let the Enemy Starve First" (Nash 1996, 497–98).

17. See, for example, anthologies on global justice edited by Deen Chatterjee (2004) and Thomas Pogge (2001a).

18. For an account of the history and strength of myths of American exceptionalism, see Richard T. Hughes, *Myths America Lives By* (2003).

19. Addams's critiques evidently had an effect. As President of the Woman's Peace Party (WPP) and a founding member of the American Union Against Militarism (AUAM) she and others protested Wilson's military interventions in Mexico in 1916. Knock writes, "Although the evidence is not altogether conclusive, it appears that the crucial factor in averting war was a series of extraordinary steps taken by the AUAM and the WPP" (Knock 1992, 82).

20. Addams refers to Tolstoy's writings on "bread labor" (Addams 1922/2002, Chapter 5) and his belief that Russian peasants had an instinctual love for working the land. She attributes the "instinct for workmanship" to Veblen (Addams 1922/2002, 23–24). Veblen published *The Instinct of Workmanship and the State of the Industrial Arts* in 1914.

5

Food Fights

A Feminist Perspective

Victoria Davion

Food availability, food safety, and health are feminist issues which raise concerns ranging from local to global. Seventy percent of the world's population earn their livelihood producing food and, of these, a majority are women. It is women who are most often responsible for food shopping and for determining what their families will eat in situations where there is choice. In situations where food is scarce, it is often women and girls who eat last, or not at all (Shiva 2000). Issues of food availability are tied to those of human population and consumption, which in turn inevitably lead to debates over reproductive freedom, another perennial feminist concern. Finally, issues of food availability and safety raise questions about trust and the construction of knowledge, which are major topics in feminist epistemology and feminist ethics.

While I was writing this essay, there were food recalls in the U.S. on organic spinach, organic carrot juice, bagged lettuce, and tomatoes sold to restaurants. These recalls led to a flurry of newspaper articles and books on food issues, including a front page article in a recent edition of *The New York Times* that presented the results of the Hannaford supermarket chain's analysis of the nutritional value of foods labeled as "healthy." According to Hannaford's three-star rating system, seventy percent of the foods analyzed, "including many if not most of the processed foods that advertise themselves as good for you, received no stars at all" (*New York Times*, 6 November 2006). This is because many foods that are advertised as healthy because they are high in fiber have other problems such as containing too much fat, sugar, or salt. Such foods include V8 vegetable juice, Campbell's Healthy Request Tomato Soup, and most Lean Cuisine and Healthy Choice frozen dinners.

In this paper, I offer a feminist analysis of the ways in which issues of trust, ignorance, and fear have emerged in contemporary debates over the safety of genetically modified foods. I focus on arguments aimed primarily at U.S. consumers, and conclude by discussing the more global implications of my analysis. I begin with a feminist critique of arguments against the safety of GM foods based on the idea that such foods are "unnatural." I then examine two typical mainstream arguments, aimed at U.S. consumers, in favor of the safety of GM foods. The first argument is that, because most of us trust the government to regulate the industrial meat industry, we should also trust the government to regulate GM foods. The second is that GM foods are no less safe than organic foods, which themselves really aren't any safer, more environmentally friendly, or more cruelty free than their non-organic counterparts. Thus, these two arguments in combination purport to show that neither those of us who eat industrially produced meat nor those of us who eat organic foods have any good reason to reject GM foods. I focus on these particular arguments because they are typical of the mainstream philosophical debates, and because they raise crucial feminist issues such as trust, the construction of knowledge (and ignorance), and choice.

I shall conclude by arguing that comparisons with industrial meat production and organic foods do not offer convincing reasons for U.S. consumers to trust GM food, but rather point to a critique of large-scale industrial food production that has a variety of implications from local to global. Many who support the development and distribution of GM food argue that those who oppose it are not really concerned with its safety, but rather with critiquing capitalism and globalization more broadly. For example, in "Dr. Strangelunch: Why We Should Learn to Love Genetically Modified Food" (Pence 2002b), environmental journalist Ron Bailey, an avid supporter of GM food, writes, "As one tracks the war against green biotech, it becomes clearer that its leaders are not primarily concerned about safety. What they really hate is capitalism and globalization" (Bailey 2002b, 112). I shall argue that recent "food fights" reveal that concerns about food safety, capitalism, and globalization are profoundly interconnected. Hence, fears over the safety of GM foods are justified at all levels from local to global, even if such foods are not radically different from other industrially produced foods, because the systems in place to regulate industrially processed foods are themselves untrustworthy. Furthermore, many arguments urging people to trust GM foods based upon their existing food "choices" imply a neoliberal model of autonomous consumer choice that is highly problematic from a feminist perspective.

FEMINIST ETHICS AND GM FOODS

As I have already stated, questions about food safety and availability are obviously feminist. Feminism is concerned with issues that directly affect women. The fact that women comprise the majority of the seventy-five percent of the world's population that earns their livelihood producing food makes food production a major feminist concern. The fact that it is women and girls who often eat last or not at all when there isn't enough to go around makes food availability a major feminist issue. The fact that when there are choices to be made about what to eat, it is most often women who have the responsibility to choose wisely makes food choice a major feminist issue. For example, it is most likely to be women who are left wandering around supermarkets wondering about the nutritional value of foods in response to a survey like Hannaford's. Similarly, it is most likely women who will be left wondering whether to purchase GM foods, or whether organic foods are better than others, when such choices are available.

In addition to those mentioned above, debates over the safety and promise of GM foods raise other important feminist concerns. Contemporary debates have focused on whether GM foods are safe, where safety is often associated with the concepts of "nature" and the "natural." Hence, many who argue against the safety of GM foods argue that they are radically different than other foods and are therefore "unnatural" and unsafe, while many who argue in their favor maintain that GM foods are not radically different from other foods and are therefore not "unnatural" or unsafe.

Ecological feminists have supplied useful critiques of the ways in which terms such as "nature" and "natural" have functioned within traditional western frameworks. They argue that mainstream Western culture has devalued nature as "other," seeing it as inferior to "reason" and "culture." Understanding these prevailing attitudes toward nature requires understanding the reason/nature value dualism that underlies dominant western traditions. A value dualism is a disjunctive pair in which the disjuncts are seen as exclusive, oppositional, and radically different, and in which higher moral value is placed on one of the disjuncts. For example, in a reason/ nature dualism, whatever is associated with reason is thought to have a higher moral value than whatever is associated with nature. There are numerous dualistic pairs within traditional frameworks, including masculine/feminine (where masculinity is associated with reason), civilized/ primitive (where civilized is associated with reason), and light/dark (where light is associated with reason). Val Plumwood argues, however, that reason/nature is the central dualism that serves to legitimate the others in dominant western frameworks. Hence, ecological feminists argue that dualistic thinking legitimates and justifies a variety of oppressions (Plumwood 1993; Warren 1990).

Ecological feminists disagree about how to respond to dualistic thinking, and in particular to the reason/nature dualism. Some argue for a strategy of reversal, where that which is associated with nature is given higher value (Salleh 1984; Swimme 1990). Similarly, some of the contemporary debates concerning the safety of GM foods, although not explicitly feminist, associate being "natural" with being superior. Hence, many proponents of GM foods argue that genetic modification is just another step in plant breeding, rather than something radically different or "unnatural." For example, Norman Borlaug, former director of the Rockefeller Foundation's Mexican wheat program and winner of the 1970 Nobel Peace Prize for work done to improve food production around the world, states, "Thanks to the development of science over the past 150 years, we now have the insights into plant genetics and breeding to do what Mother Nature did herself in the past by chance or design. Genetic modification of crops is not some kind of witchcraft, rather it is the progressive harnessing of the forces of nature for the benefit of man" (in Pence 2002b, 77). Seeing genetic modification as an extension of what "Mother Nature" has already done is supposed to allay fears that it is a radical departure from past methods of food production and therefore "unnatural."

Others disagree, arguing that the products of genetic engineering are not extensions of traditional breeding methods, but something radically different, produced in a completely different way. According to Helena Norberg-Hodge et al., "This new technology manipulates organisms in a fundamentally different and hazardous new way, precisely because it allows us to transcend reproductive limitations imposed by nature, and because anticipated effects can never be certain" (in Pence 2002b, 203). Thus, on both sides of the debate, being "natural" is equated with being safe, legitimate, and otherwise acceptable.

Thus, both sides in this debate seem to appeal implicitly to a strategy of reversal, arguing that whatever is "natural" is superior to that which is not. Therefore, the debate within ecological feminism over the usefulness of the strategy of reversal offers some insight here. Many ecological feminists, including myself (Davion 1994), have argued that it is best to try to reject the categories that underlie dualistic thinking, rather than pursuing strategies of reversal. I have more recently argued that one can clearly see the problems with reversal in contemporary debates over another kind of genetic modification, reproductive cloning. Many critics of reproductive cloning argue that cloning is "unnatural," or that it "violates the natural order," because it produces life in a radically different way from what we are inclined to see as "natural." However, I argue that appeals to glorified conceptions of "nature," although they purport merely to describe "nature," are actually prescriptive, telling people what they ought to do. Feminists should beware of such appeals because they have often been used to justify hatred and oppression, as in the idea that homosexuality is wrong because it is "unnatural." Focusing on whether reproductive cloning is "natural" sidetracks the more important issues of possible risks and discussions of social justice (that is, of who will benefit from the development of such technologies) (Davion 2006). The same point applies to the GM food debates. Because the concept of what is "natural" is itself socially constructed, deciding whether GM foods should be considered "natural" really tells us very little, if anything, about what to do. Concerns about the safety of such foods (including those of health, the environment, and social justice) are best expressed in other ways, and ecological feminist analysis is relevant in showing why.

FOOD, FEAR, AND FEMINISM

Recently, the issue of genetically modified food has been the subject of much food anxiety. Martin Teitel and Kimberly Wilson's best-selling book, *Changing the Nature of Nature*, which is aimed at first-world consumers with a variety of food choices, begins:

> Imagine yourself one morning on a modern jetliner, settling into your seat as the plane taxis toward the active runway. To pass the time you unfold your morning newspaper, and just as the plane's rapidly building acceleration begins to lift the wheels from the ground, your eye catches a front-page article mentioning that engineers are beginning a series of tests to determine whether or not the new-model airplane that you are in is safe. . . . That situation would never happen, you say to yourself. People have more foresight than that. Yet something we entrust our lives to far more often than airplanes—our food, is being redesigned faster than any of us realize, and scientists have hardly begun to test the long-term safety of these new foods. (Teitel and Wilson 1999, 1)

The problem is clear, Teitel and Wilson suggest: we are being exposed to a new level of risk, vastly out of line with what we normally accept, and something needs to be done about it. People have not responded to the problem because most of us are unaware of it. Nobody would fly in airplanes that are untested, at least under normal circumstances (though I might if I were starving to death and the plane was heading towards food), and so we should object to being placed at a clearly unreasonable level of risk in our foods. The plane analogy is captivating and immediately raises several questions. What exactly are GM foods? Do they pose unacceptable levels of risk? How are these risks distributed? And, importantly, why are most of us so ignorant about them?

I begin with the seemingly simple question of what GM foods are. Genetically modified foods are produced by identifying genes that code for a specific characteristic in one species, and transferring those genes to another species: for example, taking a gene or gene sequence from a flounder and splicing it into the genetic material of a tomato or strawberry, in order to produce frost-resistance in the fruit. One of the most controversial and well-known examples is soy that has been genetically engineered to make it resistant to the herbicide Round-Up, thus supposedly allowing farmers to spray the herbicide without killing the soy plants. Another example is *Bt* corn that has been genetically modified to contain the bacterium *Bacillus thuringiensis*, making it resistant to insect pests including the European corn borer (Newton and Dillingham 2002).

There are major ecological concerns about such transgenic crops. First, they can produce large amounts of pollen which might alter the genetic structure of wild relatives. This in turn could result in marked loss of biodiversity, produce "weedy," resistant, out of control crops, or result in the creation of super-pests which are more and more pesticide-resistant. GM crops encourage the creation of monocultures and their related risks. One major risk is that farming one type of crop exclusively increases the probability of being totally wiped out, should conditions for the health of that crop deteriorate. The potato blight in nineteenth-century Ireland is an often cited example.

In addition to environmental concerns, there are worries about GM crops' unpredictable negative effects on the health of humans and other animals. For example, Monarch butterfly caterpillars died when force-fed milkweed from pollen from *Bt* corn. Critics worry that relevant data on safety within the U.S. is not produced by the federal agencies themselves, but by those seeking approval, that is, those with private interests (Ho 1997; Shiva 2000; Teitel and Wilson 2001).

Many fear increasing globalization where transnational corporations push for global trade agreements making it difficult or impossible for people in many nations to reject importation of foods created in ways they find immoral or unsafe. Within this larger economic context, farmers are becoming industrial employees, and small farms are being wiped out, both locally and globally, which in turn leads to the losses of diversity, control, indigenous knowledges, and local food cultures. (Monsanto currently owns nearly half of the world's seed supply, and Dupont owns much of the rest.) Loss of control by ordinary people over what they grow or what they eat, and even of the ability to know what they are growing or eating, remains a central theme for critics of GM food.

For those concerned with the loss of control to private, transnational corporations, another major issue is patenting. Large corporations prospect for useful genes in crop varieties indigenous to developing countries, patent seeds with improved varieties of those genes, and sell them back to poor farmers. Critics have also objected to the creation of "terminator seeds," which cannot be saved from season to season, thus requiring farmers to buy seeds from seed companies each year. This increases the farmers' dependence upon large corporations, undermines the traditional practices of seed-saving common in developing countries, and threatens religious practices in which seeds are worshipped. In response to intense criticism, Monsanto has decided not to produce such seeds (Norberg-Hodge et al. 2001; Ho 1997; Shiva 2000).

A major issue in the debate is whether GM foods have been adequately tested for safety. In their argument aimed at U.S. consumers, Teitel and Wilson compare GM foods to an untested airplane to suggest that such foods carry risks that those of us with alternatives should rationally choose to avoid. However, according to a report issued by the House Sub-committee on Basic Research:

> No product of conventional plant breeding . . . could meet the data requirements imposed on biotechnology produced by U.S. regulatory agencies . . . Yet, these foods are widely and properly regarded as safe and beneficial by plant developers, regulators, and consumers. The report concluded that biotech crops are "at least as safe [as] and probably safer" than conventionally bred crops. (in Pence 2002b, 105)

Such profound disagreement raises issues about trust, choice, and the construction of knowledge, topics that have been central in feminist ethics and epistemology (Alcoff and Potter 1993; Frye 1983; Harding 1986).

One typical way that these issues are raised in arguments in favor of GM food safety is exemplified by Gregory Pence's approach in *Designer Food* (2002). I shall therefore focus on Pence's arguments because they are typical, and because they are deeply problematic from a feminist perspective. Discussions of the safety of GM foods often compare its risks to risks of industrially produced meat and myths about organic food. The basic argument is that because people choose to trust these foods, they should also choose to trust GM foods.

Pence offers a version of the popular argument that it is irrational to worry about GM vegetables if we trust the government to regulate industrially produced meat. His argument is thus aimed primarily at U.S. consumers who choose to eat such meat. Pence argues that given the risks the average meat eater in the United States is willing to take, the risk of eating GM foods should seem, by comparison, very low indeed. Because most of us eat meat, Pence suggests that the risks involved in eating industrially produced meat are a reasonable comparative standard. Too many critics imply that genetically modified foods should be totally risk-free, which Pence rightly points out is problematic. Obviously, people accept various levels of risk constantly. The right question to ask is whether the level of risk posed by GM foods is unacceptable. On the question of what a reasonable standard of risk for average U.S. consumers should be, Pence states:

> Well, most people eat meat and even if they feel eating meat is wrong or unhealthy, most do not think it is *unsafe* to do so. Whether this belief is true or not is a different question. For now, all that matters is that most people allow their children and grandparents to eat all kinds of meat, eat it themselves, and trust our system of food to deliver it to them safely. If the same system can do the same or better with GM plants, these same people should have no problem buying and eating GM veggies. (Pence 2002a, 97)

Assuming his readers are relatively ignorant about the industrial production of meat, Pence goes on to educate his readers about such production and the risks involved therein.

Several pages are devoted to educating readers about current conditions within the meat industry, documenting major problems that are not solved because politicians are "in bed" with private interests. Given this fact combined with the huge demand for meat, it is impossible for the industry to produce safe products. The facts are that only a dozen huge meat companies control slaughterhouses, packing plants, and feed lots for all American fast food restaurants. Producing the huge amount of meat required requires maintaining huge feeding lots and giving cows antibiotics and steroids to prevent illness and promote massive weight gain. Killing rates in assembly lines are as high as three hundred cows per hour, and the lines can only be stopped if an inspector smells or sees a rotten carcass. Rendering systems often cut into the spinal cord, which means a BSE outbreak would be transmitted to huge amounts of beef. Feces on the feet of cattle contaminate meat and *E. Coli* infects most hamburger lots. As a result of these conditions, the industry now takes the position that it is the consumer's duty to prevent sickness by cooking hamburger well, rather than the industry's duty to sell safe meat (Pence 2002a, 98).

In addition to the fact that industry standards are problematic, the industry often fails to comply even with those existing weak standards. Hence, in 2001, a hidden video camera in a Washington state slaughterhouse showed live cattle chained upside down, moving down a processing line while still conscious. Workers testified that between ten and thirty percent of cattle at the plant were processed while still conscious, in violation of Federal law. There are also environmental concerns in that huge facilities produce lagoons filled with animal feces and urine. The result of all of these conditions is that, according to the CDC's *Emerging Infectious Diseases*, diseases caused by food cause 76 million cases of gastrointestinal illness, 325,000 cases of serious illness resulting in hospitalization, and 5,000 deaths each year (Pence 2002a, 100). The reason that there is not an adequate system to weed out rotten meat is political: "the fox guards the hen house" (2002a, 102). Federal inspectors are only permitted to consult with companies and "suggest" that meat be recalled. Even more alarmingly, if a company does decide to pull an infected lot from the public, it is under no legal obligation to inform the public of the recall, nor must the USDA inform the public of a recall of infected meat from a fast-food restaurant (2002a, 101). Companies know in advance when inspectors are coming, and thus "meat inspectors have no real jobs anymore" (2002a, 102). The situation does not seem to be improving. In 1987 there were twelve thousand inspectors; in 2000 only seventy-five hundred. Bills that would have restored the USDA's power to order recalls and increased the authority of meat inspectors were defeated in 1996, 1997, 1998, and 1999 (2002a, 102).

One obvious point is that the argument clearly does not hold for people who reject industrially produced meat. Many feminists, such as Carol Adams (1990), reject all meat consumption on the basis of animal cruelty. Other critics have focused on the intersecting forms of oppression involved in large-scale industrial meat production. For example, those who slaughter poultry, mainly women of color, often suffer a variety of illnesses, including carpel tunnel syndrome, due to the huge numbers of chickens they must kill per hour (Cuomo 1998). Some reject industrially produced meat due to the pollution that results from factory farms, as documented in the Pence quotes above. And there are those who reject industrial meat for all of these reasons.

What is more interesting from a feminist perspective is the assumption that those who currently eat industrially produced meat in the United States freely "choose" to do so, and that a better understanding of the risks involved in eating industrialized meat should cause people to "choose" to accept GM foods, rather than to reject industrialized meat. This analysis assumes that people's choices about what to eat are free in a neoliberal sense. However, feminists have long argued that the kind of freedom implied by neoliberalism is nonexistent, especially under conditions of oppression (Bartky 1990; Card 1996b; Meyers 1989). It is worth remembering here that the majority of people who are responsible for choosing which foods to buy, for themselves and for others, are women.

In addition, there are crucial issues of race and class involved in the social construction of food options. Given this, it might be perfectly consistent for many people to continue to buy and consume industrially processed meat while rejecting GM foods. Industrially produced meat is both extremely convenient and cheaper than many alternatives, as those who try to avoid it are well aware. Someone who gives in to the coercive pressures of convenience and/or price in the case of industrially produced meat could certainly maintain that it would nonetheless be a mistake to develop a system making an additional kind of problematic food coercively convenient and cheap. For many poor people, both within the U.S. and elsewhere, it might make perfect sense to continue to eat industrialized meat while opposing the further development of GM produce. The idea that people have the freedom to consume only foods that they believe to be safe is just too simple. It could be completely rational for people whose food choices are limited due to their socio-economic status to eat industrially produced meat while not trusting its safety and not wanting to see their choices even more limited by being forced to consume more foods they don't trust.

In short, many people simply do not have the luxury to consume only foods that they feel are safe, and arguments such as Pence's rely on the assumption of such luxury. Food "choices" are contextual and limited, and are certainly not unproblematically free in the way Pence's arguments imply. This is a key feminist insight that clearly challenges neoliberal assumptions about freedom of choice. Once the absence of free choice is revealed, the argument that it is necessarily irrational to eat industrialized meat while objecting to GM foods collapses. For people making decisions about what to eat, both in the U.S. and in other parts of the world, the matrix of "choice" is much more complicated.

Another typical argument offered by GM food proponents focuses on organic foods. Once again, I shall use Pence's version as an example. According to this argument, many people have naïve and mistaken beliefs about much organic food, picturing organically grown food and GM food as complete opposites. However, organic food may expose people to more, not fewer risks from outbreaks of dangerous *E. Coli*. These outbreaks come not only from tainted beef but from fresh fruit juices, raw milk, lettuce, and minimally processed produce (Pence 2002a, 2). Certainly, the recent organic spinach recall indicates that organics are not necessarily safer. Like many organic foods currently widely available, the recalled spinach was industrially farmed and industrially processed. In industrial processing, spinach from many different fields is processed in the same location, which creates the possibility for microbes from a single field to contaminate large amounts of food. By contrast, when food contamination occurs in smaller-scale operations, it has the potential to affect many fewer people. Thus, when consumers assume mistakenly that the organic food they buy was grown locally by small farmers, they may well overestimate the safety of those foods.

In addition to the myth of small local production, there are myths about the relative safety of workers employed at organic farms. For instance, the organic pesticide Rotenone, derived from the roots of several tropical plants, is approved for use by organic farmers and is regularly used on tomatoes, pears, and apples. In 2000, Rotenone was shown to cause Parkinson's disease-like symptoms. Farm workers' risk of developing Parkinson's is seven times the national average (Pence 2002a, 3).

Finally, although Pence does not mention it, he could have used issues of animal welfare in organic food production to bolster his argument. In his recent book, *The Omnivore's Dilemma*, Michael Pollan reveals in horrifying detail how many of the meat producers claiming to produce cruelty-free meat, and the organic supermarkets that sell such meat, are lying. For example, Petaluma Poultry, which produces organic broilers, claims that its "farming methods strive to create harmonious relationships in nature, sustaining the health of all creatures in the natural world" (Pollan 2006, 135). In reality, although Petaluma Poultry feeds its chickens certified organic feed, the chickens are raised in conditions otherwise similar to those of other industrial poultry farms. For example, although their chickens are advertised as free range, the truth is that the birds are not allowed outside until they are at least five or six weeks old due to fears that they will catch diseases, and they are slaughtered two weeks later.

Other disturbing examples include dairies that advertise that their Holsteins are provided with "an appropriate environment including shelter, and a comfortable resting area . . . sufficient space, proper facilities, and company of their own kind" (Pollan 2006, 135). In this case, it turned out that access to a pasture was not deemed to be part of "proper facilities" for cows. In fact, much organic milk comes from factory farms where cows never see pasture and are confined to "dry lots" where they are fed organic grain. Hence, the reality is that while many large organic markets, such as Whole Foods, display books and pictures about small farms and philosophies of small farming, much of the organic food available to U.S. consumers is industrially produced. For example, Earthbound Farms grows eighty percent of the organic lettuce sold in the U.S. Paradoxical products such as the organic T.V. dinner contain as many as thirty-one ingredients—including guar, xanthan gum, carrageenan, and "natural grill flavor"—that come from far away farms, labs, and processing plants including two other countries (Pollan 2006, 140). Such industrially produced organic foods clearly contradict the comforting narratives promoted by large organic markets, and bring the ethical and epistemological issues involved in eating such food clearly into focus.

As in the case of industrialized meat, Pence's conclusion is that organic food is not what people think it is, and GM food is no worse. However—again, as in the argument regarding industrially produced meat—other conclusions are both more plausible overall and more attractive from a feminist point of view. Those with a relatively wide range of food options could reasonably attempt to opt out of industrial organics in favor of more locally produced food. If, as it seems, the underlying issue is the industrialization of our food supply, the conclusion may not be that we should avoid organic, but rather that we should avoid industrialization, when possible. Of course, the extent to which this is a live option depends upon a variety of factors including race, class, gender, and social location that arguments such as Pence's, once again, clearly overlook. Feminist analysis again reminds us that no choices are completely free: we make our choices within a social framework of options. Taking this insight into account also reveals another possible response, namely that it might be totally rational to buy and consume industrial organics, depending upon one's particular concerns and the options available. While one might prefer a chicken that was humanely raised, one might still prefer an antibiotic-free chicken to one pumped full of drugs, regardless of the cruelty issue. Finally, another conclusion based on disturbing facts about industrialized meat and industrialized organics is available. One might accept that industrial food is problematic, continue to eat it as the least-bad option given one's concerns, and yet be opposed to further industrializing food production by developing GM foods, which are clearly industrial products, whether or not they are "natural."

This seems to be a very reasonable response to the facts about industrialized food presented above. Suspicion of industrial food production can only be strengthened by the recent astonishing comments of A. Elizabeth Sloan, President of Sloan Trends, which tracks the food industry. In response to Hannaford's claim that over seventy-eight percent of foods sold in U.S. supermarkets deserve no stars for nutrition, Sloan said that food manufacturers deserve credit for trying to make products healthier. However, they cannot go too far in removing fat, sugar, and salt, she claimed, because food manufacturers that go too far produce foods that "don't taste good." "Nothing is healthy if you get right down to it, except mother's milk," Sloan continued, "and that's probably got too much fat" (*New York Times*, 6 November 2006). Of course, it is industrial food manufacturers that have molded our tastes so that foods low in fat, sugar, and salt do not taste good to us—another clue that they do not have the best interests of consumers in mind in producing our food.

THE PROMISE OF GM FOODS

One of the most important and disturbing issues about GM foods concerns whether such foods are the answer to feeding starving people, and to helping cure diseases caused by poor nutrition, particularly in developing countries. Many people who promote GM foods argue that those who fear the risks involved in the production of such foods have the luxury to demand very low risk levels, while those starving people who will benefit the most from GM foods pay the price. This is a constant theme in mainstream literature promoting GM technologies. Hence, proponents of GM foods often accuse those who oppose them of hard-heartedness. According to Norman Borlaug, the previously cited Nobel Peace Prize winner and staunch proponent of biotechnology, "Indeed extremists in the environmental movement, largely from rich nations and/or privileged strata of society seem to be doing everything they can to stop scientific progress in its tracks" (in Pence 2002b, 78). In a similar vein, environmental journalist Ronald Bailey notes that "the apparent willingness of biotechnology's opponents to sacrifice people for their cause disturbs scientists who are trying to help the world's poor" (in Pence 2002b, 102).

What should feminists make of the promise of GM foods for remedying global starvation and malnutrition, given the tremendous contention over its potential benefits and risks? Among the many profound disagreements that constitute this debate, I found remarkable agreement on one important issue. Ronald Bailey grants that anti-GM food activists Vandana Shiva and Mae-Wan Ho "make the valid point that there is enough food today to provide an adequate diet for everyone if it were more equally distributed" (in Pence 2002b, 105). GM food proponent and U-C Davis biologist Martina McLaughlin agrees that "the real issue is inequity in food distribution" (in Pence 2002b, 105), and Norman Borlaug grants that "very serious equity barriers exist in the access of the poor to food, and these must be addressed in the world community" (in Pence, 2002b, 78).

If both proponents and opponents of GM food can agree that the major causes of starvation involve issues of inequity, politics, and culture, what reason do we have to believe that, if new biotechnologies are developed, they will be used to help feed the starving? Those in favor of biotech solutions overlook the obvious fact that feeding the starving has never been a high priority within global industrial capitalism, even in situations where there is enough food to do so. We have absolutely no reason to trust that, as transnational corporations slowly gain control over the world's food supply, those corporations will suddenly make feeding hungry people a high priority. Even if it is the case that in some utopian world, biotechnology could be expected to fulfill a promise to feed hungry people, we have no reason to expect it to do so in *this* world, and therefore, no reason to have any faith in its supposed "miracles." Further industrialization of our food can be expected to deliver the same goods it has been delivering so far: unsafe, unhealthy food, offering consumers fewer options rather than more. As we have seen, the "neoliberal" choices about food implied in arguments such as Pence's simply do not exist anywhere. Hence, the idea

that such choices can be extended to desperate people in so-called developing countries is highly dubious.

CONCLUSION

Feminist philosophy has much to offer in critiquing typical positions
within current debates over GM foods. First, I have used ecological feminist
insights to argue that appeals to whether GM foods should be considered
"natural," which commonly appear on both sides of the debate, are ultimately unhelpful and highly problematic. Appeals to social constructions
of "nature" don't provide any useful information, and have been used in
the service of oppression. I then showed how some fairly typical mainstream philosophical arguments in favor of GM food employ a neoliberal
conception of "free choice" which is rejected by many feminists. And that,
once the notion of "choice" is appropriately limited and contextualized,
these arguments fail. Finally, I have argued that questions about GM food
safety and of the promise of GM food to feed starving people, cannot be
separated from critiques of the institutions that regulate food safety and
distribution. These include industrialized global capitalism. Hence, proponents of GM foods who argue that its critics really aren't concerned with
safety, but actually hate industrial capitalism and globalization, have
missed the boat. Issues concerning the potential safety of GM foods cannot
be separated from critiques of the institutions that regulate and distribute
food institutions that are part of industrialized global capitalism. Feminist
analysis clearly shows how these issues are inseparable. Therefore, we
shouldn't expect GM foods to be safer or more fairly distributed than other
food, if such foods are to be regulated by the same overall system that currently allows the production of unhealthy, unsafe, industrialized foods, and
also allows huge numbers of people to starve to death when there is currently enough food to feed them.

6

What Is Poverty?

Peter Higgins, Audra King, and April Shaw

INTRODUCTION

On November 10, 1999, *The Onion* reported a dramatic reduction in the rate of poverty in the United States, in the following article titled "Eight Million Americans Rescued from Poverty with Redefinition of Term."

> Approximately eight million Americans living below the poverty line were rescued from economic hardship Monday, when the U.S. Census Bureau redefined the term. "We are winning the war on poverty," said bureau head James Irving, who lowered the poverty line for a four-person family to $14,945. "Today, millions of people whose inflation-adjusted total household income is less than $16,780 are living better lives." Said formerly poor Jackson, MS, motel housekeeper Althea Williams: "I never dreamed I'd ever become middle-class. America truly is the land of opportunity." (*The Onion* 1999)

What this satirical example demonstrates is the need for philosophical examination of the concept of poverty, and of certain related questions such as: Is poverty increasing or decreasing? Are there certain groups that tend to be disproportionately overrepresented among the poor, and is such group-associated poverty becoming more or less common? Philosophers have spent little time attempting to answer these questions, perhaps because, as one might imagine, there is apparently little to say philosophically about them. Rather, it may seem, at first glance, that empirical investigation is all that is required to find answers to these questions. Instead, philosophers have focused, to the extent that they have been concerned with poverty at all, on what moral obligations persons and social institutions have with respect to the prevention and amelioration of poverty.

While it is true that answering these questions requires empirical work, that empirical work cannot be done before some more conceptual questions are answered: for instance, "What is poverty?" and "Does one's likelihood of being poor depend in part on one's social identity relative to others and to institutional structures of domination?" In this paper, we defend certain answers to these questions, and we argue that an adequate definition of poverty must account for the ways in which a person's social position affects both her economic welfare and her ability to make use of the resources she has. We maintain, by applying this desideratum, that some common understandings of poverty are inadequate, and that furthermore, they fail to yield empirical data about poverty that accurately represents who is poor, and who is getting poorer. To satisfy our criterion, and to reflect accurately who is poor, we must understand poverty as the deprivation of certain human capabilities. That is to say, a person is poor if, for any reason, she is unable to do certain things or achieve certain ends.

METHODOLOGY

To be in a position to defend one conception of poverty over others, one must first provide the criteria by which the different conceptions will be evaluated. For this reason, in what immediately follows, we argue that a satisfactory definition of poverty will fulfill three important desiderata: empirical adequacy, conceptual precision, and sensitivity to social positioning. Having explained each criterion in this section, we will then apply them to actual conceptions of poverty, including our own.

Empirical Adequacy

Perhaps the most important and least controversial desideratum for a good definition of poverty is that it be empirically adequate; that is, that it include all and only those who are actually poor. In this regard, we will argue that some definitions of poverty are too broad (i.e., they tend to include those who are not poor). Moreover, and perhaps more significantly, we will contend that those definitions of poverty that are currently most influential are entirely too narrow—they exclude many who are in fact poor. Some definitions of poverty, we will maintain, are both too broad and too narrow.[1]

Conceptual Precision

An adequate definition of poverty must be conceptually precise, by which we mean that it must distinguish the concept and the phenomena of poverty from other concepts and phenomena that are correlated with or causally related to poverty, but not constitutive of it. Some conceptions of poverty appear to include in the definition of poverty factors that serve to cause and/or exacerbate poverty, such as political and social exclusion. Conceptually, it is incoherent to include the causes of poverty in the definition of poverty since, first, this would lead to an infinite regress, and second, it would imply that poverty is self-caused or uncaused—a troublesome thought for anyone who is concerned to reduce the incidence of poverty. At the practical level, such lack of precision in how one conceives of a phenomenon may result in inadequate policies or strategies for dealing with the phenomenon. If one's aim is to reduce poverty, then one must be able to distinguish poverty from phenomena that are correlated with or causes of poverty.

Sensitivity to Social Positioning

What it is for a particular conception to be *adequate* depends on the epistemological and methodological framework in which an analysis is conducted. A primary aim of feminist research is to uncover and eradicate domination and subjugation on the basis of the socially constructed category of gender (as it intersects with race, class, ethnicity, sexual preference and so on). Thus, the values, interests, and assumptions that constitute an adequate feminist methodology will also treat this aim as paramount.

Broadly speaking, feminist philosophy is defined by its aim to expose and amend gender bias within mainstream philosophy. A feminist methodology begins with the recognition that dominant philosophical frameworks are often grounded in narrow, often male-biased assumptions about human beings' relations to each other and to nature. Such distorted views function to create and reinforce social relations of domination and subordination. Because partial and biased assumptions are often masked as neutral and are invisible to those embedded in dominant frameworks, a chief aim of feminist methodology is to expose and transform these distorted assumptions so as to more adequately reflect reality as it is experienced by *situated* individuals.

That is, rather than purporting to embody a neutral or positionless perspective, conceptions, policies, and strategies should be based on ideas and beliefs that are consistent with the experiences of persons understood as positioned within historical, social, material, cultural, and/or religious contexts. Individuals are not isolated units whose experiences can be understood independently of the situation in which they are embedded. Given this, an adequate conception of poverty must reflect the interdependent, interrelated character of individuals with one another and with nature, as well as the social institutions and relations in which they are *situated*.

Understanding poverty as it actually occurs requires recognizing the ways in which multiple factors interact to create and reinforce a state of severe deprivation in which a person is unable to satisfy her most basic needs. Thus, an adequate definition of poverty will incorporate an understanding of how a person's position (socially, culturally, locally, etc.) affects not only her vulnerability to material deprivation, but also whether and how she is able to convert resources to the satisfaction of basic needs. As we will demonstrate throughout the paper, factors such as whether a person has access to state-subsidized services, the costs of goods within her community, her membership in marginalized groups as determined by relations of power in the local, national and global community, her position within the household with regard to power and responsibility, as well as her particular nutritional needs relative to her age, sex, health, etc., are all profoundly important to determining her ability to fulfill her basic needs.

ALTERNATIVE CONCEPTIONS OF POVERTY

Poverty as a Lack of Income

Currently, the World Bank's empirical data on poverty are the most comprehensive estimates on the rate of poverty.[2] They define poverty as "the inability to attain a minimal standard of living," which they identify as anyone whose income has less purchasing power than $1/day, as it is calculated within a particular country in a particular year (World Bank 1990). Yet both the method employed by the World Bank and the conception of poverty on which it is based are fundamentally flawed, resulting in miscalculation of estimates of the global poor (Pogge & Reddy 2003).

Thomas Pogge and Sanjay Reddy point out that the value of a nation's currency as it is used for the national poverty line is determined on the basis of the aggregate consumption pattern of that country, with no division between categories of commodities (Pogge & Reddy 2003, 5). This aggregate consumption model is problematic because goods that are necessary for meeting one's basic needs, such as cheap food, are counted in the same category as services that are "extra"/supplements to one's quality of life. Yet, in general, the economic level of those who consume "supplemental" services is such that they are already able to satisfy their basic needs. In short, no matter how cheap a haircut or a taxi ride becomes, the worst-off must first put their resources to securing food and shelter. If the price of these "supplemental" services drops, while the price of basic goods remains the same or increases, then the poor are not in any sense better off. Unfortunately, in failing to distinguish between goods necessary to fulfil basic needs and services that enhance overall quality of life, the World Bank model does not account for intra-country differences in consumption, resulting in an inadequate account of poverty.[3]

It could be argued that, while the World Bank's method has some fundamental flaws, the best way of defining poverty is nevertheless in terms of "lack of income." Yet foremost among the problems with this definition of poverty is that it is both too broad and too narrow at the same time. In other words, on this definition, certain people are counted as poor who are able to satisfy their basic needs, and others who cannot are not counted as poor. For example, a person who has a high income but who nevertheless cannot provide herself with adequate nutrition or who has no access to basic medical services (because, for instance, she is not permitted by governing social norms and institutions to leave her home alone, or perhaps because she lives in a rural area) would not count as poor despite the fact that she is not able to meet her basic needs.

Additional problems arise from some problematic assumptions income-based definitions of poverty tend to make. For instance, such models tend to view the household solely as a sphere of consumption, with each household counting as a "single unit of consumption" (Jaggar 2006). The problem is that these methods fail to disaggregate within the household, which presupposes equal distribution of income within the household.[4] This ignores the fact that social relations of power based on gender most often result in the "gendered division of authority" (Ibid.), in which women tend to occupy an inferior position within the household, a position in which they have little, if any, control over the allocation of income and resources; insofar as women are seen as less valuable or inferior, women's needs tend to be seen as secondary and negligible. As Amartya Sen points out, this is further compounded by the fact that women often view their own self-interest and well-being in relational terms, that is, their own interest is seen as directly related to the well-being of the members of their family (Jackson 1998). Thus, when there are limited resources within a household, women often forgo fulfilling their own needs to provide for those of their children, spouses, etc. That most societies, as well as the global economic community, are hierarchically structured in a way that subordinates women has crucial implications for people's ability to access and to use commodities to satisfy their basic needs. However, most income-based methods fail to attend to the influence of gendered social positioning and the concomitant contextual factors in its conception of poverty.

Ravi Kanbur and Lyn Squire suggest a third problem for income-based definitions of poverty, namely that "economically marginalized groups tend to be socially marginalized as well," so that they are disadvantaged with respect to both resources and power (2001, 2).[5] They are right to assert that poverty often manifests as a form of powerlessness. However, the relationship between social marginalization and economic marginalization is much more profound and complex than Kanbur and Squire acknowledge. Individuals are always and everywhere entrenched in a web of power relations, such as racism, sexism, ethnocentrism, classism, heterosexism, etc., that either advance or hinder their life prospects. Where one is positioned relative to social structures of power will not only shape one's ability to access resources, such as income, but will affect one's ability to convert those resources into the fulfillment of basic needs. Income-based definitions of poverty assume that lack of income is the only obstacle to the fulfillment of one's basic needs. However, this assumption overlooks how other institutitional forms of inequality limit individuals' ability to fulfill their basic needs. For example, an immigrant may have a relatively high income, but due to her marginalized social position, may lack the mobility necessary to fulfill her basic needs. To the extent that an individual belongs to multiple marginalized groups, her ability to have command over resources is significantly diminished, leaving her more vulnerable to poverty than others.[6]

Poverty as Lack of Resources

An alternative to the World Bank's income-based definition, a resourcist approach, may be used to provide a meaningful grounding for the development of a poverty line. A resourcist definition of poverty sees it as (in Paul Spicker's words) "lack of material goods or services . . . that people require in order to live and function in society" (Spicker 1999). For example, in 1995, the UN defined poverty as "a condition characterized by severe deprivation of basic human needs, including food, safe drinking water, sanitation facilities, health, shelter, education, and information. It depends not only on income, but access to services" (Ibid, 152).[7] This conception is based on the idea that each person requires a certain basket of goods in order to "live and function in society."

One may wonder, however, whether the resourcist approach sufficiently accounts for how individuals' needs differ. Insofar as poverty is defined in reference to a single basket of goods, it may fail to account for individuals with increased needs, such as the elderly, the sick, children, and pregnant women, as well as for those who care for these persons, and so on. Insofar as differently situated persons relate to resources differently, measuring poverty on the basis of a single basket of goods does not capture the varying adequacy of those goods for those with different needs—thereby resulting in underestimation of poverty. In particular, resourcist approaches to defining poverty neglect the fact that individuals who are members of marginalized groups tend, as a result of their socially imposed marginalization, to convert resources into functionings at lower rates than those who are not marginalized. As such, this type of definition systematically overlooks the poverty experienced by members of marginalized groups.[8]

The resourcist definition of poverty misses what is important for avoiding poverty: not having resources per se, but rather, having command over resources. Amartya Sen makes a similar point, using the example of owning a bike: "The commodity ownership or availability itself is not the right focus [for conceiving of poverty] since it does not tell us what the person can, in fact, do. I may not be able to use the bike if—say—I happen to be handicapped" (Sen 1983).

Poverty as Inequality

On an inequality approach to poverty, people are poor if they are among the least well-off in a society. (This can in principle be understood in any terms—income, material resources, social exclusion, or capabilities fulfillment—but it is normally understood in terms of income.) That is, those individuals who occupy the worst-off positions, relative to the material status of others in a particular society, are counted as poor. O'Higgins and Jenkins explain:

> Virtually all definitions of the poverty threshold used in developed economies in the last half-century or so have been concerned with establishing the level of income necessary to allow access to the minimum standards of living considered acceptable in that society at the time. In consequence, there is an inescapable connection between poverty and inequality: certain degrees or dimensions of inequality . . . will lead to people being below the minimum standard acceptable in that society. (Spicker 1999, 156)

Thus, an inequality approach does not conceive of poverty as being any absolute state of life in which individuals are deprived of particular needs or resources, but rather merely as a situation of deprivation relative to others' material position. Yet, as Spicker points out, this view of poverty implies that a reduction in the resources of the better-off is a reduction of poverty, even if the absolute status of the worst-off has not changed. But this clearly would not be a reduction in poverty, and so an inequality-based definition of poverty is unsatisfactory. In addition, on such a definition it would be nearly impossible to eradicate poverty, since some are almost always worse-off than others. It is odd to say that someone is poor simply because she has less than others if she, for example, obtains adequate nutrition, has protection from adverse climatic conditions, and has access to basic medical services.

This definition also implies, counterintuitively, that there could not be a society in which the majority of people are poor. That is, since "worst-off" entails falling below some average, this group would, by definition, need to be less than half the population. The counterexamples show that an inequality-based definition of poverty is both too broad (since someone may be among the worst-off and yet still be able to live "decently" in an affluent society) and too narrow (since someone may not, for example, be able to obtain adequate nourishment in a society in which more than half of the population cannot obtain adequate nourishment, and so would not be counted as poor).

Poverty as Social Exclusion

Another definition that is cited among international development agencies is the view of poverty as a type of "social exclusion" (Narayan et al., 2000). For example, in the World Bank's *Voices of the Poor*, poverty is defined as "vulnerability to social risks," "powerlessness," or exclusion "from participation in the normal pattern of social life" (Spicker 1999, 154).

Obviously an understanding of such factors is vitally important for the development of anti-poverty strategies and for the analysis of social institutions, especially as the most marginalized members of society experience them. However, our worry is that this type of definition does not reflect what is constitutive of poverty per se. Rather, it seems to explain the impact of the interaction of various social injustices—including poverty—on those who are adversely affected by them. Vulnerability, powerlessness, and exclusion are both created and reinforced by poverty, as well as by various institutions of social, cultural, political and/or economic domination. Given the multidimensional, interactional nature of social injustice, any policy seeking to eradicate it will necessarily require examining this complex web. However, this does not entail that the various social factors are indistinguishable and/or that they can or should all be subsumed under the label "poverty" (Pinker 1999).[9] Furthermore, it would be conceptually incoherent to identify such factors as causes of poverty, while at the same time defining them as part of poverty itself.[10] Thus, while we advocate examining these factors as crucial to human development and poverty alleviation, we reject them as a central defining feature of poverty.

POVERTY AS CAPABILITIES DEPRIVATION

Defending Capabilities

Any reasonable definition of poverty must take into account how a person's social position affects both her economic welfare and her ability to make use of the resources she has (whether income or actual goods and services). Although the alternative conceptions of poverty we have discussed are problematic for various reasons, each, most importantly, fails to meet this desideratum—that a definition of poverty must consider how a person's membership in marginalized and/or dominant social groups affects her ability to utilize resources.

In virtue of this criterion, we propose that poverty be defined in terms of a person's capabilities, where this refers to a person's positive freedom.[11] In other words, in order to determine if a person is poor, one ought to consider what that person is able to do or what that person can achieve. A person will count as poor if, for any reason, she is unable to do certain things or unable to achieve certain ends.[12] Poverty, then, on our account, is the deprivation of certain capabilities or positive freedoms.

Defining poverty as "the deprivation of certain capabilities" meets the above criterion in the following way. As we have mentioned in our criticisms of alternative definitions of poverty, a person's material needs can vary in complex ways depending on her social position, among other things. Often, for example, a person who is a member of a marginalized group will have greater difficulty in converting resources (whether income or material goods) into functionings—that is, in making use of her resources—than a person who is otherwise similarly socially situated but not a member of the same marginalized group. To give a specific example, the nutritional needs of a person who works intensively for long periods each day will be higher, other things being equal, than the nutritional needs of a person who does not perform such work. Thus, for example, many women's nutritional needs are greater than they would otherwise be because of the domestic labor that they perform (on top of any paid labor they may also do); however, because that domestic labor is unremunerated, it does not afford them additional resources for meeting those heightened nutritional needs.

There are countless ways in which one person's needs will vary from another's as a result of their respective social positions, each of which shows the inadequacy of defining poverty as falling below some standardized income level, or as having less than some standardized basket of goods. For example, a person who has a physical disability will often need a higher income than a person who does not have a physical disability, but who is otherwise similarly socially situated, in order to achieve the same level of material well-being.[13] (One reason among many for this difference is that an automobile, which may be necessary in certain places in order to obtain food and other basic needs, will cost more if it is made to accommodate a person with a physical disability.)

Defining poverty as "deprivation of certain capabilities" has additional advantages over other common definitions. Consider again Amartya Sen's contention that "commodity ownership or availability is not the right focus" of defining a minimal standard of living (i.e., poverty assessment), because what is most important is "what the person can do" with those commodities (Sen 1983). On this approach, someone's lacking certain material resources is seen as morally significant *because* such deprivation prevents him or her from being able to do certain fundamental things. This approach, unlike others we've considered here, stresses *why* material deprivation is so important: it reveals the normative implications of such deprivation for human well-being, as well as its inexorable link to the circumstances of particular persons, including their social positions within particular contexts.[14]

As a result, accurately assessing poverty requires examining factors like the availability of state-subsidized services, the costs of goods and services within a particular context, and individuals' needs relative to their situations, including their identities relative to institutional structures of power. In most social contexts, factors such as class, gender, race, age, sexual orientation, ethnicity, ability, and the like systematically disadvantage individuals in ways that affect their ability to access and convert material resources into capabilities. To the extent that a person's social identity influences her ability to function, or to fulfill her basic needs, it must be considered in any adequate assessment of poverty. This set of variables is most fully incorporated by a capability-based definition. Such a definition not only captures the significance of cross-country, intra-country, and intra-household variations in costs, power, etc.; it also underlines Alison Jaggar's point that power structures systematically limit the life prospects of individuals who belong to social groups undervalued by such structures, thus disproportionately increasing an individual's vulnerability to poverty (Jaggar 2006).

Following Sen, the model we advocate is absolute in terms of the capabilities whose lack defines poverty, but relative to individuals in terms of the particular goods and services (and levels thereof) needed to achieve those capabilities (Sen 1983, p. 160). So, while the concept of poverty appeals to a context-independent set of capabilities, we recognize that the resources that one needs in order to satisfy these requirements vary according to the context. As we have stressed thus far, intra-country variations in commodities and prices, as well as other contextual (social, political, historical, etc.) factors that influence an individual's ability to use goods to satisfy her needs, must be accounted for by whatever methods are used to assess poverty. Delineating a universally applicable list of elementary capabilities provides a stable and consistent benchmark for measuring poverty rates, as well as for assessing poverty-reduction strategies. Furthermore, such a global list allows for more uniform modifications to national poverty lines as needed to reveal any variations in the cost of basic necessities. Finally, by establishing a universal conception of poverty, the normative and moral importance of poverty is more firmly grounded.

Although it would be quite an undertaking to provide a definitive list of capabilities the deprivation of which constitutes poverty, we would nonetheless like to make some preliminary suggestions. Most importantly, it should be kept in mind that, while the notion of capabilities is often invoked in development theory and as part of theories of justice, in the current context we are concerned with capabilities only insofar as they are relevant to the concept of poverty.[15] For this reason, and to remain consistent with our criticisms of other conceptions of poverty (most notably, that of poverty as social exclusion), we believe that the list of capabilities whose deprivation constitutes poverty should be rather limited and narrowly drawn. For example, this list should include items such as "the capability to be adequately nourished," "the capability to live free of avoidable and easily treatable diseases," and "the capability to be protected from climatic conditions." For the purposes of this paper, we are agnostic about what methods ought to be employed in order to generate a more complete list of poverty-relevant capabilities. Nevertheless, both for conceptual reasons and because eradicating poverty requires an accurate understanding of the phenomena, we believe that such a list should be constructed in a way that avoids conflating poverty with other social ills.

For example, one feature of Sen's argument that we reject is his apparent support of "the capability to live without shame" and the capability for social participation as capabilities the underfulfillment of which constitutes poverty (Sen 1983). This rejection is justified by an argument similar to the one we used against the "social exclusion" definitions of poverty: namely, including such items in the list of the basic capabilities used to identify poverty results in a conception that is too broad. Such conditions, while important, signify multiple injustices and social issues which are related to, but should not be conflated with, poverty.

Objections

Broadness

Most objections to our thesis take the form of counterexamples that aim to show that our account of poverty as capabilities-deprivation is too broad. Imagine, for example, that a billionaire has been kidnapped, restrained, and denied access to adequate nutrition, shelter, and medical care. This person, one might think, will be characterized as poor by our definition of poverty; yet intuitively, one may object, this person, though the victim of moral wrongdoing, is incorrectly identified as poor.[16] Similarly, one can imagine a person who, as a result of a gambling addiction, no longer has the ability to provide nutrition, medical care, and shelter for himself. Again, the gambling addict seems to count as poor on our definition, and this again may seem intuitively inaccurate. As such, our definition is too broad and must be rejected.

There are multiple counterexamples that all, in a similar way, attempt to demonstrate that our definition of poverty is too broad. Nevertheless, no such counterexamples, we argue, provide sufficient grounds for rejecting our definition. This is so for three reasons. First, similar counterexamples apply, in slightly modified forms, to the other alternative definitions we have considered in this paper. This is because the only way to avoid such counterexamples is to add a set of necessary conditions specifying the *cause* of an individual's material deprivation. The intuitive force, if there is any, behind the case of the kidnapped billionaire has to do with the fact that the cause of her material deprivation is not of a kind normally included within the concept of poverty. But none of the currently popular definitions of poverty (lack of income, lack of resources, being the least well-off, and being socially excluded) take the cause of an individual's material deprivation to be relevant to whether or not she is poor. As such, this line of objection, even if the counterexample is successful, does not count as a reason to reject a definition of poverty in terms of capabilities-deprivation any more than it counts a reason to reject alternative definitions of poverty. (For example, the kidnapped billionaire would also be considered poor on a resourcist definition of poverty, since she is deprived of all of her resources.)[17]

Does this mean that an adequate definition of poverty should take into account the cause of a person's material deprivation? We believe this would be a mistake. Even if concerns about over-broadness could be addressed by adding a set of necessary conditions that specify certain kinds of causes of a person's material deprivation, such necessary conditions would be highly likely to result in an overly narrow definition of poverty. That is, for every person who is allegedly not poor, but who is "mistakenly" counted as poor on a definition of poverty that is not cause-sensitive, there will be at least as many who are actually poor, but who would not be counted as poor on any similar definition of poverty that does require material deprivation to have certain kinds of causes. It seems reasonable to assume, at the very least, that two definitions are equally inadequate if one is too narrow and the other is too broad, provided that the degrees of narrowness and broadness are similar. Furthermore, as we will argue below, in the case of defining poverty, it is better for a definition to be too broad than too narrow. For this reason, we deny that an adequate definition of poverty should take account of the causes of a person's material deprivation.

Secondly, though we consider poverty in general to be morally problematic, our definition does not entail that, if a person is poor, certain others have a moral obligation to alleviate his or her poverty. For example, while our definition does indeed require us to say that the kidnapped billionaire is (suddenly) poor, it does not require us to say that his poverty is as morally troubling—or that it imposes on anyone the same kinds of ameliorative obligations—as more ordinarily caused forms of poverty. Much the same qualification applies to the case of the gambling addict. We believe that this clarification substantially mitigates the force of the counterexamples.

Third and finally, we wish to call into question the methodological assumptions behind the use of counterexamples (such as the case of the kidnapped billionaire) as methods for critiquing various philosophical positions. Specifically, we argue that improbable cases, such as the case of the kidnapped billionaire, are too rare to constitute decisive objections—certainly in this context, and perhaps in many others. As we have argued throughout this essay, alternative definitions of poverty systematically underrepresent poverty among, and thereby entrench the oppression of, women and members of groups marginalized along lines of race, age, and ability, among other things. These actually existing people are systematically excluded from definitions of poverty that are entirely too narrow, and as a result, attempts to alleviate poverty, such as promoting economic growth defined in terms of Gross National Products, continually fail to improve these people's material conditions. Under these circumstances, we believe very little weight, if any, should be given to improbable cases like that of the kidnapped billionaire, whom we are more than willing to call "poor" if the alternative is a definition that systematically underrepresents poverty among women and members of other marginalized groups. Other things being equal, narrowness is a more serious vice for a definition of poverty than is broadness, as it is better to include a few kidnapped billionaires in the definition of poverty than to exclude many thousands or even millions of people whose social identity makes them more vulnerable to material deprivation. In summary, we do not think that the kidnapped billionaire case shows that our definition of poverty is too broad; but even if our definition is too broad, the extent to which it is too broad is significantly less than the extent to which competing accounts are too narrow.

Empirical Adequacy

This objection relies on a counterexample meant to demonstrate that resourcist definitions of poverty are more empirically adequate than capabilities-based definitions. Imagine two societies, A and B, the members of both of which are deprived of their capability to be adequately nourished. In society A, the cause of the individuals' capability-deprivation is a lack of food resources, whereas in society B, individuals, though they are relatively resource-rich, are undernourished, and so deprived of their capabilities, because they have extremely high metabolisms. Since, in both cases, individuals are deprived of the relevant capability, the individuals of both societies will, counterintuitively, count as poor on our definition. But in fact, only the individuals of society A are poor, according to the resourcist. So, our definition must be rejected in favor of a resourcist definition of poverty.[18]

However, the apparent force of this objection relies both on the underdescription of the case and on its improbability. The counterexample trades on the impression of the two groups as geographically and socially isolated societies. Imagine, alternatively, that the two groups are not composed of members of geographically isolated societies, but rather, more realistically, of different social groups in the same geographical area—that, for example, group A is composed of resource-deprived men, while group B is composed of pregnant women, whose nutritional needs are greater than those of the non-pregnant and who therefore, despite having somewhat greater food resources than the members of group A, are nonetheless unable to meet their nutritional needs. Even if one were inclined to believe that our account mistakenly identified the members of society B (in the original counterexample) as poor, what force the counterexample has, if any, is significantly diminished by reconstructing the counterexample in more realistic terms. It does not seem counterintuitive (to us at least) to say that the pregnant women in group B are poor even if they have somewhat greater food resources than the resource-deprived men in group A (whom we would also, of course, consider poor.)

Second, since (as discussed above) our definition of poverty does not entail that if a person is poor, certain others have a moral obligation to alleviate that poverty, our account allows one to say (though we ourselves probably would not) that the poverty of the members of group B is less morally significant than that of members of group A. This consideration diminishes the force of the counterexample.

Third, there is an equally forceful counterexample to the resourcist definition which supports our definition of poverty in terms of capabilities-deprivation. Imagine two groups, A and B. The members of group A are resource-deprived, and so unable to meet their nutritional needs. The members of this group will be considered poor on both the resourcist and capabilities-based definitions of poverty. The members of group B also have scarce food resources, but are able to meet their nutritional needs due to their extremely low metabolisms. The members of group B will not count as poor on the capabilities-based definition (since they are able to nourish themselves), but they will count as poor, counterintuitively, on the resourcist definition (because they lack the specified resources). Whatever force the original pro-resourcist counterexample may have had is neutralized, it seems to us, by this re-imagined version.

Finally, the central problem with this objection, which both our first and third responses suggest, is that (like the resourcist position itself) it requires determining what the needs of the "standard" person are. Since the resourcist approach to defining poverty depends on specifying a single basket of goods or set of resources that a person needs in order to avoid or escape poverty, a defender of the resourcist account must identify who the "standard" person is, and then determine what his needs are, in order to generate the list of resources that are to comprise the single basket of goods. However, the needs of individuals vary significantly, for both idiosyncratic and systemic social reasons. In the original version of the counterexample, the members of society B are said not to lack food resources, despite the fact that they are unable to meet their nutritional needs. But the claim that members of society B do not lack food resources depends on assuming a single basket of goods, conceived of in reference to the needs of some "standard" person whose needs, and thus whose required resources, are less than the needs of the members of group B. In the first reconstructed version of the counterexample, the members of group A are resource-deprived men, and the members of group B are pregnant women who, despite having a greater quantity of resources than the members of group A, are nonetheless unable to meet their nutritional needs. The only way for the resourcist to maintain, as she must, that the members of group A are poor, while the members of group B are not, is to assume a single basket of goods based on the needs of some "standard" person whose needs are less than those of a typical pregnant woman (perhaps the men in group A), while taking the needs of the pregnant women of group B to be an exceptional case. For these reasons, we do not find this objection to be compelling.

Practicality

The final objection concerns the practicality of the capabilities-based definition of poverty as a guide for poverty-reduction. As we have noted throughout the paper, an important advantage of this understanding of poverty is that it recognizes the ways in which an individual's social position can affect her ability to function in society. However, one might object that this very feature of the capabilities model renders it an impractical approach to assessing and measuring poverty. For example, it requires taking into account differences among individuals such as gender, race, age, and disability (and perhaps even metabolic rate and location). Given the resources and time that such an approach appears to require, the practical problems involved in measuring poverty would be insurmountable. This suggests that, as a practical guide to poverty reduction, the capabilities model fails.

One should keep in mind, however, that all definitions of poverty are individualized in a certain sense. Even income-based definitions of poverty require that the income of all individuals (or households, as the case may be) be measured in order to determine whether a person is poor—and, if so, how poor he or she is. (Furthermore, the income model is, at this level, even less practical than it initially seems, for the following reason. While in affluent western states, sufficient infrastructure exists for conducting census surveys, and most income earning occurs in the formal economy, i.e., is indicated in tax records, the same is not true in other parts of the world which, by no coincidence, tend to contain the highest proportion of the world's poor. As such, accurately measuring the income of individuals is not as easy as it seems at first glance.) Similarly, measuring the rate of poverty according to a resourcist definition would also require taking stock of the quantity and type of resources owned by individuals. So in this sense, a definition of poverty in terms of capabilities is no more individualized, and thus no more impractical, than any definition of poverty. However, the capabilities model is individualized in a sense that other definitions are not: while the list of poverty-relevant capabilities is universal (as noted previously), the quantity and type of resources an individual must have command over (not merely legally possess, as in the resourcist model) will vary from one individual to the next depending on their respective social positions. In other words, the threshold of poverty for the capabilities model will vary among individuals. It is for this reason that the capabilities model is thought to be less practical than other models for measuring the rate of poverty globally.

Even with this consideration in mind, however, the capabilities model is not significantly less practical than other definitions of poverty. The work required to determine the thresholds of poverty for different groups of people, based on their particular social positions, though it must be highly empirically informed, is primarily conceptual. Furthermore, similar models already exist in other areas of inquiry and are highly effective. For example, the medical field has been able to capture differences among individuals, thereby improving their ability to target and anticipate the medical needs and vulnerabilities of differently situated persons. The success of these strategies depends upon evaluating factors such as metabolism, age, sex, height, etc. This shows that measuring and responding to such individual differences is not an unrealistically daunting endeavor.

Additionally, in our view, there is little value in knowing for its own sake the most empirically and conceptually ideal meaning of "poverty." Rather, a definition of poverty is valuable primarily to the extent that it helps identify who is poor, and for what reasons, so that strategies for eradicating poverty can be most effective. As we have argued, however, other definitions of poverty systematically misrepresent and underestimate the rate of global poverty, particularly among women and members of other marginalized groups. As such, even if these other definitions of poverty are more conducive to the practical measurement of poverty—a claim we have denied—they will nonetheless ultimately fail to result in data about poverty that accurately represent who is poor, and who is getting poorer. That is, at best, they allow us to arrive more efficiently at a drastically inaccurate measurement of poverty. Furthermore, even if a definition of poverty in terms of capabilities-deprivation is less conducive to the practical measurement of poverty (which, again, we deny), this implies that, if adopted and employed to measure poverty, our definition would risk underestimating the rate of global poverty. In other words, at worst, the practical deficiency of the capabilities model would have the same result as the application of other definitions of poverty for accurately identifying the poor. And since this represents the worst-case scenario for the capabilities model, and since, if our previous argument is correct, the capabilities model is no less conducive to the practical measurement of poverty than any other definition, we maintain that this objection presents no reason to reject the understanding of poverty in terms of the deprivation of certain human capabilities.

CONCLUSION

In "The Poorest of the Poor" (2006), Alison Jaggar calls attention to a vital limitation in mainstream literature on global justice: namely, the failure to recognize and analyze women's disproportionate representation among the global poor (the global *feminization of poverty*). Among other things, mainstream literature on poverty is increasingly focused on the role of global economic institutions and affluent countries in exacerbating global inequality and poverty. Yet, insofar as women's overrepresentation is unanalyzed by such theorists, the systematic gender biases of the economic order will also go unnoticed. This omission, however, may be due, at least in part, to the restricted and problematic nature of available poverty estimates, which tell us little about the actual distribution of poverty. In order to determine whether and to what extent women constitute the majority of the world's poor, we first need an accurate conception of poverty. This conception must account for the ways in which one's context, including her social position relative to social relations of power, influences her ability to use resources in a way that allows her to fulfill her basic needs. Unless a definition of poverty includes such concerns, measurements of poverty will continue to be inadequate and, thus, strategies for alleviating poverty—perhaps especially the poverty of women—will be misguided.

NOTES

1. The project of defining a term is inevitably beset by the problem of circularity, particularly to the extent that empirical adequacy is invoked as a desideratum of definitional adequacy. Insofar as empirical adequacy requires that one already know who is poor, our application of this criterion, one may object, is question-begging. However, this objection applies to any case where empirical adequacy is used to test a definition, since one must know the particulars in advance to know the definition, and one must know the definition in advance to know the particulars. As such, all attempts to define "poverty" will be equally encumbered by the problem of circularity; to object that our attempt to justify the understanding of poverty as capabilities-deprivation is circular, then, is to object to the very project of defining "poverty" (and, for that matter, to the project of defining any word).

2. The World Bank's poverty line is arbitrary insofar as it is produced without accounting for many factors that affect whether or not $1/day is sufficient for fulfilling one's basic needs. As we shall argue, the World Bank's poverty line is generated without attention to, among other things, cost of living differentials within countries, the unequal distribution of income within the household (e.g., the impact of gender inequality), as well as neglect of the increasing trend of global consumption toward services over goods. It is in this sense that we characterize the poverty line as "arbitrary."

3. In addition, the World Bank's income-based method ignores the extent to which an income's adequacy for attaining basic necessities will depend on certain key features of one's situation. One important factor is the extent to which one's country provides state-funded public services, such as healthcare and education. Whether someone's circumstances are characterized by unsanitary drinking water, market-based healthcare and education, and the like will have tremendous impact on her standard of living. While an income of $1/day *may be* sufficient for someone who lives in a society that provides quality healthcare and education, as well as public utilities and the like, at no cost, it is far from clear that it would be sufficient in a society in which any or all of these services were provided by the market. This shows that the World Bank lacks a meaningful concept of what basic necessities persons need in order to attain a minimal standard of living. Consequently, one sense in which the World Bank's generation of a baseline income is arbitrary involves its failure to represent the actual resources individuals require to survive.

4. It is possible, however, for any definition of poverty to employ a method of measuring poverty that considers a household a single unit of consumption, and so in principle this can be a problem for any definition.

5. As we will show in the following sections, this is also a problem for other conceptions of poverty that overlook the impact of one's position in relation to social relations of power on one's ability to convert resources into fulfillment of one's basic needs.

6. Different social identities, as they relate to marginalized groups, relate to structures of domination in different ways, which affects their particular experience of this domination, as well as the character of the domination itself. There is no unified experience of racist, sexist, classist, ageist, or heterosexist oppression. Rather

the different features of an individual's identity interact so as to produce a unique experience of sexism, racism, etc. Alison Jaggar once compared this interactional nature to the character of infused tea. The infusion of different flavors yields a unique tea, the character of which is something beyond the addition of the parts. Similarly, the interacting of various structures of domination yields an experience that cannot be understood by separating the different "types" of oppression. Also see Angela Harris (1990).

7. While Spicker classifies the UN's model differently (1999, 152), it seems that a resourcist approach more accurately captures the UN's definition.

8. Why can't a resourcist approach define poverty in reference to multiple baskets of goods? Conceptually, we argue, it is not possible to do this without essentially altering the meaning of poverty offered by the resourcist approach. If a resourcist wished to account for individuals' varying ability to make use of resources by, say, conceiving of the poverty of the elderly in terms of a different basket of goods than that required by the young, she would need to specify some independent standard in terms of which the needs of the elderly could be differently determined relative to the young. For example, she might say that a person is poor if she lacks the resources to be able to function in society in certain ways; since the elderly in general need a greater amount of resources to be able to function in certain ways than do the young, the quantity and type of resources (or basket of goods) needed by the elderly to escape poverty would be greater than that of the young. In this way, the defender of the resourcist approach could justify conceiving of poverty in reference to multiple baskets of goods. However, in doing so, the defender of the resourcist approach has invoked an independent standard to judge whether some basket of goods is adequate to avoid or escape poverty; in this case, that was "to be able to function in society in certain ways"—i.e., capabilities. Hence, it is not possible for a resourcist approach to define poverty in reference to multiple baskets of goods while remaining a resourcist approach.

9. Robert Pinker (1999) argues that while these factors are causally related to poverty, they are not identical to them.

10. In a similar vein, Jaggar (2006) states that such broad definitions "risk using poverty as a catch-all for a range of varied problems and injustices that deserve more direct consideration and precise analysis."

11. Following Amartya Sen's use of the term in *Development as Freedom.*

12. An individual may not be able to meet her needs due to individual shortcomings such as a gambling habit, and although she will still be counted as poor, we do not regard such poverty as imposing justice-based demands for poverty reduction on an institutional, national and global level. For an extensive and persuasive argument on the importance of distinguishing between institutional, or formal, versus informal harms, see Pogge (2003).

13. It is important to note that we are only addressing capabilities as they are required to meet *basic needs*. For instance, a person with a physical disability who has adequate nutrition and housing may not be able to satisfy other needs such as expensive surgery based on her available resources, yet this would not count as poverty. Similarly, lack of access to certain forms of medical treatment such as medicine and/or surgery required for AIDS or cancer treatment may be unjust for various reasons, but is itself not a mark of poverty.

14. We wish to point out, however, that our account differs from Sen's in two important respects. First, as we discuss below, we diverge from Sen concerning what types of capabilities ought to be included in a list of capabilities the lack of which constitutes poverty. More significantly, our justification for the capabilities-based definition of poverty is markedly different from Sen's. While Sen emphasizes the need for a definition that most accurately represents what he takes the concept of poverty to refer to, we are concerned that a definition of poverty take into account various institutional and individual factors that make women and members of other marginalized groups more vulnerable to poverty than otherwise similarly socially situated individuals.

15. In this respect, among others, our account differs from Martha Nussbaum's (2000) work on capabilities. Nussbaum's work defends capabilities as part of a complete theory of the good, and perhaps of a complete theory of justice, while we merely wish to invoke capabilities in order to define poverty. Our account also diverges from Nussbaum's both in terms of the items we wish to include in the list of relevant capabilities (predictably, given our divergent goals), and in terms of our methodological or justificatory process for defending capabilities.

16. Thanks to Uwe Steinhoff for this example.

17. It may appear that the case of the kidnapped billionaire is a counterexample in favor of income-based definitions of poverty, since what is counterintuitive about claiming the kidnapped billionaire is poor is that she has a very high income (as opposed to what we have claimed—that what is counterintuitive about saying the kidnapped billionaire is poor is that the cause of her material deprivation is not appropriately relevant to the concept of poverty). As such, one might claim, income-based definitions of poverty are best because they would not incorrectly characterize the kidnapped billionaire as poor. However, we believe that any meaningful definition of poverty in terms of lack of income would, to the contrary, find the kidnapped billionaire to be poor. This is because a person's income is important only to the extent that she can actually make use of it. For this reason, we argue, this counterexample might be more appropriately described as the case of the kidnapped former billionaire; that is, she is no longer a billionaire if she cannot make use of her billions. If a definition of poverty in terms of lack of income requires, as we believe it must to be meaningful, that a person be able to make use of her income (rather than merely requiring that she have a certain amount of money in her bank account), then the kidnapped billionaire will also count as poor on an income-based definition of poverty. As such, the counterexample does not work to the advantage of income-based definitions of poverty. In addition, we believe this consideration supports our claim that the intuitive force behind the counterexample concerns the cause of the kidnapped billionaire's material deprivation, not her high income.

18. Thanks to Thomas Pogge for this example.

3

PERSONS AND STATES

7

Nussbaum versus Rawls

Should Feminist Human Rights Advocates Reject the Law of Peoples and Endorse the Capabilities Approach?

Alyssa R. Bernstein[1]

Two widely respected contemporary philosophers have recently presented importantly different theoretical conceptions of human rights: John Rawls in *The Law of Peoples* (1999, hereinafter "LP") and Martha Nussbaum in *Frontiers of Justice* (2006, hereinafter "FJ"). Since Nussbaum makes incisive criticisms of Rawls's view and defends a list of human rights that differs markedly from his, these two conceptions of human rights initially appear incompatible. However, in fact they are not significantly incompatible, or so I will argue. If they were, it would be unfortunate, because both theories can be of great value to the oppressed and their allies in advocating that their human rights be respected and secured.

Women and girls continue to suffer significant discrimination in all parts of the world, despite progress made in the twentieth century, including the adoption by the United Nations General Assembly of the Convention on the Elimination of All Forms of Discrimination against Women (CEDAW) in 1979.[2] The number of states that have ratified this convention is greater than the number of states ratifying almost any other convention (Dairiam 2004, 3).[3] However, many of the ratifying states have declared reservations; many of these reservations are stated in broad terms and apply to the most important parts of CEDAW; and few states have fully incorporated CEDAW into their domestic legal systems.[4] Moreover, compounding the wrong of discrimination and unequal treatment, in many parts of the developing world women and girls suffer severe deprivation. Not only is their quality of life lower than that typically enjoyed by members of wealthier societies, and lower than that typically enjoyed by male members of their own societies, but many females are deprived relative to any plausible universal standard of basic human rights. Clearly, getting states to ratify conventions and treaties is not enough: governments must be persuaded, assisted, pressured, or forced—whether by their own populations, foreign human rights advocates, non-governmental organizations, or other state governments and international organizations—to secure at least the most basic human rights for all members of their society and to change discriminatory laws, policies, and practices.

Persuasive arguments for human rights, made in public as well as private forums, can raise awareness and generate motivation and pressure for change. Although it may not be essential for effective political action, clear thinking about human rights can facilitate such action, and at the very least "it can help to unmask the arguments of dictators and their allies" (Donnelly 2003, 3). Moreover, shared understandings and reasoned convictions among human rights advocates can strengthen their solidarity and make their collective efforts more effective. However, philosophers continue to disagree about what human rights are and how they are to be justified and specified.

Nussbaum provides powerful arguments that everyone, female as well as male, is entitled to the fundamental requirements of a life with dignity, as specified in her list of ten Central Human Capabilities; she contends that "a society that does not guarantee these to all its citizens, at some appropriate threshold level, falls short of being a fully just society" (FJ 75). However, Nussbaum's Capabilities Approach (hereinafter "CA") lacks, and needs, a well-developed account of a certain proper subset of human rights— namely, those that are internationally enforceable. In this paper I will argue that such an account can be derived from Rawls's Law of Peoples (hereinafter "LP"), if the latter is reconstructed and interpreted as I propose; so understood, LP evades Nussbaum's criticisms and does not in fact conflict with CA. As I interpret LP, it provides powerful arguments supporting the claim that the international community should recognize a state's government as legitimate, and should regard that state as therefore immune from coercive humanitarian intervention by other states, *only if* it secures basic human rights for all its members, whatever their sex or gender.

In the next section of this paper I briefly explain Nussbaum's conception of human rights, and in the following section I briefly explain Rawls's. I then argue that Nussbaum misinterprets LP. In the remainder of the paper I contend that insofar as LP and CA address different questions about human rights, the two views do not conflict. If my arguments are correct, then oppressed women and their allies can draw arguments from both LP and CA to advocate that the full range of women's human rights be respected and secured.

NUSSBAUM'S VERSION OF
THE CAPABILITIES APPROACH

Nussbaum has been writing about capabilities since the late 1980s, further developing a theoretical approach to assessing quality of life that Amartya Sen had introduced into the field of economics several years earlier.[5] This approach, CA, has become highly influential: it is used by a number of international agencies and non-governmental organizations, including the United Nations Development Program, which employs a capability metric to determine each country's score on the Human Development Index for its annual *Human Development Reports*.[6] Nussbaum's version of CA differs from Sen's, as she points out, "in its emphasis on the philosophical under-pinnings of the approach" (which she understands partly in terms of Aris-totle's ideas of human functioning and Marx's use of these ideas), as well as "in its readiness to take a stand on what the central capabilities are."[7]

In Nussbaum's view, CA can provide "definite and useful guidance, and prove an ally in the pursuit of sex equality, only if we formulate a definite list of the most central capabilities, even one that is tentative and revisable" (CFE 36). Therefore she has formulated such a list.[8] Each item on the list is a category of capabilities, each of which Nussbaum explains briefly.[9] She argues that the capabilities on this list ground "a set of basic entitlements without which no society can lay claim to justice" (CFE 36). Does she regard these basic entitlements as basic human rights? Her answer to this question seems to be "no and yes," with an increasing emphasis on the "yes" in recent years. If CA is a conception of human rights, then in order to assess it one should compare it to other contemporary conceptions of human rights and consider whether it does better the work that such conceptions should do. Such a comparison is also appropriate even if CA is not a conception of human rights, since Nussbaum has claimed that CA is "in some ways superior to" the "familiar human rights paradigm" (CFE 36). I will compare CA with John Rawls's conception of human rights, but before doing so, I will briefly present Nussbaum's account of capabilities, focusing on her account of the relationship between capabilities and human rights.

Capabilities and Human Rights

Nussbaum distinguishes three kinds of capabilities. *Basic capabilities* are "the innate equipment of individuals that is the necessary basis for developing the more advanced capability" (CHR 289). Non-basic, or *advanced*, capabilities are either internal or combined. *Internal capabilities* are "states of the person herself that are . . . sufficient conditions for the exercise of the requisite functions" (CHR 289). *Combined capabilities* are "internal capabilities *combined with* suitable external conditions for the exercise of the function" (CHR 290, italics in original).

According to Nussbaum, basic capabilities are closely related to human rights, understood as rights that people have whether or not their circumstances enable them to exercise or enjoy these rights. We use the term "human rights" in this sense when we say that people "have a right to X," even when their society does not secure such a right to them. Human rights in this sense typically "are thought to derive from some actual feature of human persons, some untrained power in them that demands or calls for support from the world" (CHR 293). To declare a human right, so understood, is to assert that all persons have an urgent, morally justified claim to have a certain *advanced* (i.e., *internal* or *combined*) capability secured to them, for the reason that they are human and/or that they have certain *basic* capabilities. Nussbaum explains it as follows:

> The right to political participation, the right to religious free exercise, the freedom of speech, the freedom to seek employment outside the home, and the freedom from unwarranted search and seizure are all best thought of as human capacities to function in ways that we then go on to specify. The further specification will usually involve both an internal component and an external component: a citizen who is systematically deprived of information about religion does not really have religious liberty, even if the state imposes no barrier to religious choice. On the other hand, internal conditions are not enough: women who can think about work outside the home, but who are going to be systematically denied employment on account of sex, or beaten if they try to go outside, do not have the right to seek employment. (CHR 292–293)

Here, by saying that women in such circumstances do not have the right to seek employment, Nussbaum is saying that they lack the relevant combined capability to function: they are not able to seek a job outside the home, even though their basic capabilities give them an urgent, morally justified claim to have that combined capability secured to them.

According to Nussbaum, combined capabilities "are the *goals* of public planning," in the sense that the state should respond to its citizens' human rights by undertaking to enable the citizens to have combined capabilities (CHR 293, italics in original). "It is in this sense," she writes, "that capabilities and rights should be seen as equivalent" (CHR 293). Summarizing her view, Nussbaum says:

> capabilities as I conceive them have a very close relationship to human rights, as understood in contemporary international discussions. In effect they cover

the terrain covered by both the so-called first-generation rights (political and civil liberties) and the so-called second-generation rights (economic and social rights). And they play a similar role, providing the philosophical underpinning for basic constitutional principles. (WHD, 97)

Note that Nussbaum has distinguished two related notions. Human rights in one sense (HR1) are grounded directly in basic capabilities and constitute urgent, morally justified claims to advanced capabilities; here, the advanced capabilities are understood as the contents or the objects of the human rights, as what they are rights *to*. When human rights (HR1) are recognized in international laws and policies, they are human rights in an additional sense (HR2). Note that international legal or political recognition does not necessarily entail domestic legal recognition. Therefore, even when international declarations assert that constitutions should secure certain advanced capabilities, people may not actually have those capabilities.

Note also that Nussbaum's assertion of the equivalence of rights and combined capabilities may be misleading, if by "equivalent" we take her to mean "interchangeable" or "identical." Combined capabilities are not identical with human rights in either of the two senses of "human rights" distinguished above. Capabilities are not rights but instead the grounds, contents, or objects of the rights. However, one familiar and plausible interpretation of the idea that everyone has human rights is the idea that all governments ought to secure certain combined capabilities for everyone; that is, that these capabilities should be the goals of public planning.

Nussbaum's Publications on CA and Human Rights

Nussbaum discusses the relation between capabilities and human rights most extensively in the article "Capabilities and Human Rights" (1997), which in her later works she cites, summarizes, and revises. She explains that she and Amartya Sen favor CA partly because they find "the language of rights" unsatisfactory: despite its prevalence and its moral resonance, it lacks theoretical and conceptual clarity, and many important theoretical questions about rights remain unresolved (CHR 273–275). Nussbaum thinks the language of rights is "not especially informative . . . unless its users link their references to rights to a theory that answers at least some of these [important] questions" (CHR 275). She and Sen have offered CA as such a theory.

In *Women and Human Development* (2000) Nussbaum argues for her own version of CA, including its list of the central human capabilities. She also distinguishes between a stronger and a weaker use of CA. In its weaker use it "specifies a space within which *comparisons of life quality* (how well people are doing) are most revealingly made among nations" (WHD 6, italics in original). In its stronger use it provides the philosophical basis for an account of fundamental constitutional principles establishing "a bare minimum of what respect for human dignity requires," which "should be respected and implemented by the governments of all nations" (WHD 5).

In *Frontiers of Justice* (2006) Nussbaum argues that constitutions should require that all of the central human capabilities be secured to each and every citizen, "at least up to the threshold level," and that an appropriate threshold level for each capability can be determined via "the judicial process" (FJ 175). Before I present my account of LP, I want to take a closer look at what Nussbaum says in FJ about several of LP's main topics: societal justice, governmental legitimacy, state sovereignty, and humanitarian intervention. Nussbaum discusses these topics in light of her distinction between justification and implementation.

Nussbaum on Justification and Implementation

According to Nussbaum, societies should aim at raising all of their citizens above a certain threshold level for each of the central human capabilities: the level "beneath which . . . truly human functioning is not available to citizens" (WHD 6). Although attaining this goal may not make a society just, she says, it will make it far more just than any society now is (WHD 75). Every national constitution should be based on the fundamental political principles provided by CA; however, implementation of these principles must be left largely to the "internal politics" of each nation (WHD 105). Although the same moral norms apply to all nations (FJ 257–260), she emphasizes that to say that we can *justify* the same norms for all nations is not to say that we are morally entitled to *implement* these norms everywhere (FJ 260).

Nussbaum says that the fullest justification for implementing CA would be a worldwide reflective-equilibrium-type consensus. However, even before such a consensus is reached, pro-CA nations may appropriately "commend this norm strongly" to other nations, and even make CA part of international as well as national law by endorsing international treaties, covenants, or conventions based on it (WHD 103–105). They may also try to convince or compel other nations to do likewise, e.g., via diplomatic exchanges and aid policies. Furthermore, pro-CA national governments and international agencies may, in especially grave cases, justifiably employ economic or political sanctions intended to compel nations to implement CA-based constitutional principles (WHD 104). Nussbaum acknowledges that a nation may fail to secure all of the capabilities up to their threshold levels because it is unable to do so, e.g., due to dire poverty and disease. However, she does not think such cases raise any new questions of justice, but only "a purely practical question what to do next," for "[t]he question of justice is already answered: justice has not been fully done here."[10]

Nussbaum points out that the modern human rights movement "uses persuasion in most cases and urges forcible intervention in a very small number of cases," thus recognizing the distinction between justification and implementation (FJ 256). Here "implementation" evidently means employment of some form of pressure or coercive force, by nations acting alone or in concert, in order to compel (rather than persuade) another nation to change its policies and practices. When and why is implementation, so understood, permissible according to Nussbaum? Her answer is brief and unclear, and she offers little argument to support it. In general, Nussbaum says, "one should respect the sovereignty of any nation that is organized in a sufficiently accountable way, whether or not its institutions are fully just" (FJ 256). As long as a nation, though imperfect, is "still above a certain threshold of inclusiveness and accountability," respect for the nation's citizens and for their state as an expression of their human autonomy should lead other nations to "refrain from military intervention into the affairs of that nation," and to "negotiate with its duly elected government as a legitimate government" (FJ 256).

What is a "sufficiently accountable" way of organizing a nation, according to Nussbaum? At various points in the text, she seems to suggest that only procedurally democratic regimes can be sufficiently accountable and thus legitimate.[11] However, at other points Nussbaum expresses agreement with Rawls, who denies that only states with democratic regimes can, in principle, have the right against coercion by other states.[12] Moreover, Nussbaum does not systematically and fully address what reasons may justify state actions or policies aiming to compel other states to respect human rights. No conception of human rights should be regarded as complete and satisfactory unless it adequately addresses this issue, both because the term "human rights" figures in justifications for international actions and policies, and because such actions and policies can have such important consequences for people's lives.

Above I suggested that Nussbaum's claim that there is a "basic distinction" between justification and implementation means that, although there may be conditions in which we are not morally entitled to implement CA by means of coercive force, this implies neither that CA is not justifiable nor that it is not justifiably implemented by other means (FJ 262). This interpretation is supported by the fact that Nussbaum criticizes Rawls for holding (she claims) the contrary position (FJ 255). She accuses him of conflating the question of whether a nation is "worthy of respect" as a member in good standing of the Society of Peoples with the question of whether we should "refrain from intervening in that nation to seek the implementation of our own moral standards" (FJ 255). But these are distinct questions, she argues:

> We may think that the standards of a given nation are defective, and that we can justify as applicable to that nation a more extensive menu of basic rights and liberties than it now recognizes, thus making justified criticisms of that nation, without thinking that we have the right to intervene in its affairs, either militarily or through economic or political sanctions. (FJ 255–256)

In fact, however, Rawls does distinguish these questions; Nussbaum is mistaken in confidently asserting the contrary.[13] In LP Rawls undertakes to answer several related questions which presuppose and employ (1) the distinction between a fully just society and a decently well-ordered society, and (2) the distinction between societies that meet all of the criteria of decency (and are thus entitled to the rights of members in good standing of the Society of Peoples) and states that do not (whether because they are unwilling or because they are unable). LP takes a clear and consistent position on the question of whether only states with democratic regimes can have immunity from coercive intervention by other states, and it addresses this issue directly and systematically, as part of a broader inquiry into universal human rights. If my interpretation of LP is correct, Nussbaum misunderstands its aims as well as its arguments, and her criticisms therefore miss their target.

RAWLS'S CONCEPTION OF HUMAN RIGHTS[14]

Liberals regard all non-liberal societies as unjust, at least to some degree and in some respects, including in particular that their form of government is not democratic. However, it seems clear that such a judgment does not by itself constitute even *prima facie* moral justification for liberal societies to employ coercive force to compel any or all non-liberal societies to adopt a democratic form of government. Yet it also seems clear that if there are grave and widespread violations of basic human rights in a society, this does provide at least *prima facie* moral justification for the use of some form of coercive force by other states to stop those violations. So liberal societies face the question of what principles should govern their relations with other societies, in order to (a) try to ensure that all societies secure human rights for the people they govern or affect, while at the same time (b) minimizing the risks of war and (c) allowing all societies to govern themselves, work out solutions to their own problems, and progress toward their own social ideals in their own ways, free from undue interference. In LP Rawls takes initial steps toward determining where a just system of international law would set the limits of states' rights of self-determination and non-intervention.

Rawls develops his conception of human rights (more precisely, his conception of internationally enforceable basic human rights, hereinafter "IEB-HRs") in the context of his conception of the moral basis of a just system of international law, which he calls "the Law of Peoples." In his long essay by the same name,[15] he defends a set of principles of international cooperation as suitable for inclusion in the foundation charter of a Society of Peoples (the nucleus of a law-governed international community that can develop into a fully just global order). These principles, among which is one requiring that all societies honor human rights, constitute the moral basis and framework of a system of international law that can develop into a just system of global public law.

Clearly, it is necessary to specify the meaning of the requirement that all societies honor human rights. To do so requires specifying both the sense and the reference of the term "human rights," as it is used in the statement of this principle. To specify its reference requires developing a list of human rights that would be suitable for use in interpreting an enforceable legal requirement that all societies honor human rights. The sense of the term "human rights," as Rawls uses it in LP, is that of internationally enforceable basic human rights, understood as urgently important rights that all individual persons may validly claim and that all governments are obligated to respect, because no government can plausibly claim legitimate authority unless its legal and political system ascribes such rights, and no society can plausibly claim to be just unless it has a legitimate government. These rights are grounded in principles of justice that apply to all governments and that set constraints on their use of political power in making and implementing foreign as well as domestic policy. To determine which rights belong in this category, one would have to determine which principles of justice apply to all governments. In LP Rawls undertakes this task. In doing so, he reasons from liberal premises and considers what principles should guide the foreign policy of liberal-democratic states. However, he argues that these are principles which all decent societies can endorse as constituting the moral basis of international law and as applying to international relations among all societies.

Societal Justice and Governmental Legitimacy

Taking a bottom-up or "at-least" approach, Rawls starts from the idea that a just society has at least a legitimate government, which must be understood as at least a system of law such that the people governed are not merely forced but instead obligated to obey it. Thus he develops an argument aiming to show that at least a proper subset of the basic rights of the citizens of a fully just liberal-democratic society are universal and internationally enforceable basic human rights: that all individuals are entitled to claim them, that all governments are obligated to respect and secure them, and that the international community may and should enforce them worldwide (via appropriate procedures and measures), for moral reasons that do not depend on states having explicitly committed themselves to respect and secure these rights.[16] Rawls aims to show this by means of arguments that no government can reject while plausibly claiming legitimacy.

In developing his conception of a fully just liberal democratic society, which he calls Justice as Fairness (JF),[17] Rawls analyzes the idea of fair social cooperation among individual human beings who are members of the same society, all free citizens of equal political status. He argues for two fundamental, general principles of societal justice,[18] which are to guide and constrain the citizens of a democratic society (i.e., one characterized by popular sovereignty) in using the coercive powers of their government domestically. These two principles are to constitute its foundation charter.

Analogously, in LP Rawls argues for certain fundamental, general principles of fair social cooperation among legitimately governed states,[19] which are to guide and constrain the international uses of their coercive powers. These principles spell out some of the logical implications of an abstract idea of social cooperation among states aiming to establish a just and stable system of international law. The principles are to be included in the foundation charter of such a legal order.

To determine whether the set of internationally enforceable basic human rights is coextensive with the set of the basic rights of the citizens of a fully just liberal democratic society, Rawls takes a top-down approach. He starts from JF and asks whether *all* of the basic rights of such a society's citizens, i.e., the rights specified by JF's two principles of justice, should count as basic human rights. His answer is no, not all of them: internationally enforceable basic human rights are a proper subset of those citizens' rights.[20]

Rawls emphasizes that certain long-standing principles of international conduct (i.e., that states are to observe a duty of nonintervention, and that states have the right of self-defense but no right to instigate war for reasons other than self-defense) have rightly been revised in recent years[21] to allow for intervention in cases of "grave violations of human rights" (LP 37). In developing his conception of the moral basis of a just global system of public law, Rawls further modifies these principles by substituting the term "peoples" for the term "states"; thus, he puts the normative idea of a well-ordered society under a legitimate government (an ideal to which he refers using "peoples" as a technical term) in place of the idea standardly used in political science (particularly in realist international-relations theory) according to which a state is a rational, self-interested collective agent that mainly aims to acquire and retain military, economic, and diplomatic power over other states. He imagines the governments of peoples setting up a system of international law, and argues that all and only peoples, which are societies under governments satisfying criteria of decency which include honoring certain basic human rights, are entitled to the rights traditionally ascribed to all states.[22]

The Criteria of Decency

Rawls's first criterion of decency requires nonaggressiveness vis-à-vis other societies. His second criterion comprises three conditions of governmental legitimacy, one of which requires respect for the basic human rights. Rawls's justification of his second criterion of decency may be summarized as follows. A system of laws must meet certain conditions if it is to be viable. However, if those to whom the laws are applied have *bona fide* moral duties and obligations to obey them, the legal system must meet not only the conditions of viability but also a further condition: the officials of the government must be trying in good faith to govern justly and to ensure that the laws accord with their conception of justice and its idea of the common good of the society.

Furthermore, argues Rawls, a society's political and legal system can be regarded as morally defensible, and the society as well-ordered, only if the political and legal system is structured so as to ensure that everyone's fundamental interests (as it understands them) are secured. In addition, the governing conception of justice must understand the fundamental interests of those to whom the laws are applied in a way consistent with recognizing them not only as human beings but also as moral persons, for their being moral persons is entailed by the very idea of a political and legal system ordered in accordance with a conception of justice that imposes *bona fide* moral duties and obligations upon them. This holds for women as much as for men: to require anyone to obey laws is to recognize them as persons with the requisite capacities for moral as well as prudential reasoning, judgment, and action. Thus everyone, regardless of gender, is equally entitled to the universal human rights for which Rawls argues.

A Sketch to be Further Developed

Rawls presents his proposed list of internationally enforceable basic human rights as an incomplete, abstract sketch.[23] It functions mainly to indicate that the list of human rights appropriate for inclusion in a Law of Peoples would largely agree with classic bills of rights, but that not all of the rights listed in the UDHR should be classified as permissibly enforced internationally, in principle, on moral grounds independent of official commitments to secure them. Rawls's proposed list can be variously interpreted, since each of the rights on the list is described only briefly and abstractly. And it can get expanded if suitable arguments for further rights are developed. Although LP is in some respects merely a sketch, it provides strong arguments for excluding certain rights from the category of IEBHRs, as well as strong arguments for including a number of rights in this category; it also shows how to develop such arguments regarding other rights.

HOW NUSSBAUM MISINTERPRETS LP

In the rest of this paper, I present some of Nussbaum's main criticisms of LP and show that they do not apply to it as I interpret it. I will focus on two key points, each of which will require some discussion. Nussbaum asserts that (1) Rawls conflates justification with implementation, and that (2) Rawls unjustifiably excludes "burdened" societies from the Society of Peoples, thus in effect denying that they are entitled to assistance from wealthier societies.

Regarding point (1), Nussbaum asserts: "Rawls clearly thinks that if we conclude that another nation has defective norms we will intervene in some way, whether militarily or through economic and political sanctions."[24] She bases some of her harshest criticisms on this interpretation.[25] However, it is contradicted not only by my interpretation of LP but also directly by Rawls's text.

What Rawls clearly thinks is that any society that is not a liberal democracy has norms that are defective in some way. He says this more than once and in more than one way.[26] With regard to the question of justified intervention, Rawls argues that we must take note of the morally significant differences among four kinds of non-liberal societies: (1) aggressive "outlaw states," which refuse to comply with any reasonable Law of Peoples (LP 4, 5, 48, 80–81, 90); (2) non-aggressive societies that are willing but unable to secure their people's basic human rights;[27] (3) nonaggressive societies that secure their people's basic human rights but deny them any "meaningful role in making political decisions";[28] and (4) decent, well-ordered societies that not only secure their people's basic human rights but also enable them to play a "substantial role" in making political decisions, although not within a democratic structure in which they are all citizens with equal political rights (but instead within, e.g., a reasonable form of consultation hierarchy) (LP 4, 71–75). Rawls argues that liberal societies should recognize *only* non-liberal societies of type (4) as entitled to *bona fide* membership, i.e., full membership in good standing, in the Society of Peoples (LP 61, 80). However, since societies of type (3) secure their people's basic human rights (at least those on the list in LP), other societies cannot justifiably intervene or coerce them to reform. More generally, when a society's domestic political, economic, and social institutions secure its people's basic human rights, it is unjustifiable for other societies to intervene militarily or even to impose economic or diplomatic sanctions.[29] Contra Nussbaum, Rawls clearly *does not* think that "if we conclude that another nation has defective norms we will intervene in some way, whether militarily or through economic and political sanctions."[30]

Regarding point (2), Nussbaum says that according to Rawls, "burdened peoples" will "on account of their poverty" not "be part of the Society of Peoples" (FJ 239, 247). She evidently ascribes to Rawls the view that better-off societies may or even should exclude worse-off societies from the Society of Peoples in order to avoid having to assist them. But in fact, Rawls holds the contrary view: "Well-ordered peoples have a *duty* to assist burdened societies" (LP 106, italics in original). Since burdened societies have dysfunctional political, economic, and/or social institutions, they do not meet the criteria of decency and cannot engage in international cooperation guided by the Law of Peoples, as the well-ordered societies can. What this means is not that well-ordered societies may simply exclude burdened societies and disregard their needs, but rather that the former must undertake to assist the latter to reform or rebuild their institutions so that they meet the criteria of decency.[31]

Nussbaum does acknowledge[32] that Rawls holds that all well-ordered peoples have a duty to assist the burdened societies. However, she mentions this only briefly and inaccurately: "For Rawls, such assistance chiefly entails helping [the burdened societies] to develop stable democratic institutions, which he takes to be the main ingredient of their eventual prosperity" (FJ 247). In fact, Rawls holds that well-ordered peoples should provide diverse forms of assistance, including but not limited to financial and material aid. Rawls makes it very clear that assistance to burdened societies may require much more than merely giving money: "What must be realized is that merely dispensing funds will not suffice to rectify basic political and social injustices (though money is often essential)" (LP 108–109). A "burdened society," as Rawls defines the term, is one that "lack[s] the political and cultural traditions, the human capital and know-how, and, often, the material and technological resources needed to be well-ordered" (LP 106). Therefore burdened societies typically need not merely additional material resources, but also other kinds of assistance. Rawls emphasizes that no matter how and why the society is burdened, "the duty of assistance is in no way diminished" (LP 108).

What kinds of nonmaterial assistance does Rawls think well-ordered societies should provide to burdened societies, in addition to material resources? High on the list is helping them to educate their populations and to acquire needed technology (LP 106). Also high on the list is helping the policymakers in resource-poor countries to understand how to avoid overburdening their nation's lands and economy with an unsustainably large population (LP 108). If a country needs to change some of its institutions or practices, well-ordered societies may be able to accelerate and support the reform efforts of its governmental and non-governmental organizations. However, there is, as Rawls says, "no recipe, certainly no easy recipe, for well-ordered peoples to help a burdened society to change its political and social culture" (LP 108).

One form of assistance that well-ordered societies can and should offer, Rawls emphasizes, is human-rights advocacy. They should demand that callous and corrupt rulers respect at least the basic human rights. Referring to Sen's work,[33] Rawls says that "insisting on human rights will, it is to be hoped, help to prevent famines from developing, and will exert pressure in the direction of effective governments in a well-ordered Society of Peoples" (LP 109).

As mentioned above, Rawls holds that one of the crucial elements determining whether resource-poor countries can be well-ordered is the country's population policy (LP 108). This provides a further reason for burdened societies to respect human rights, he contends: "A decisive factor here [regarding population pressure] appears to be the status of women" (LP 109–110). Referring to China's harsh policies and contrasting them with those of the Indian state of Kerala (which rapidly reduced its birth rate by empowering women to own and manage property, to acquire education, and to vote and participate in politics), Rawls says that "the simplest, most effective, most acceptable policy is to establish the elements of equal justice for women" (LP 110). Well-ordered societies, when advocating that burdened societies respect human rights, can point this out and urge them to "pay particular attention to the fundamental interests of women" and to reform the country's political procedures in whatever ways are "necessary to prevent violations of the human rights of women" (LP 110).

Rawls explains that the aim of the duty of assistance is "to help burdened societies to be able to manage their own affairs" and "to realize and preserve just (or decent) institutions" (LP 107, 111). As noted earlier, meeting Rawls's criteria of decency does not necessarily require that a society's government be procedurally democratic. So the text of LP contradicts Nussbaum's assertion that for Rawls, assistance to burdened societies "chiefly entails" helping them "to develop stable democratic institutions" (FJ 247). It also contradicts Nussbaum's assertion that Rawls uses Sen's theory "to deny that richer nations need to give economic aid to poorer nations" (FJ 316).

THE APPEARANCE OF CONFLICT
BETWEEN LP AND CA

Rawls's LP and Nussbaum's CA initially appear to conflict. This is so not only because Nussbaum contends that they conflict, but also because both theories are conceptions of human rights and global justice, yet each presents a different list of human rights. However, the appearance of conflict is largely, if not entirely, misleading. Both CA and LP are incomplete conceptions of human rights and global justice, each focusing on different important questions about human rights.

Rawls develops his open-ended list of human rights as a proposed answer to the following question: Which rights must be included on a list of urgently important human rights suitable for use in interpreting an enforceable international legal requirement that all societies honor human rights? He does not fully answer this question; instead he indicates a method for answering it, and he takes a number of the initial steps of the reasoning for us, thus generating his proposed provisional list of internationally enforceable basic human rights.

Nussbaum develops her open-ended list of human rights (or, in her terms, central human capabilities to which everyone is entitled) as her proposed provisional answer to the following question: What are the central human capabilities implicit in the idea of a life worthy of human dignity, such that every society should aim to raise all of its members above the threshold level of each of these capabilities, and should establish a constitutionally guaranteed social minimum based on these threshold levels? Clearly this question is quite different from Rawls's; unsurprisingly, her answer is different as well.

These different questions are associated with different inquiry-specific aims which exert opposing pressures on each philosopher's list of human rights. Rawls's aim in LP is to develop a principled general justification for international use of coercive force to stop grave violations of basic human rights, without weakening too much the prohibition on non-defensive war. The latter concern acts as a constraint keeping Rawls's list of basic human rights shorter than the list of the basic rights of citizens of liberal-democratic societies, and much shorter than Nussbaum's list of central human capabilities.

Nussbaum, on the other hand, aims to develop a justification for advocating that we, and in particular those of us wielding power (whether in governments or non-governmental organizations), undertake to secure for everyone worldwide a social minimum of such a kind and at such a level that everyone can enjoy at least a decent human life and possibly also a flourishing one. This aim functions to lengthen her list of human rights.

CONCLUSION

Nussbaum rightly claims as an advantage of CA that "by focusing from the start on what people are actually able to do and to be, it is well placed to foreground and address inequalities that women suffer inside the family:

inequalities in resources and opportunities, educational deprivations, the failure of work to be recognized as work, insults to bodily integrity" (FJ 290). However, her claims that CA is a better "model of global development" than LP, and that CA is a more promising "way of thinking about the goals of development in this increasingly interdependent and interconnected world" than is LP, are partly true and partly false (BSC 2004, 4). In determining what the goals of development should be, we must consider what structure a just global order would have. According to both Nussbaum and Rawls, it would be an order of politically independent states regulating their relations with each other according to the requirements of a just system of international law. So in determining what the goals of development should be, we must consider what moral principles would ground and structure a just system of international law. But CA does not do this, whereas LP does. On the other hand, Nussbaum's list of the central human capabilities arguably provides good guidance to those undertaking to interpret lists of abstractly formulated basic rights (such as LP's list or the lists that may be included in international declarations or national constitutions) that are to be implemented in laws and policies.

Advocates for the human rights of women and girls need clear and well-justified replies to challenging questions, including: (1) Why should states respect and secure the rights listed in CEDAW? (2) Are the states that have ratified CEDAW obligated to implement it, not only in virtue of the fact that they (or their former political representatives) have ratified it, but also for moral reasons that are independent of such ratification? (3) Are the states that have not ratified CEDAW obligated morally, if not legally, to respect and secure the rights listed in it? (4) When, why, and how may the international community or any of its component agents (individual or collective) justifiably pressure or coerce a state (whether or not it has ratified CEDAW) to respect any or all of the rights listed therein? LP offers partial answers to the first three questions, in abstract and general terms (i.e., without specific reference to CEDAW) and with reference to only some of the rights it lists (those corresponding to the IEBHRs on LP's list). CA proposes different partial answers to the same questions, also in general terms, but with reference to all of the rights listed in CEDAW, and on the basis of different arguments. Regarding the fourth question, LP provides most of the necessary components of a good abstract answer to it, while CA has comparatively little to say.[34]

CA does provide powerful arguments for securing the human rights of women and girls. These arguments are based on CA's central claims: that all human beings are entitled to respect, that all governments should enable their people to live lives worthy of human dignity, and that the ideas of human dignity and respect should be fleshed out in terms of Nussbaum's list of central human capabilities.[35] However, to the extent that CA's conception of the responsibilities of government or its interpretations of the ideas of respect and human dignity are open to reasonable dispute, so are arguments based on them. Therefore advocates for the human rights of girls and women have reason to base their arguments not only on CA but also on LP. And they can do so without inconsistency since, as I have argued, CA is not significantly incompatible with LP.[36]

LP is a basis and source of especially powerful arguments for respecting and securing the basic human rights of women and girls. They are especially powerful in that they employ premises presupposed by any government that sincerely and plausibly claims to exercise legitimate political authority (i.e., claims that the people it requires to obey its laws are not merely coerced but instead obligated to obey them), and that requires not only men but also women to obey its laws. To regard women as obligated to comply with legitimate laws is to regard them as capable of doing so, thus capable of carrying out the necessary reasoning: it is to regard them as possessing the powers of rationality and reasonableness to at least the minimum degree necessary for compliance with legitimate law.[37] A government claiming legitimate political authority over women cannot consistently require them to exercise powers of reasoning and judgment, yet deny to girls and women the conditions and resources necessary for developing and exercising those powers.

NOTES

1. For helpful comments and editing suggestions I thank Todd Bastin, Nathaniel Goldberg, Casey Haskins, Mark LeBar, Francis Longworth, Wendy Parker, and James Petrik, as well as the editors of this volume, Peggy DesAutels and Rebecca Whisnant. I presented a shorter version of this paper at the 2006 meeting of the Eastern Division of the American Philosophical Association; I thank my fellow panelists and the audience for their helpful questions and comments. For financial assistance facilitating my research, writing, and public presentation of this paper, I thank Ohio University's Institute for Applied and Professional Ethics and in particular its director, Professor Arthur Zucker.

2. See, for example, World Economic Forum (2005). Feride Açar, Chairperson (1997–2004) of the United Nations Committee on the Elimination of Discrimination Against Women, has stated that "No country in the world has fully implemented the human rights of women, and full *de jure*, let alone *de facto*, equality has not been achieved anywhere in the world" (Açar 2004, 30).

3. As of November 2, 2006, 185 states had ratified CEDAW. The USA is not among them: it signed the treaty in 1980 but has not ratified it (http://www.un.org/womenwatch/daw/cedaw/states.htm, read in January 2006).

4. CEDAW has more reservations than any other human rights treaty (Açar 2004, 21).

5. Here I will limit my attention to Nussbaum's version of CA, discussing Sen's

only in relation to hers and only as she characterizes the relationship. For an account of the relation between Nussbaum's and Sen's views, see Crocker (1992) and (1995); also see Nussbaum's (2003) "Capabilities as Fundamental Entitlements: Sen and Social Justice" (hereinafter "CFE").

6. Nussbaum expresses dissatisfaction with this: "The use of capabilities in development is typically comparative merely, as in the *Human Development Reports* of the UNDP" (CFE, 35).

7. *Women and Human Development* (2000), 70 (hereinafter "WHD").

8. Nussbaum (1997) has been revising and specifying the list so that it may "do real work guiding public policy" ("Capabilities and Human Rights" [hereinafter "CHR"], 277). One revised version of the list appears in CHR, 287–288, another in WHD, 78–80; the latest version, entitled "The Central Human Capabilities," appears in FJ, 76–78.

9. The categories are: (1) *"Life.* Being able to live to the end of a human life of normal length . . ." (2) *"Bodily Health.* Being able to have good health, including reproductive health . . ." (3) *"Bodily Integrity.* Being able to move freely from place to place; to be secure against violent assault . . ." (4) *"Senses, Imagination, and Thought.* Being able to use the senses to imagine, think, and reason—and to do these things in a 'truly human' way . . ." (5) *"Emotions.* Being able to have attachments to things and people outside ourselves . . ." (6) *"Practical Reason.* Being able to form a conception of the good . . ." (7) *"Affiliation."* (7A) "Being able to live with and toward others . . ." (7B) "Having the social bases of self-respect and non-humiliation . . ." (8) *"Other Species.* Being able to live with concern for and in relation to animals, plants, and the world of nature." (9) *"Play.* Being able to laugh, to play, to enjoy recreational activities." (10) *"Control over One's Environment."* (10A) *"Political.* Being able to participate effectively in political choices that govern one's life; having the right of political participation, protections of free speech and association." (10B) *"Material.* Being able to hold property . . . ; having the right to seek employment on an equal basis with others . . ."

10. FJ, 175. What she means by this is not clear. Is she saying that situations in which nations are unable to secure all of the capabilities of all of their citizens up to their threshold levels raise only practical, not moral questions? This would be an implausible view, so I hesitate to attribute it to her. The most plausible construal seems to be that the infeasibility or even moral impermissibility of implementing her conception of justice at a particular time and in a particular country undermines neither its justification nor its applicability to that country.

11. In addition to the passage from FJ, 256, quoted above, there are several other passages. For example: "Consider . . . the case of a nation that fails . . . to offer women equal property rights. . . . So long as this nation is above a certain threshold in terms of democratic legitimacy, much though one might deplore the inequalities of women under that state's constitution, it would not be right to intervene in coercive ways" (FJ, 258). Commenting on the genocide and mass rapes in Gujarat, India, in March 2002, Nussbaum says that there were arguments both for and against intervention, and that one argument against was the following: "So long as democratic processes in India are robust, as they were and are, we should prefer to allow them to take their course, out of respect for these processes themselves and

the citizens involved in them, in the hope that over time duly elected officials and duly appointed courts will bring the offenders to book and prevent further abuses . . ." (FJ, 259).

12. Here are two examples: "What is the threshold of legitimacy? A reasonable accountability of government to people: and here Rawls's conception of a 'reasonable consultation hierarchy' may offer good guidance." (FJ, 259). "At this point Rawls might say that I have conceded his basic point: that we should treat nations as decent members in good standing of the Society of Peoples on a much weaker showing of liberal freedom and equality than we would demand within a liberal society. And indeed Rawls and I have converged in some respects on a set of practical principles." (FJ, 261).

13. "Rawls *clearly* thinks that if we conclude that another nation has defective norms we will intervene in some way, whether militarily or through economic and political sanctions" (FJ, 255, emphasis added).

14. In this section I briefly summarize ideas and arguments which I develop more fully in Bernstein (2004), (2006), (2007a), and (2007b).

15. It appears in the volume entitled *The Law of Peoples*, which includes a long essay entitled "The Idea of Public Reason Revisited."

16. I do not interpret Rawls as holding that states may legitimately act to enforce rights merely because the rights are justifiable via sound moral and philosophical arguments, even though they are not recognized in positive law.

17. See *A Theory of Justice* (Cambridge, Mass.: Harvard University Press, 1971/ 1999), *Political Liberalism* (New York, N.Y.: Columbia University Press, 1993/1996), and *Justice as Fairness* (Cambridge, Mass.: Harvard University Press, 2001). Hereinafter "TJ," "PL," and "JF," respectively.

18. "(a) Each person has the same indefeasible claim to a fully adequate scheme of equal basic liberties, which scheme is compatible with the same scheme of liberties for all; and (b) Social and economic inequalities are to satisfy two conditions: first, they are to be attached to offices and positions open to all under conditions of fair equality of opportunity; and second, they are to be to the greatest benefit of the least-advantaged members of society (the difference principle)" (JF, 42–43).

19. The principles of LP are as follows (LP, 37): (1) Peoples are free and independent, and their freedom and independence are to be respected by other peoples. (2) Peoples are to observe treaties and undertakings. (3) Peoples are equal and are parties to the agreements that bind them. (4) Peoples are to observe a duty of nonintervention. (5) Peoples have the right of self-defense but no right to instigate war for reasons other than self-defense. (6) Peoples are to honor human rights. (7) Peoples are to observe certain specified restrictions in the conduct of war. (8) Peoples have a duty to assist other peoples living under unfavorable conditions that prevent their having a just or decent political and social regime.

20. I develop this argument in Bernstein (2006).

21. This is not to say that they have been revised for the right reasons or in precisely the right ways.

22. Here I disagree with Nussbaum's understanding of the term "a people" as used in LP (FJ, 243). For a lucid discussion of Rawls's use of this term, see 423–424 and 427 of Samuel Freeman's excellent review essay (2006). I encountered Free-

man's review after having written and publicly presented the present paper; I was pleased to see both that we agree and also that he does not present the arguments I present in this paper. Freeman discusses LP and Nussbaum's criticisms of it on 421–427 of his review.

23. "Among the human rights are the right to life (to the means of subsistence and security); to liberty (to freedom from slavery, serfdom and forced occupation, and to a sufficient measure of liberty of conscience to ensure freedom of religion and thought); to property (personal property); and to formal equality as expressed by the rules of natural justice (that is, that similar cases be treated similarly)." LP, 65, footnotes suppressed.

24. FJ, 255. Nussbaum earlier made an almost identical statement in "Beyond the Social Contract: Capabilities and Global Justice," in *Oxford Development Studies* 32:1, March 2004, 10 (hereinafter "BSC 2004").

25. FJ, Ch. 4, section iv: "Justification and Implementation."

26. "A decent hierarchical society . . . does not treat its own members reasonably or justly as free and equal citizens, since it lacks the idea of citizenship" (LP, 83). "To repeat, I am not saying that a decent hierarchical society is as reasonable and just as a liberal society" (ibid.).

27. Rawls describes these societies as "burdened by unfavorable conditions," in that their "historical, social, and economic circumstances make their achieving a well-ordered regime, whether liberal or decent, difficult if not impossible" (LP, 4, 5, 90, 106).

28. Rawls describes these societies as "benevolent absolutisms" (LP, 4, 63).

29. The rights in the special class that Rawls calls "human rights" have three roles: (a) they "set a necessary, though not sufficient, standard for the decency of domestic political and social institutions;" (b) if a society fulfills them, then other societies lack adequate justification for coercive intervention; (c) they "limit admissible domestic law of societies in good standing in a reasonably just Society of Peoples." (LP, 80).

30. FJ, 255. Note that Nussbaum says "will," not "should." If we interpret her statement as a prediction or as a statement of an empirical law of some kind, we find even less support for it in the text of LP.

31. Rawls says: "the long-term goal of (relatively) well-ordered societies should be to bring burdened societies . . . into the Society of well-ordered Peoples" (LP, 106).

32. She acknowledges it on 247 of FJ, then denies it on 316 of the same book.

33. Sen has written about empirical research showing that famines do not occur in countries with political and legal systems that meet certain criteria, foremost among which are democracy and a free press. Sen argues that the main cause of famines is not a sudden sharp drop in food production but the failure of the country's government to take action to prevent starvation by distributing and supplementing the country's supply of food. See Sen (1981) and Sen and Dreze (1989).

34. It is important to keep in mind the difference between judging that interstate coercion is in principle justifiable in certain kinds of cases, and judging that in some particular case coercive force should be used. One can endorse LP while opposing the use of coercive force when other means of securing human rights

would be sufficiently effective. On this topic see, for example, Nickel (2006). However, there is an especially strong moral case for respecting and securing a particular basic human right if a sound argument shows that a law-governed international community such as LP's Society of Peoples could justifiably include that right in its foundation charter.

35. The capabilities approach "considers the account of entitlements not as derived from the ideas of dignity and respect but rather as ways of fleshing out those ideas" (FJ, 174).

36. Here I have argued that CA and LP are not significantly incompatible. Samuel Freeman (2006) argues in support of the broader claim that CA is "more complementary to, rather than competitive with, Rawlsian contractarianism than [Nussbaum] intends."

37. Here I am using the terms "rational" and "reasonable" to draw a distinction like that drawn by W. M. Sibley, according to Rawls's summary of Sibley's view: "[K]nowing that people are rational we do not know the ends they will pursue, only that they will pursue them intelligently. Knowing that people are reasonable where others are concerned, we know that they are willing to govern their conduct by a principle from which they and others can reason in common; and reasonable people take into account the consequences of their actions on others' well-being." (PL, 49, note 1).

8

When Being Human Isn't Enough

Reflections on Women's Human Rights

Serena Parekh

Women are half the world's population, yet they do two-thirds of the world's work, earn one-tenth of the world's income, and own less than one-hundredth of the world's property.

—United Nations, *State of the World's Women*, 1979

Gender inequality in the developing world . . . is the greatest single source of human rights violations today.

—Nicholas Kristof, *New York Times*, March 28, 2006

INTRODUCTION

It has now become almost trite to say that we, in the West, live in a human rights culture. But what precisely is meant by this claim? In the most general sense, it means that the legal norms of human rights have infiltrated our culture to such an extent that society-wide debates on topics as diverse as euthanasia, immigration, health care and even gun registries often appeal to human rights.[1] Further, it means that we are a culture which almost universally ascribes to and espouses human rights norms. Yet despite this almost universal acceptance of human rights, which human rights are worth protecting and for whom remains entirely in question, notwithstanding our formal agreement to various international treaties which outline human rights (such as the UDHR, ICCPR, and ICESCR).[2]

In this paper I want to look at the question of whose human rights are considered worth protecting and why. A central assertion of this paper is that our human rights culture, and human rights institutions more generally, have largely failed to protect women from the specific violations that they, as women, commonly experience. This, in turn, is because the violations that women experience are not, or are only rarely, considered—both by international law and by cultural attitudes—to be genuine human rights violations. Domestic abuse, rape, and sexual harassment of the everyday variety that most women experience in their lives by spouses, relatives, boyfriends, and bosses are not generally considered human rights violations. Human rights theory has failed to incorporate the specific violations that women face as women, and as such, it has failed to arrive at a practice which reliably protects women's safety and dignity. While proponents of CEDAW[3] and other grassroots women's rights groups have made tremendous strides in recent years, much work nonetheless remains to be done in reformulating our conception of human rights to include the rights of women against these gender-specific violations.

Let me put the problem in another way. Imagine an ethnic group whose members are found throughout the world, in every country, state and community, in much the same way that Jewish communities could be found in every part of Europe before the Second World War. Imagine that the members of this group live in conditions that are consistently inferior to those of nonmembers. In less developed countries, members of this ethnic group are more likely to be illiterate, to have less access to education and health care, to have less effective legal recourse, and to be less well nourished than nonmembers. In developed countries, members of this group are consistently paid less than nonmembers for the same job, are less likely to occupy positions of power and authority, and are more likely to face discrimination and harassment in the workplace because of their membership in this group (Nussbaum 2000, 1).[4] Everywhere in the world, the odds that members of this group will be violently sexually assaulted at some point in their life are virtually the same: 1 in 3.[5] Add to this the estimate by experts that 80 to 100 million members of this group are thought to have "disappeared" in recent years, having probably been killed at birth or shortly thereafter (Bunch 1995, 16).[6]

The group described above, of course, is women. The point of that description is that abuses of women's human rights are so systematic and entrenched that they do not even appear as human rights abuses—not even in our "human rights culture." If the group described above was any other group—the Kurds, Jews, Aboriginals—policies, laws, and cultural attitudes which lead to this disturbing state of affairs would undoubtedly be criticized as human rights violations. That is, when such treatment affects both men and women, we are more ready to see the discriminatory and violent treatment as a human rights issue. Traditional human rights theory has failed to see such cruel treatment of women as a problem of human rights, and hence to put women's suffering on par with more universally condemned treatment such as torture of political prisoners or genocide. This failure has served to keep women's oppression largely hidden in the international arena despite the fact that the principle of nondiscrimination is deeply entrenched in international documents like the UDHR, ICCPR, and ICESCR, as well as in most domestic law, and is well accepted within our culture.

In this paper, I attempt to explain this phenomenon. I begin by addressing a number of feminist views on women's human rights, looking in particular at how they account for the gap in human rights theory described above. I contend that, although these theories contain important feminist insights, they are nonetheless not fully adequate to the task of accounting for the problem described above. To fill in the story, I turn to an author the relevance of whose work to this topic is less immediately obvious—Hannah Arendt.

Arendt never considered herself a feminist and, as such, she never addressed this topic directly. There are, nonetheless, at least two good reasons for considering Arendt's work in this context. First, Arendt's life gave her firsthand knowledge of what it means to be denied one's human rights. She was a German Jew born in 1906, who became an adult during the Nazi rise to power. During that period she fled Germany for France, where she worked with Jewish refugees for a number of years. Just prior to the Nazi occupation of France, she, her husband, and her mother fled to America where she eventually became a well-known intellectual, scholar and teacher. Nonetheless, the experience of being stateless for eighteen years never left her. Second, Arendt studied philosophy with two of the most important philosophers of the 20th century, Martin Heidegger and Karl Jaspers. Consequently, her understanding of human rights are infused with these two elements—a rigorous philosophical education, and eighteen years of statelessness. Drawing on Arendt's first major work, *The Origins of Totalitarianism*, I argue that her theorizing about statelessness and rightlessness in the 20th century can help us understand why certain groups can be routinely and gravely harmed without having these harms recognized as human rights violations.

The people that Arendt had in mind in her writings were those left stateless before and during the Second World War. For her, stateless people were also rightless, in that they were rendered unable to claim their rights as human rights. This was so for two reasons. First, they did not have a state or government to appeal to, and no government in the world stood up for their rights. Second, because of a history of racism and ethnic hatred in the form of anti-Semitism, they did not belong to any particular society in a way that enabled others to see them as fully human. Rather, they were seen as abstractions—each a human being in general, not a person in particular—and this is what prevented them from effectively claiming their rights.

According to Arendt, the ability to make human rights claims is predicated on this latter kind of belonging. To belong in this deeper sense means to be judged by one's actions and opinions, not by one's biological givenness. That is, it means to be seen in one's unique individuality. Paradoxically, only by being seen and judged as the particular individual that one is can one truly be seen as a human being (and thus as a subject of human rights). Hence, being judged by *who* one is, not merely *what* one is, is a precondition for one's ability to claim human rights.

Based on that analysis, I argue that women, like stateless people, are treated according to a biological given—femaleness—and consequently are not seen and judged according to their words and deeds. Consequently, they do not fulfill the conditions of belonging that allow them to be seen as fully human and hence able to make legitimate claims to human rights. For Arendt, simply being seen as human is not enough to enable one to make effective claims to human rights. Applying Arendt's analysis of stateless people to women will, I believe, shed some light on the problem of women's human rights.

FEMINIST ANALYSES OF THE GENDER GAP IN HUMAN RIGHTS

There are two primary feminist explanations of why women, although they supposedly have inalienable human rights, experience so many rights-violations and of why the latter are not typically recognized as violations of human rights. The first view is that the subject of human rights is male, that is, because men wrote the various declarations and demands for human rights, it is men's experiences and values that have come to define human rights. According to Peterson and Parisi, women are not included in the liberal, western definition of an individual that underlies human rights discourse (Peterson and Parisi 1998, 114). In particular, human rights were traditionally conceived as the rights of citizens who were, for the most part, men. They are the rights that men needed in order to be protected from other men. For example, the right to have one's private property protected is one of the oldest and most entrenched rights, originating in John Locke's articulation of it as a natural right (along with life and liberty). Yet for most of history, women were not even allowed to own property. As the quotation which began this paper illustrates, even when women are legally entitled to own property, the conditions of male dominance continue to bring it about that women own less than one-hundredth of the world's property.

Hence the right to private property can be understood to benefit men significantly more than it benefits women. Yet because the language of human rights is supposed to be universal and the subject of human rights a depersonalized, dehistoricised, and disembodied person, this particular fact of history is ignored, as is the historical oppression that underlies it.

As Wolper and Peters explain, the traditional human rights formulations are made on a normative male model and applied to women as an afterthought and, we might add, only at women's insistence (Peters and Wolper 1995). One important consequence is that women's rights came to be seen as "special interests," different from and less important than genuine human rights. The slogan "women's rights *are* human rights" is meant to criticize this assumption and to assert that the specific violations that women face as women are violations of human rights. Although much work is being done to rectify this, women's rights are still largely considered secondary to so-called human rights.

The second explanation of the gender gap in human rights proceeds by deconstructing the idea of the public and the private.[7] On the traditional view, human rights violations by definition occur in the public realm and are committed by state actors. For example, police brutality can be considered a human rights violation because the action in question is done by somebody who is engaged by the state, while gang violence, committed by private citizens against each other, is not. On this view, violations of women's dignity such as domestic abuse and sexual assault are unlikely to be seen as human rights violations, since they are committed mostly in the private realm by non-state actors. So while these acts might be officially illegal, they are not considered human rights abuses.

Arati Rao argues that women's human rights abuses will never be adequately redressed until the private realm is considered a realm of human rights violations. The Universal Declaration of Human Rights, for example, leaves untouched the human rights violations that occur against women in the private sphere and within the family. It upholds the family as "the natural and fundamental group unit of society . . . entitled to protection by society and the state."[8] In so privileging the family, it implicitly assumes that unjust power can only be employed by the state, thus ignoring the abuses of power that occur in the home.[9] According to Rao, the private realm must be recognized as a legitimate area of human rights concern. Further, she argues that, rather than seeing the private and the public as two entirely distinct spheres, we ought to recognize that the private sphere and domestic life are at the heart of civil society (Rao 2001, 516).

This way of dividing legitimate human rights (as rights against public-sphere violations by state actors) from "women's rights" has been criticized by other feminists as well. As Charlotte Bunch argues, this view assumes that the state is not responsible for violations of women's rights in the private sphere, even when such abuses are often condoned or sanctioned by the state (even though the perpetrator may be a private citizen). In other words, there are ways in which the public reinforces oppression in the private sphere, however indirectly. Further, relegating women's oppression to the realm of the private means that women's oppression is not seen as political; it is seen as the actions of a few individuals, rather than as a systematic or structural problem (Bunch 1990 and 1995). The state then cannot be held accountable for legitimating and sustaining a gender hierarchy, and for entrenching power relations that disadvantage women. Peterson and Parisi (among others) insist along similar lines that the state plays a role in perpetuating gender economic inequality by (1) not legislating equal pay or not enforcing existing equal pay rights; (2) promoting welfare policies that discourage women from working in the public sphere through lack of training, jobs, and child care provisions as well as through inadequate wages; and/or (3) not creating or enforcing nondiscrimination laws governing hiring and promotion, and thus sustaining male dominance in the economic arena (Peterson and Parisi 1998, 149).

ARENDT ON RIGHTLESSNESS

It is clear that our conception of human rights assumes a male subject, and that the privileging of men's human rights is further entrenched by the artificial public/private divide. As helpful as these explanations are, however, they do not explain why the exclusion of women's rights from "human rights" continues to such a degree that it is not even recognized as such. I will argue below that this persistence is partially explained by the way that women are seen and understood.

When you lack an ability to call the violations of your dignity *human* rights violations, you are in a condition that Hannah Arendt called "rightlessness." Though you may have human rights in theory, in practice you are not recognized as the subject of legitimate human rights claims. In the section below I will argue that women, like stateless people, lack a kind of belonging that makes them recognizable as bearers and legitimate claimmakers of human rights. The same reasons that Arendt gives for why the stateless lack "the right to have rights" can, I argue, be applied to the situation of women around the world. Like the stateless, women are denied a fundamental dimension of humanness that would enable them to be recognized as makers of legitimate human rights claims. I will argue that to *belong* means not only to have citizenship or an official status within a country, but also to be seen and understood by others in a certain way. In particular, it means being judged on the basis of your words and deeds, and not on the basis of what you are in general, in the abstract (i.e., a woman or even a human being). This is what Arendt refers to as "the right to have rights." It is only by acquiring the right to have rights that women, like stateless people, can overcome their situation of rightlessness.

This section will proceed as follows. First I will show why human rights are tied to political belonging, that is, why being stateless entails being rightless. Second, I will argue that what the rightless lack is more than just citizenship, but the deeper kind of belonging articulated above. I explain why this kind of belonging is so essential for human rights, why seeing people as abstractions is so dangerous, and why this is particularly so for women. Finally I will conclude by discussing some implications of my argument for the women's human rights movement.

Response to a Common Criticism

Before we delve into the heart of Arendt's work, let us look at a common criticism that is often levied against Arendt and that may seem particularly relevant to the present discussion. Arendt has been more often criticized than praised by feminists, and one of the primary grounds of such criticism has been Arendt's perceived praise of the public realm and deprecation of the private. For Arendt, one speaks and acts, thus disclosing one's identity, in the public realm, while in the private realm one looks after the necessities of life. The private realm is where many women live much of their lives, taking care of the family, being wives, mothers, daughters, etc.[10] The public realm, on the other hand, is traditionally a masculine realm, dominated by men. Thus, Arendt is criticized for implicitly devaluing women's activities in the private sphere and uncritically praising the activities of men, from which women have been traditionally excluded.

If this reading of Arendt is correct, then my use of Arendt above would be legitimately subject to question. But this criticism of Arendt rests on a misreading of her view. First, while Arendt does place a heavier ontological weight on the public realm, she does not devalue the private realm and hence women. Indeed, the private realm has a particular dignity for Arendt, though people often overlook her recognition of this dignity. In the section on labor in *The Human Condition*, her most important philosophical work, Arendt takes great pains to explain the importance of the private sphere. Without this realm, she argues, there could be no genuine public; thus the public is in fact *dependent* upon the private. She even writes that the most elemental kind of happiness is to be found in the private realm.[11] Her point is only that this realm is ontologically incomplete, and it must be supplemented with, not surpassed by, the public realm.

Second, we need not understand Arendt as suggesting that one can act and disclose one's identity only within the supposedly masculine realm of the public. Following Seyla Benhabib (2003, 126–27), I understand

Arendt's "public" not as an institution or given space, but rather as a way of interacting with the world in which your concern is for the world, the common space, rather than for the private interests that tie together family, friends, business partners, etc. To act in public is not to be seen in front of a universal audience (like CNN), but to manifest your concern for what transcends your individual life, for those aspects of the world that are shared in common. While the home is intrinsically "private," there are ways that women can and do act within the public or social arena. We only have to look at Arendt's own example of Rahel Varnhagen, the 19th-century Jewish salon keeper, to see this (Arendt 1974).[12] Thus acting in public, which Arendt deems necessary for political life as well as for an individual identity, is in principle as open to women, and generally to those socially marginalized and oppressed, as it is to men or members of dominant groups.

Political Belonging

Arendt's interest in statelessness began when she herself was a stateless person. *The Origins of Totalitarianism* was originally published in 1951, though Arendt had been working on it for years before this, when she was a stateless person in France and then the US. One of the book's themes is the history and nature of *rightlessness*, wherein people who lose their national identity also lose their ability to claim human rights. This is why Arendt refers to them as rightless, instead of merely stateless. The difference is significant. Prior to the 20th century, statelessness was always a consequence of war, and was in itself nothing new. What happened in the 20th century is that, for the first time, people who were expelled from or had to leave their countries of origin could not find any other country to accept them. For example, the Jews of Europe, having been stripped of their nationality, their property, their valuables and their cultural heritage, were seen as impoverished beggars when they arrived in other European countries.[13] For various reasons, including their impoverished state and the widespread anti-Semitism in Europe, they were not able to gain citizenship in any other country,[14] and thus they became rightless in the sense that they were unable to claim their human rights anywhere. In such a situation, "the prolongation of their lives is due to charity and not to right, for no law exists which could force the nations to feed them" (1958/1976, 296). In other words, they could not claim that their lives should be preserved because they have a basic human right to life, but rather, all they could rely on was charity, the whim of the state that was supposed to protect them.

For Arendt, this phenomenon illustrated a central paradox of human rights: *human* rights can only be enjoyed by a human being who lives within a state. Consequently, as soon as a people cease belonging to a state, they effectively lose their human rights. I do not take Arendt to be claiming that such people are truly, ontologically without the rights that belong to us by virtue of being human. Rather, she is making a very practical claim about the way we have always understood human rights. Indeed, though these rights are meant to belong to people by virtue of being human, it turns out that they can only be claimed against a state. In this sense, human rights are inextricably bound up with civil rights.

This paradox can be traced back to the writings of John Locke. For Locke, often considered the first modern theorist of natural rights, a nation was considered legitimate only to the extent that it protected the natural rights of its members. Indeed, citizens were justified in overthrowing their government if it failed to do so.[15] This idea was taken up in the French Revolution, wherein the purpose of government was understood to be the protection of the "rights of man." Because human rights were so inextricably bound up with the nation, no protection outside of the nation was thought to be necessary. No one ever thought about separating human rights from national rights. As such, since their modern beginnings in the 18th century, human rights have been tied to national belonging. Yet it still came as a surprise in the 20th century that people denied a nationality were also denied human rights.

My contention is that women are in a condition of rightlessness similar in important ways to that of the Jews prior to and during World War Two. In both cases the people in question are unable to claim their rights as *human rights*, though for different reasons. For both groups, their treatment depends on what their state and culture chooses to do with them. In other words, they are dependent on charity to take care of them, and cannot rely on rights claims. Unlike the Jews, who became rightless as a result of losing the protection of a state, women are rightless despite membership in a state. I will argue, however, that women do not *belong* to the state in a way that allows the state—the supposed guarantor of human rights—to recognize them as human. Hence the failure of most states throughout history to stand up for the rights of women, either by enforcing laws that protect women or by initiating changes in culture.

The Right to Have Rights

Arendt's observations in the 20th century showed her that human rights are ultimately predicated on something still more basic: what she calls "the right to have rights." This she describes as the right "to live in a framework where one is judged by one's actions and opinions, and the right to belong to some kind of organized community" (1958/1976, 296–297). Arendt thus indicates that the "right to have rights" includes two distinct elements; let us look at each in turn to see how women can be understood to lack the right to have rights.

The first element—belonging to a political community—is easy to understand in light of her views on statelessness. In becoming stateless, you lose your legal status and are essentially outside of the law. It is for this reason that Arendt suggests a rightless person may actually improve her situation by committing a crime, because then she must be treated within the bounds of the law. As a stateless, rightless person, there is no law to protect her and certainly no government to enforce that protection. Hence it is the loss of official governmental, legal protection which characterizes a stateless person.[16] This is why the most basic right is the right to belong to some kind of organized political community.

To overcome rightlessness in this sense, Arendt suggests that establishing citizenship is all that is needed. She writes, "The restoration of human rights, as the recent example of the State of Israel proves, has been achieved so far only through the restoration or the establishment of national rights" (1958/1976, 299).[17] Though Arendt is aware of the difficulty of repatriating millions of unwanted people, it remains the only possibility within our global nation-state system.

The second element—that of living "in a framework where one is judged by one's actions and opinions"[18]—is less straightforward. Arendt argues that "the fundamental deprivation of human rights is manifested first and above all in the deprivation of a place in the world which makes opinions significant and actions effective" (1958/1976, 296). To be rightless, as stateless people and many women are, is to be in a situation where how you are treated does not depend on what you do or do not do, but merely on *what* you are—your "mere givenness," the traits that you were born with and did not choose. To take a contemporary example, imagine two people who have applied to a school, one of whom is rejected because she is the wrong race or gender, while the other is accepted because of the way he expressed himself in a personal essay and interview (words and opinions) or on the basis of his past achievements (actions). The latter person is treated according to *who* he is, while the former is treated according to *what* she is. "What" a person is consists of traits and characteristics that are observable by other people and that the individual is aware of—being a woman, a Jew, Asian, white, etc. However, "who" a person is is revealed only in his or her speech, actions and opinions, and can neither be predicted nor controlled. Your identity in this sense is often a surprise even to yourself, and is often expressed most clearly when your story is told by others (1958/1998, 179).[19] Implied in Arendt's view is that to genuinely belong to a political community is to be judged, generally and for most purposes, according to your words and deeds.

According to Arendt, it is only when you are seen as an individual in this sense that you are truly seen as a human being. She insists that in being treated according to your "mere givenness," you are deprived of something fundamental, something distinctly human: "If a Negro in a white community is considered a Negro and nothing else, he loses along with his right to equality that freedom of action which is specially human. . . . Much the same thing happens to those who have lost all distinctive political qualities and have become human beings and nothing else" (1958/1976, 301). Paradoxically, without being seen in your individuality, you are not really seen as a human being.

It is partly for these reasons that Arendt argues that the most fundamental right on which other rights are predicated is the right to be judged by your actions and opinions, that is, to be judged according to *who* you are, and not merely *what* you are. To be recognized in both your individuality and your common humanity, I argue, constitutes the kind of belonging necessary for human rights. Both aspects of identity are necessary—to be recognized in one's sheer difference (individuality) is no better than being recognized in one's sheer generality (humanness). As Arendt puts it, "The paradox involved in the loss of human rights is that such loss coincides with the instant when a person becomes a human being in general— without a profession, without citizenship, without opinion, without a deed by which to identify and specify himself—*and* difference in general, representing nothing but his own absolutely unique individuality which, deprived of expression within and action upon a common world, loses all significance" (1958/1976, 302).

Though Arendt talks about stateless people who had become "nothing but human," she might just as easily have used the example of women, who are judged according to the expectations associated with their biological femaleness—sexual availability, procreative capacity, domestic competence, etc.—and not according to their individual words and deeds. Under such conditions it is hard to see women as fully human, and hence as bearers of human rights. This may be why abuses connected with ensuring that a woman fulfils her "womanly role"—female genital cutting, forced marriages, marital rape, etc.—are not often recognized as human rights violations. In fulfilling these roles women are not seen as human, but rather as merely women. According to Arendt's analysis of rightlessness, what is needed is not a reassertion that women are human, which nobody in principle would deny. What is required, rather, is a space in which women's individuality can be expressed through deed and word. It is only through recognizing women as individual people that each woman's humanity, and through it the humanity of women in general, becomes visible. Thus, even though women are not stateless, the lack of such recognition—and the deep belonging it engenders—renders them rightless.

Why Being an Abstract Human Being Is Not Enough

Let us look more carefully at Arendt's unorthodox assertion that simply being a human being in general is not sufficient to enable one to claim human rights. This is a somewhat surprising claim, given our traditional view of human rights: that they are the rights we have just in virtue of being human, not because of who or what we are as individuals. As Michael Perry and others have argued, this view suggests that we believe that there is something inherently valuable about being human, something which makes human beings as such sacred and inviolable (Perry 1998, 12–13). Hence, it seems reasonable to expect that mere humanness would be enough to ground effective human rights claims.

Yet what Arendt observed in the 20th century is that when a person has lost all the particular attributes that make her recognizable to us—her individuality, citizenship, social setting, etc.—we often fail to recognize such a person as *human*. Arendt writes, "the conception of human rights, based upon the assumed existence of a human being as such, broke down at the very moment when those who professed to believe in it were for the first time confronted with people who had indeed lost all other qualities and specific relationships—except that they were still human. *The world found nothing sacred in the abstract nakedness of being human*" (1958/1976, 299).[20] This is a harsh indictment of human rights as traditionally conceived, as well as a practical insight into what prevents human rights from being realized. Here she states the paradox in another way:

> If a human being loses his political status, he should, according to the implications of the inborn and alienable rights of man, come under exactly the situation for which the declaration of such general rights provided. Actually the opposite is the case. It seems that a man who is nothing but a man has lost the very qualities which make it possible for other people to treat him as a fellow man. (1958/1976, 300)

According to the traditional view, being human is sufficient to arouse others' compassion for one's suffering, and to be heard when articulating rights claims. Arendt claims, on the contrary, that one also needs to belong in such a way that others recognize one as a legitimate bearer and claimant of rights. Being human simply is not enough.

This is one way we may see the connection between the stateless and women. Women are often stripped of all forms of identity except their womanhood. Their value is supposed to arise from the fact that they are fulfilling some universal eternal role of women—as wife, mother, sexual object, etc. Yet I would argue that quite the opposite is the case: when women are stripped of individual identity in this way, it is hard to recognize them as fully human. In both cases, reducing individuals to an abstraction serves not to increase their dignity but rather to push them further away from what we can recognize as human. Much as the stateless are "nothing but human," we might say that women are "nothing but women." In this sense, women, like stateless people, simply don't "count" and hence their specific violations can be seen as less important than genuine human rights claims.

The truth that Arendt observed is that only when one is able to speak and act, and to be judged by one's words and deeds, is one genuinely seen as an individual within the larger human community; and only then are violations of one's dignity seen as unjust and impermissible. A practical example can be taken from contemporary asylum law. An asylum seeker is a person who has fled her home country from fear of persecution and asks to be considered a refugee in another country. When an asylum seeker comes to a Western country to claim asylum, he is given a hearing. What he needs to prove during that hearing is that he is being persecuted in his home country because of an opinion he holds or something he has said or done. In other words, he must show that the persecution is based on what he did as an *individual* and that he is not just one of the suffering masses seeking a better life. It is only when he can prove his individuality that he is accorded the basic *human* right of asylum. Similarly if a woman is seeking asylum, she must prove that she is being persecuted because of who she is or what she said or did. It is not enough to claim that she is being persecuted because of being a woman in general.

CONCLUSION

Having a place in a community where women can speak, act, and be recognized as individuals—rather than according to pre-given notions of womanhood—is essential for the protection of women's human rights. For Arendt, as we have seen, this kind of belonging is part of what constitutes the right to have rights. If she is correct about this, then we must reconsider how human rights are conceived. If human rights are predicated on this deeper belonging—not merely belonging to a political community, although this prerequisite can by no means be taken for granted, but belonging in such a way that you are judged according to word and deed— then our traditional methods for implementing human rights will seem insufficient. Addressing women's human rights solely in terms of law, for instance, will necessarily be ineffective if the need for this more primal belonging is not addressed.

Arendt always maintained that achieving human equality is within our power, even though it may be a struggle at the best of times. We can understand her as calling for a mediation between individuality and culture: what is important is not only that the person be a distinct, unique individual, but that she be recognized as such by her culture and community. So although it is important to resist forced community and the stifling norms often imposed therein, community itself is not a barrier but rather an essential condition for the realization of human rights. The international human rights movement ought to seek to further women's human rights not only through enforcing and changing local laws, but also by changing how women are seen (and how they see themselves) within the public or social dimension of society. Insisting on a public space for women to speak, act, and be taken seriously—to be active participants in shaping their cultures—will affect how women in general are viewed and treated. This is all the more reason why women's representation in politics, education, business, medicine is so important: it is not just a matter of abstract equality, but a prerequisite for the realization of women's human rights.

NOTES

1. The New York Times reports the following about a pro-gun rally at the United Nations: "'Crime goes down the more that citizens are armed,' said Nic Leobold, an organizer of this mini-rally. And don't fool yourself, he said: human rights are very much at stake" (Haberman 2006).

2. Universal Declaration of Human Rights (UDHR), International Convention on Civil and Political Rights (ICCPR), and International Covenant on Economic, Social and Cultural Rights (ICESCR). The US has signed both the ICCPR and the ICESCR, but it has only ratified (made part of domestic law) the ICCPR. The US has signed the UDHR, but because the UDHR is a *declaration*, not a convention (which is legally binding), it does not require ratification.

3. Convention on the Elimination of All Forms of Discrimination Against Women. This convention was adopted by the United Nations on December 18, 1979 and has been ratified by 170 countries. The United States is one of only 21 countries that have not ratified the convention (other non-ratifying countries include Afghanistan, Iran, and Sudan). The US remains the only industrialized country that has not ratified the treaty.

4. Also see the US Bureau of Labor Statistics and US Census Bureau for statistics concerning women's pay relative to men's.

5. From a UN Report by the Commission on the Status of Women, February 2000. See http://wc.studentaffairs.duke.edu/vdaystats.html. The estimate that 1 in 3 women will experience sexual assault in her lifetime applies to countries as diverse as the US and India. While no country improves on this number, some are far worse (such as Turkey where 80% of women encounter sexual assault).

6. From the work done by Amartya Sen. This number was calculated by comparing ratios of males and females in different regions in Asia.

7. For a philosophical analysis of the public/private distinction, see Elshtain (1997).

8. *Universal Declaration of Human Rights*, Article 16-3.

9. For instance, Thomas Pogge insists that human rights violations must be state-sponsored: "Human rights can be violated by governments, certainly, and by government agencies and officials . . . —but not by a petty criminal or by a violent husband" (2001b, 192).

10. See Honig (1995) for a number of essays on this topic.

11. For example, she writes that "The 'blessing or the joy' of labor is the human way to experience the sheer bliss of being alive which we share with all living creatures," and further, that "the blessing of life as a whole, inherent in labor, can never be found in work. . . . The blessing of labor is that effort and gratification follow each other as closely as producing and consuming the means of subsistence, so that happiness is a concomitant of the process itself." It is this happiness which is "the felicity with which earthly life has always been blessed" (Arendt 1998, 106–108).

12. Arendt's second book, which she completed when she left Germany in 1933, is a biography of Rahel Varnhagen, a German Jew who despite her lack of wealth, cultivation, and beauty ran one of the most important *salons* in Berlin. It introduces a number of themes that Arendt takes up throughout her life—the dangers of assimilation, the meaning of being a minority and a pariah in society, and the possibility of action in conditions of social constraint. In this work Arendt suggests that even though Varnhagen was relegated to only the private and social realms, she was still able to act and define her identity.

13. "The official SS newspaper, the *Schwarze Korps*, stated in 1938 that if the world was not yet convinced that the Jews were the scum of the earth, it soon would be when unidentifiable beggars, without nationality, without money, and without passports crossed their frontiers. And it is true that this kind of factual propaganda worked better than Goebbels' rhetoric" (Arendt 1976, 269).

14. For a more detailed history of how stateless people were treated in the interwar years, see Arendt 1976, chapter 9.

15. See Locke 1980, chapter XIX.

16. Since Arendt's writing a number of conventions and laws concerning stateless people—refugees, asylum seekers, internally displaced people (IDPs), forced migrants—have emerged. Yet I would argue that refugees remain fundamentally in the situation that Arendt described. Not having their own state against which they can claim their human rights, they can claim them either against their host country (i.e., the country where they happen to find themselves, even though they may lack legal status there) or against the United Nations, and specifically the body that is assigned to protect them (the UN High Commissioner for Refugees). Yet in neither case are refugees and asylum seekers able to claim their full human rights as enumerated in the Universal Declaration of Human Rights. Further, people who remain in their countries of origin but have essentially lost their legal status, IDPs, are in an even more precarious situation since they lack any external help. Stateless people in the 21st century remain one of the fundamental human rights challenges.

17. Arendt notes that the Jewish problem was only settled at the end of the war with the foundation of Israel. This, however, meant colonizing and conquering a territory and leaving a new group of people (approximately 700,000 to 800,000) stateless and rightless. In other words, restoring human rights by restoring national rights is, at best, only a partial solution.

18. There is a tension on this subject in Arendt's work. At times, she appears to be saying that all that is needed to overcome rightlessness is to be a member of a political community, no matter how marginal. She writes, "even slaves still belonged to some sort of human community; their labor was needed, used, and exploited, and this kept them within the pale of humanity. To be a slave was after all to have a distinctive character, a place in society—more than the abstract nakedness of being human and nothing but human" (1976, 297). However, despite this statement, what she stresses more deeply is the need to be judged according to word and deed, which the slave, of course, was not.

19. She stresses that "who" a person is is "implicit in everything somebody says and does. It can be hidden only in complete silence and perfect passivity, but its disclosure can almost never be achieved as a willful purpose" (1998, 179). That we reveal who we are through all our words and actions supports my earlier claim that action in Arendt's sense is not limited to men or those who occupy the elite public arena.

20. Italics added.

9

"A Woman's Body Is Like a Foreign Country"[1]

Thinking about National and Bodily Sovereignty

Rebecca Whisnant

Violations of national sovereignty and of bodily (especially sexual) sovereignty are routinely merged in rhetoric and metaphor: we speak of *virgin territory*, of Israeli troops *penetrating* deeper into Lebanon, of the *rape* of Iraq. Such connections, according to Jane Caputi, are "open secrets" within mainstream U.S. culture: "Nuclear warheads, chainsaws, handguns, SUVs, and space rockets: All are regularly and often risibly flaunted as invasive and destructive phalli. Everyone gets the joke, but lots of us are not laughing" (2004, 395). Taking the metaphor in the other direction, actual rapes are often called invasions, and penises are described as weapons (both by those who celebrate, and by those who decry, their use as such). When those on opposite sides of the political and moral fence perceive similar connections—as, for instance, with the sexualized metaphors commonly employed by both supporters and opponents of U.S. wars—further investigation of those connections seems warranted. Thus, in this essay, I reflect on the overlapping and divergent meanings of national sovereignty and bodily sovereignty, particularly the bodily sovereignty of women.

Note: This essay contains graphic descriptions of hardcore pornography, which may disturb some readers.

Both forms of sovereignty have lately been dismissed by some critics as anachronisms, no longer relevant or useful in navigating our increasingly complex and globalized world. In the field of international relations, some contend that given the transnational character of key challenges (such as terrorism and global warming), the increasing power of multinational corporations and of supranational organizations (from the UN to the WTO), and the move toward liberal cosmopolitanism in scholarly circles, the theoretical and practical significance of national sovereignty is declining precipitously. Jean Cohen observes that, according to some critics, "the background conditions of the international [political] system allegedly no longer involve a baseline of separation, autonomy, and defined territorial and jurisdictional boundaries, but rather [of] connection, interaction, and interpenetrating networks and institutions" (2004, 7).[2]

Meanwhile some postmodern theorists, without necessarily using the language of bodily sovereignty, emphasize the increasing irrelevance of "organic bodies" and the permeability and artificiality of bodily boundaries. Donna Haraway, for example, famously offers the "cyborg," which she calls a "hybrid of machine and organism" (1991, 149), as a model or metaphor for the contemporary subject. In previous eras, Haraway contends, "female embodiment seemed to be given, organic, necessary" (1991, 180). She suggests, however, that such a view of female embodiment—or, for that matter, of male or human embodiment—is outdated and naïve: "Why should our bodies end at the skin, or include at best other beings encapsulated by skin?" (1991, 178)

I believe, in contrast, that sovereignty—that of nations[3] and of persons' bodies—has continuing moral importance. Claiming such sovereignty, and criticizing its abrogation, is essential to the project of dismantling patriarchy and imperialism in their many interconnections.[4] More specifically, I will argue herein that a certain tradition of radical feminist thinking about women's bodily sovereignty can help us understand the meaning and locus of sovereignty in general, and in turn to draw some tentative conclusions about the grounds and limits of national sovereignty.

THE DEATH OF NAURU

Nauru, a tiny island in the remote reaches of the South Pacific, is on the brink of total economic and ecological collapse. After nearly a century of selling off the island's phosphorus-rich soil for use as fertilizer in the West—first under colonial duress, later as a desperate attempt to survive in the global economy—Nauru is left with nothing more that it can produce or sell. "The people have dug up and sold off the interior of their homeland," as the writer Jack Hitt puts it (2004, 322), leaving that interior gutted and barren, a gaping lifeless pit.

Here Hitt describes his first view of "Topside," the abandoned mining range that now occupies all but the narrow shoreline encircling Nauru:

> Brian [his driver, a native Nauruan] turns up a dirt road. Right away, as we slip behind the outer scrim of trees, shrubs, and ground cover, all things green disappear to reveal a sight both terrible and spellbinding. The road itself becomes a kind of levee laid atop an expanse of pure ruination. . . . The small atoll has essentially been tonsured. The sickly collection of water-starved vegetation on the periphery . . . mask[s] the horror that lies just on the inside of that ring of trees and scrub: The entire interior has been cut down, and the underbed of phosphate strip-mined so deep that the only things remnant are the coral bones of the atoll as it might have existed a million years ago. It's a haunting landscape of dug-out stone channels. With all the topsoil and phosphate gone, what's left are sinuous canals marked by sunbleached limestone towers and coral outcroppings. . . . Old filthy trash blows around this blistering desert, the shredded plastic bags snagging on a bit of coral, the weightier garbage eventually sinking into the ruts where the rot managed to service the root system of a few brave weeds. . . .
>
> There is no breeze, just fine talc, airborne and stagnant like particulate suspended in the stillness of a laboratory vacuum. It seems to crackle and pop in the heavy birdless air. The emotional sensation of just standing there is one of intense, primal fear, like I could be murdered. . . . Brian sits still and stares straight ahead . . . as if his chiseled profile is part of the tour: an expression of shame I have never before seen. (2004, 330–332)

With what was once lush tropical forest now gutted and despoiled, utterly incapable of producing or sustaining life, Nauru must import everything its citizens need—even water. As their desperation grows, the Nauruans consider their dwindling options for economic survival: from extracting residual phosphate from the limestone pinnacles of Topside, to slicing up and polishing those pinnacles and selling them to Westerners as coffee tables, to selling the country's phone code to be used for phone sex lines.

Truly, Nauru has nothing left to sell—except, Hitt observes, "its very sovereignty." After a mere thirty-plus years of independence from a succession of colonial powers, Nauru

> has no choice but to root through the last valuable trinkets of their independence—a UN seat, a batch of "embassies," a passport stamp, bank regulations, a vote on certain international councils. And Nauru trades them with the same brutal, hard-core capitalist spirit that they learned at the knee of their teachers—the factory managers at the phosphate plant. (2004, 343)

NATIONAL SOVEREIGNTY

Although national sovereignty has been variously understood, its commonly accepted meaning as it pertains to the modern nation-state system is "supreme authority within a territory" (Philpott 2001, 16). Sovereign authority is "supreme" in that it trumps all other authorities within the territory: for instance, because the federal government holds sovereign authority within the U.S., the Supreme Court can overturn laws passed by the legislatures of Vermont, Ohio, or California. Sovereign authority is more than coercive power; a holder of sovereignty is thought to rule legitimately and by right. Unlike classical (or Westphalian) sovereignty—the absolute authority of a state or ruler over those living in a given territory—national sovereignty in most contemporary contexts is seen as held properly by a nation's people, who vest their sovereign authority in a government whose rule over them is thus limited and provisional (Dahbour 2006, 111).

National sovereignty is typically thought of as both internal and external: the sovereign exercises governing authority within the nation's borders, and also claims rights against invasion or other undue interference by outside powers. In fact, internal sovereignty seems to *require* external sovereignty: it is difficult to see how a nation can be governed (or govern itself) effectively if it cannot rely, minimally, on freedom from invasion by other nations. In a system of sovereign nations, then, each nation claims a right against external interference and control, at least partly because such a right makes internal governance possible.

One obvious and direct way to violate a nation's external sovereignty is by invading its territory—sending troops across its borders, for instance, or bombing its cities from the air. However, as the sad story of Nauru indicates, there are other ways to subvert the sovereignty of a nation or people. To understand the process by which Nauruan sovereignty has been effectively destroyed, we must trace its history a bit farther back (McDaniel and Gowdy 2000). Native Polynesian and Micronesian people lived peacefully and self-sufficiently on Nauru for many centuries, until Germany annexed the island in 1888. Nauru's fate was further sealed in 1900, when a British company discovered its rich reserves of phosphate and quickly moved to gain mining rights. With the two world wars came a succession of colonial powers, including a brutal Japanese occupation during World War II. A period of trusteeship thereafter led finally to Nauruan independence in 1968; thus for the past four decades, Nauru has been officially a sovereign nation.

The course of events described earlier demonstrates, however, that even when a nation gains formal sovereignty, the historical context and surrounding conditions can still render the nation, practically speaking, at the mercy of more powerful others—that is to say, functionally not a sovereign entity. Although Nauruans managed to live for centuries (pre-1888) without selling anything to the West, the intervening period of colonial extraction and occupation has rendered them now incapable of doing so. D.A. Clarke describes this process as follows:

> At first the native people were *forced* to submit to the extraction of their local resource . . . under mailfist colonial rule. But after enough of the island ecology is disturbed, and the balance of population and food economy warped by the monetist/capitalist colonial trade, the populace becomes dependent upon the outside trade and no longer have to be forced at gunpoint to destroy their island; they do it themselves, in what the neoliberals are pleased to call "free choice in a free market."[5]

Thus, meaningful external sovereignty requires more than mere formal independence and freedom from (current) military invasion and occupation. The locus of control over the Nauruan economy, and hence over the daily lives of Nauruans, is now outside Nauru itself, in that Nauru has been reduced to a state of abject economic dependence on western "markets" (that is, on the desires of comparatively wealthy westerners for certain goods and services). This relation of dependent subservience surely explains, at least partially, why the Nauruans eventually sell off elements of that formal sovereignty: given the underlying economic relationships, such "sovereignty" does them little good.

THE WORLD OF PORNOGRAPHY

I am creating, with two other feminist scholars, a new educational slide-show on pornography.[6] Thus, regrettably, I must spend time surfing and culling images from internet pornography—surveying its vast, dizzying landscape of splayed, shaved, sullied, mocked and, above all, multiply and aggressively penetrated female bodies.

Here a man pushes four fingers deep into a woman's mouth, to distend and stretch it. (On other sites, dental instruments are used.) Here, on a site called "Suck Me Bitch," a penis is shoved into a woman's mouth sideways, pushing out her cheek in a distorted and seemingly painful manner. Her eyes look puzzled and afraid.

The genre known as "gag factor" is enormously popular. A site called "Gag On My Cock" promises "fresh new gag victims" weekly, and boasts that "we fuck them in the face 'til they cry!" A few young women are shown wearing "gag on my cock" T-shirts and smiling; the accompanying text reads, "Can these fuck toys be any dumber? They think the T-shirts are a fucking joke . . . stupid hoes, the joke's on them!" The images of fellatio on the front page show men holding women by the throat, yanking their heads back by their hair, and even holding the women's noses so that they can't breathe. The image that's front and center on the page shows a young woman with a penis in her mouth and a man's hand pushing her forehead back so that she's looking straight at the camera. She is crying, her mascara running down her face.

A fascination with multiple penetration is pervasive. It is not uncommon to see a woman fellating one man while two others simultaneously penetrate her vaginally and anally. (In the argot of the business, this is known as "airtight": every hole is plugged.) When the penetrations are not simultaneous, they are sequential: oral, vaginal, anal, performed by one or more men while they call the woman abusive names and declare that she loves it. At the scene's end, all the men ejaculate in the woman's face or on her breasts, leaving her soaked in semen.

On the front page of the "Altered Assholes" site, women's stretched and inflamed anuses are displayed, in some cases with a man's hands roughly pulling the woman's buttocks apart, to ensure that the camera captures the full extent of the damage. The promotional copy for a DVD called "Anally Ripped Whores" reads, "We at Pure Filth know exactly what you want . . . chicks being ass-fucked till their sphincters are pink, puffy and totally blown out. Adult diapers just might be in store for these whores when their work is done."

This is the world of contemporary, mainstream, so-called gonzo pornography.[7] In this world, women have no boundaries and no privacy: no part of any female body is off-limits to male inspection, evaluation, use, and abuse. What is fetishized is penetration not merely as border crossing, not even as forceful border crossing, but as border *obliteration*—the kind of bodily invasion that permanently alters the body, so that what was formerly an effective boundary to the body no longer is. That women's bodies have an interior realm, one that is sometimes inaccessible to men and that is clearly distinguishable from their exterior, is treated as an intolerable affront. Foreign objects are introduced into women's bodies, while repeated violent penetration brings what's inside out: women gag, drool, vomit, lose bowel control. Having spent a bit of time in this world, one starts to suspect that if some men could turn women inside out entirely, they would.[8]

After looking at pornography, I want to hide—to cover myself, tuck myself away. Although I believe that pornography reliably produces (and reproduces) bodily and sexual shame in women, such shame is not what motivates my desire to hide. Rather, I've seen that my own privacy and internality as a woman are under a massive, all-fronts assault. It is a stealth assault, hidden in plain view, as it were, and often called something else, like "freedom" or "sex."

BODILY SOVEREIGNTY

A person's body is her territory—not something she merely owns, but something she *is*. In much the way that peoples typically require and seek sovereign territory to support and make possible their common life, a person must have effective sovereignty over her body in order to enact fully her humanity and her particular identity as a person. As Marjorie Reiley Maguire puts it,

> Our body is . . . not like a house that we inhabit. Our body is the very fabric of our personhood. It is through our body that we weave the person we are, and, to a large extent, it is our body that will determine the kind of person we can become. If another being controls our body, we have no possibility of self-determination, perhaps the most basic right of a person. (1989, 12)

To violate a person's body, then, is to violate *her*. In their classic feminist analysis of rape, Marilyn Frye and Carolyn Shafer point out that, given the intimate conceptual connection between bodies and persons, to invade a person's body against her will is essentially to deny that there is a person there at all (1977, 340).

Contemporary radical feminism, as I understand it, is distinguished above all by the view that the systematic deprivation of bodily sovereignty defines the oppressed condition of women as such. As Andrea Dworkin once put it, "I think that women's fundamental condition is defined literally by the lack of physical integrity of our bodies. I think that our subordinate place in society begins there" (1993, 139). Jane Caputi claims along similar lines that "control of women's sexual and reproductive capacities is the core patriarchal practice" (2004, 393). She points out that, tellingly, the most common misogynist slurs are "based in an open contempt for personal, political, and sexual female sovereignty" (2004, 393). In this section and the next, I will not attempt to defend this view in any definitive way, but rather to state it clearly and draw out some of its implications.

According to the radical feminist view I am outlining, patriarchy systematically denies the bodily sovereignty of women as such, by defining our bodies as existing *for* the use and benefit of others—men, and by extension fetuses and children—and then constructing institutions, from marriage to prostitution and more, that serve to normalize and enforce this definition. Within the ideology of patriarchy, a woman's body cannot be *her* sovereign territory precisely because it is the "virgin" (at first) territory for someone else to conquer and annex. Consider, as a contentious but nonetheless useful instance of this view, Andrea Dworkin's much-maligned analysis of sexual intercourse (1987). She observes that intercourse—an act defined by the legal and philosophical systems of patriarchy as both obligatory and definitive of women's status—is a physical border-crossing, an entering of women's bodily territory. Her point is not that such border-crossings are *inherently* violating or oppressive, independently of social context, but rather that when patriarchy makes intercourse definitive of "real woman-hood" (itself defined as subordinate), it thereby defines women as inherently penetrable; as Jane Caputi puts it, intercourse so understood "positions women as space to be invaded" (2004, 395).[9] Women are thus defined as *by nature* lacking in bodily sovereignty—indeed, as becoming most truly and fully women precisely in the abrogation of such sovereignty.

It is not only with respect to sexual penetration that women's bodies are treated as inherently violable and manipulable. For instance, the eagerness of many within patriarchal medical establishments to tinker with, cut into, and reorganize women's breasts, uteruses, genitals, hormones, and so on—often to the detriment of women's physical and emotional health—has been well documented by feminists.[10] Furthermore, it is not only women as such whose bodies are interpreted as devoid of sovereignty. The bodies of colonized people as such are subject not only to rape but to myriad other extreme physical violations. According to Andrea Smith,

> Because Indian bodies are "dirty," they are considered sexually violable and "rapable," and the rape of bodies that are considered inherently impure simply does not count. . . . the history of mutilation of Indian bodies, both living and dead, makes it clear that Indian people are not entitled to bodily integrity. (2005, 10)

Such mutilations, carried out in innumerable massacres of Indian communities during the era of U.S. settlement and expansion, ranged from scalping and decapitation to disembowelment. Andrew Jackson personally supervised the massacre of eight hundred Creek Indians, seeing to it that his men cut off the victims' noses as records of their kills and sliced off long strips of their flesh to tan and use as bridle reins (Jensen 2002, 246).[11] Similarly, lynchings of black men and women in the United States often included bodily (especially sexual) mutilation and the taking of "trophy" body parts from the victims.[12]

The radical feminist emphasis on women's bodily sovereignty is sometimes assumed to entail that violations of same (such as rape) are patriarchy's most important or most damaging manifestations, meriting more of our analytical and activist attention than, say, women's exploitation as workers (Baber 1987). Such comparative judgments, however, are neither necessary nor the point. The point is rather that the denial of women's bodily sovereignty is "the system's heart" (Dworkin 1983, 227): that which underlies and makes possible patriarchy's myriad other manifestations.

Claudia Card makes this kind of point, for instance, when she says that the terrorist institution of rape "underlies women's willingness to do whatever work men find suitable for women to do" (1991, 296). The analysis under consideration does suggest, however, that a full understanding of what bodily sovereignty is, and a continuing attempt to claim it (in both sexual and reproductive arenas, perhaps among others), must remain central to any effective feminism. It also explains why women's attempts to claim control over our bodies and their unique capacities, and to deny men access to and control over our bodies, so often inspires male resentment. (In a telling reversal, such attempts are frequently said to involve women's exercising illegitimate *power* over men.) In short, women's claims of bodily sovereignty inspire male rage and backlash, in pornography and elsewhere, precisely because the denial of such sovereignty is the central dynamic of patriarchy itself.

METAPHYSICAL CANNIBALISM

Radical feminists have analyzed at length the personal annexation, and subsequent exploitation, that men systematically visit upon women in patriarchy. As part of her definitive philosophical account of such annexation, Marilyn Frye describes as follows the endpoint of patriarchal seasoning (as of a girl or woman to sexual slavery):

> the woman or girl now serves herself only by serving [the master], and can interpret herself only by reference to him. He has rent her in two and grafted the raw ends to himself so she can act, but only in his interest. She has been annexed and is his appendage. . . . The slave's substance is assimilated to the master—a transference Ti-Grace Atkinson called "metaphysical cannibalism." (1983, 65)

Frye goes on to point out that much the same result can be achieved via the institutionally and ideologically supported power of perception and expectation. Such "arrogant" perception, she observes, "organize[s] everything seen with reference to [oneself] and [one's] own interests" (1983, 67). By getting someone else to believe that she too ought to be so organized—that, for her, being "good and healthy" means serving him—the would-be exploiter can acquire a willing servant. The patriarchal definition of women (and especially of our bodies) as *for* men is, of course, arrogant perception writ large.

The problem with such annexation, from the exploiters' point of view, is that it is inevitably partial, unstable, and insecure. This is so precisely because of the irreducible fact of bodily separateness. Persons and human bodies typically exist in a one-one relationship[13]: one body per person, one person per body. Although a person's bodily boundaries can change—my body can change size or shape, I can lose a limb, and so on—you cannot annex my living body and make it literally part of you. One reason, then, for the centrality to patriarchy of denying women's bodily sovereignty— and for many men's rage in response to women's claiming such sovereignty—is that the separateness, privacy, and internality of women's bodies is one of the few inherent, structural brakes on the patriarchal annexation and exploitation of women. Contra Haraway, it is enormously important that our bodies do, in fact, "end at the skin": in the face of metaphysical cannibalism, the separateness of our female bodies is all that stands in the way of our being eaten alive.

It is in this light that we can start to comprehend the aggression, the "extreme penetrations,"[14] and in general the intense physical cruelty and humiliation that we find in contemporary pornography, one of patriarchy's most visceral and up-to-the-minute blueprints.[15] Through such invasions— and the collective vicarious celebration thereof—some men simultaneously express their fury at women's obstinate physical separateness and their determination to nonetheless gain (or maintain) effective dominion by violating women's physical integrity. ("Face fuck her into submission!" commands one site.) From the cannibalistic perspective, moreover, if another person's body cannot literally become part of *me*, the next best thing is to make it at least symbolically *mine*. Consider the explanation offered by pornographer Brandon Iron for many men's fascination (in pornography, and increasingly outside it) with ejaculating *on* women's bodies, and especially in women's faces: "It's like a dog marking its territory. You know, why do dogs pee on fire hydrants and trees? . . . It's just like a man will leave his mark on a woman . . . you've got to let them know you were there."[16]

SOVEREIGNTY AND CONSENT

He called it "'round the world." My long-ago former husband . . . said he had heard, and believed, that it was greatly pleasurable to a man, and he wanted to do it with me. Penile intercourse in all three major orifices—anus, mouth and vagina. He had come in my mouth and vagina before, but never in my anus. I let him push his penis into my anus, and it hurt, and I didn't like it. He was angry with me for not liking it.[17]

Although an understanding of rape is essential to radical feminist analysis, radical feminists have also long insisted that bodily sovereignty is not abrogated *only* by nonconsensual uses and invasions (West 1995, Whisnant

2004). In fact, as devastating as such invasions are, their occurrence also paradoxically indicates that the victim's loss of sovereignty is not yet complete. For there to be a rape, a woman first has to refuse, and in refusing she implicitly claims some degree of bodily sovereignty.[18] Rape is, however, one of the signal means of beginning or advancing the destruction of a person's bodily sovereignty. For instance, feminist playwright Eve Ensler has said that being raped (and otherwise abused) by her father rendered her unable to "find [her] voice" for many years thereafter. Having been thus "done in" (as she puts it) at a young age, she could no longer distinguish between legitimate and illegitimate uses of her body: a man would sexually assault her, she says, "and then I would get up the next morning and have breakfast with him."[19] Women whose effective sovereignty has been thus undermined are often ideal targets for further exploitation, as misogynist radio host Tom Leykis once infamously commented on the air. Because women who have been molested as children "put out" more, Leykis reasoned, it's only rational for men to take advantage of their compliance and vulnerability: "If you think that a woman's more likely to put out or more likely to be good in bed because she has a history of abuse, is it wrong . . . to go for the gold?"[20] As D.A. Clarke observes, much the same dynamic has played out in the U.S. invasion and occupation of Iraq: having largely destroyed the country and rendered void its previous laws and other institutions of sovereignty, the U.S. then proceeded to "go for the gold," imposing "free market" rules and other conditions considered maximally advantageous to U.S. elites (personal communication, 2007).

Once a woman's (or girl's) bodily sovereignty has been significantly undermined, her formal rights of control over her body and its uses may seem to her not to be of any great importance; it thus may not seem like much of a loss to, as it were, officially sell off her sexual sovereignty. In Scott Anderson's valuable discussion of prostitution (2002), he describes it in much this way; in prostitution, he claims, a woman does not express or enact her sexual autonomy, but rather barters it away for other goods. (Capitalist ideology, of course, encourages just the opposite view: that marketplace participation is the ultimate manifestation of freedom and personal sovereignty.) And just as the Nauruans began to sell off their national sovereignty only as a last resort, a woman's right to control whether, when, and with whom she has sex is typically the *last* thing she sells, once all else is laid waste (by means consensual or nonconsensual).[21] It is no accident, furthermore, that in both cases, the sovereignty being sold off was only recently gained to begin with: Nauru entered the global "free" market at an enormous disadvantage after decades of colonial control, and those (comparatively fortunate) women who now have formal rights over the sexual and reproductive uses of our bodies won those rights only recently, after millennia of being owned outright by men—both publicly as prostitutes, and privately as daughters and wives.

Not only does a woman's nonconsent indicate her persistent claim to some degree of sovereignty, so too does what we might call her mere consent. It is most instructive that, for the husband in the quote that opened this section, his wife's consent is not good enough; he is angry because she doesn't "like it." Her liking it would (to him) indicate that total and unconditional penetrability is her natural state, her default condition; by not liking it, she implicitly claims a degree of sovereignty. The expectation that persons violated by more powerful others will display pleasure in and gratitude for the violation is, again, apparent in other contexts: surely cheering Iraqis will throw flowers at the feet of U.S. invaders—and if they don't, they must not understand the value of freedom.[22]

FAUX-SOVEREIGNTY AND TABOO VIOLATION

Much like the violation of women's bodily sovereignty, the violation of national sovereignty is widely agreed to be wrong in the abstract, but is frequently defended (or called something else) in particular instances. In both cases, belief in the sovereign equality of the less powerful is maintained in the face of its routine and manifest violation by those with power. In particular, the most casual survey of U.S. history reveals that the "sovereign equality" of nations has been honored mostly in the breach (Jensen 2004c, Mahajan 2002, 2003). "Contempt for sovereignty," observes Noam Chomsky,

> is as old as American history. . . . The sovereignty of others is of no account if they're in our way—if they're what are called "rogue" states, meaning not following orders. But our own sovereignty, and that of our client states and those that join with us, that has to be protected. None of this is new, but also, none of it matters. It's all . . . declared irrelevant. It's just facts. (1999)

National sovereignty thus functions largely as an ideological construct, deployed at the will and according to the self-serving definitions of the powerful. Powerful nations (or, more properly, the elites that control them) do as they please, and less powerful nations enjoy the formal protections of sovereignty for only so long as they obey. When they step out of line, they must be punished. To borrow a phrase painfully familiar to feminists, such nations are seen as "asking for it."[23]

The fiction of sovereign equality—whether among nations or persons—can obscure to oppressed and colonized people the existence and nature of their oppression, thus shortcircuiting their resistance. Even for those among the oppressed who perceive (perhaps dimly) the reality behind the rhetoric, such ideological mystification is crazy-making, which then has its own advantages from the oppressor's point of view. But I think there is an additional reason why, in systems of power both imperial and patriarchal, sovereignty is such a useful fiction. To illustrate this reason, I'll now return to the example of pornography.

One important element of pornography's appeal to its users is its frequent portrayal of various sexual activities as unauthorized, rebellious, and against social norms. By its very nature, pornography violates certain traditional rules governing sexuality (most obviously that of female chastity and monogamy). But the sexualizing of rule- and boundary-violation in pornography has many more dimensions. It is perhaps most evident in the wild popularity of the "barely legal" genre, in which very young-looking girls are presented for the sexual consumption of adult men, as well as in voyeur pornography in which women are presented as having been photographed or filmed without their knowledge.[24] Another increasingly popular genre that clearly illustrates the pattern of taboo-violation is what the industry calls "interracial," which is mostly code for sex between black men and white women. In this kind of pornography, the historical taboo on black men's sexual access to white women is sexualized—and so, too, is the veiled threat of retaliatory violence against black men by white men, not to mention the usually not-so-veiled message that the white woman's body has been damaged by the black man's freakishly large penis (Dines 1998, 2006).

What should we make of this fascination with the forbidden, with that which violates publicly acknowledged social and/or moral norms? According to Jane Caputi, taboo violation is central to patriarchal culture itself:

> Whether advancing upon the "final frontier" of outer space, probing the "most intimate properties of matter," taking possession of desirable and colonizable "virgin land," or staking a claim on the body of a child, patriarchal men routinely disregard any notion of taboo or limitation and continually give themselves permission to "boldly go where no man has gone before." (2004, 286)

It is hardly surprising that, in such a culture, taboo-violation itself is sexualized.[25] As Caputi puts it, "[P]atriarchal culture is about . . . eroticizing the forbidden . . . . [The] rules are made really to be broken. It's thrilling to march in without invitation, justifying everything from incest to manifest destiny to all kinds of cultural imperialism" (Caputi 1998). Seeing this point can help us understand the otherwise-puzzling importance, in our patriarchal and imperialist culture, of formally recognizing the sovereignty both of other nations and of women's bodies.[26] In short, if something is forbidden, then in doing it anyway one demonstrates one's power that much more fully. Taboo-violation by powerful groups and individuals—particularly when it takes the form of officially proscribed abuses against those less powerful—serves to reinforce, extend, and reinscribe their power.[27]

Thus, both the formal prohibition of rape and incest and the formal ideal of sovereign equality among nations demonstrate the paradoxical usefulness to oppressors of certain violations being nominally off-limits. In order to do what is forbidden and get away with it—perhaps the ultimate display of power—the thing one does must, in fact, be forbidden. The message then becomes, "We can do this *even though* it's not allowed; who's going to stop us?" To take an obvious example, the fact that its 2003 invasion of Iraq was widely opposed and in clear violation of international law actually served an important purpose for the Bush administration. To both U.S. allies and enemies, it sent the message that the U.S. government can and will do as it pleases and call it whatever it likes—so watch out. (Recall the outraged fulminating by some of the war's supporters at the idea that the U.S. should have to "ask permission," from the UN or anyone else, to unleash its military might whenever and wherever it chooses.)

The problem with taboo-violation is that, as shattered taboos give rise to new norms and reorganized realities, one eventually runs out of taboos to violate. One cannot break a boundary that is already broken, nor defile what has already been defiled.[28] The contemporary pornography industry is facing precisely this dilemma, as some of its own producers have acknowledged. For example, as anal sex has become increasingly standard in mainstream pornography, it has lost its former edge of taboo-violation, to be supplanted by double penetration, double anal, and even triple anal. Reflecting on consumers' constant pressure on him to push the envelope, porn director Mitchell Spinelli says that "People want to know . . . how many dicks you can shove up an ass." Jules Jordan, another director, agrees: "so many fans want to see so much more extreme stuff that I'm always trying to figure out ways to do something different." Pornography producers understandably wonder, as one plaintively asks, "what are [we] gonna do next?"[29]

A culture or social group that obsessively seeks the thrill of taboo violation ultimately finds itself in a dilemma that can be resolved only one way: the fewer rules there are left to break, the fewer boundaries are left intact, the more cruel and forceful the penetrations of old boundaries will be. To keep reinscribing its power, the dominant group has to re-break those boundaries, imposing additional damage, and ultimately obliterate them. It's time, in other words, for "shock and awe." This dynamic thus provides a partial explanation for the prevalence of extreme, gratuitous cruelty in both contemporary pornography and contemporary U.S. wars.

'ROUND THE WORLD: NATIONAL
SOVEREIGNTY REVISITED

With nations as with embodied persons, dispensing with the prima facie entitlements encoded in claims of sovereignty leaves us with the free play of unrestrained brute power, and with its predictably ugly results. As Jean Cohen points out, "the sovereignty-based model of international law appears to be ceding not to cosmopolitan justice but to a different bid to restructure the world order: the project of empire" (2004, 2). In this context, she contends, "undermining the principle of sovereign equality of states in the name of legal cosmopolitanism plays into the wrong hands" (2004, 11). Furthermore, national sovereignty is increasingly threatened by the brute power not only of nations with imperial ambitions, but also of multinational corporations, which roam the globe free from democratic accountability and largely outside the control of national governments.

In the face of such dangerous and escalating threats to national sovereignty, should feminists' defense of the latter be as uncompromising as our insistence on women's bodily sovereignty? My view is that, although both forms of sovereignty require defense at this historical moment, the two are not parallel in the nature and grounds of their moral importance or (therefore) in their centrality to a liberatory politics. Explaining why not requires that I return to the concept of sovereignty itself.

Sovereignty is a kind of authority that is located and traced according to the borders or boundaries of something. For most people, the term "sovereignty" calls to mind most immediately that of a nation, and here the relevant borders are territorial ones. Unlike human and animal bodies, however, nations are artificial entities, their borders ultimately just lines on a map. While the borders of persons' bodies are in some meaningful sense natural, the same is not true of nations: the only natural boundaries dividing territorial regions are provided by such things as oceans, rivers, and mountain ranges.[30] National boundaries come into being, expand, and contract—often as a result of violent conquest and annexation, the result of which is then treated as a natural or preordained entity (consider "manifest destiny").[31] The more deeply we ponder this fact, the stranger it may seem to regard these artificial entities of suspect moral origin as having rights, including those of sovereignty, in anything like the sense that persons do.

But what does it mean to say that bodies, but not states, are naturally bounded? In what important sense are bodily boundaries "natural"? Clearly, for an organism to survive and thrive, its component parts must be in certain functional relationships to each other: if a person's liver slides down into her feet, or if her body lacks a valve connecting her heart to her veins, then, qua organism, she is in trouble. Bodily boundaries are among the minimal necessary conditions for such internal functioning. Because my body is bounded—again, *pace* Haraway, because it "ends at the skin"—my heart will not pump blood into your veins, nor will my liver fly off into thin air. The boundaries of my body—and my ability to maintain those boundaries by controlling, to a significant extent, what does and does not cross them—protect and make possible my functioning as an organism.

Violations of bodily boundaries, at least when repeated or systematic, tend to undermine an organism's internal functioning. At the level of pure biology, a toxic substance that invades an organism may cause its parts to become dysfunctionally reorganized. Intentional bodily invasions such as rape, which violate the person through her body, can also yield disordered internal relations. As we saw earlier, rape and sexual abuse "seasons" victims to become alienated from their bodies; when such abuse occurs repeatedly, especially early in a victim's life, she may become skilled at dissociating or "splitting," that is, at experiencing herself as wholly disengaged from her body and what is happening to it.[32] While such dissociation can help the victim survive the violation, it can also come at the price of her own long-term wholeness and psychological functioning. The difficulties of severely violated and traumatized people are often somatic as well as psychological. As Judith Herman observes, survivors' bodily pains and illnesses (often neither explainable nor remediable by conventional means) can lead them, over time, to "perceive their bodies as having turned against them" (1992, 86); some attack their own bodies by means ranging from eating disorders and self-mutilation to compulsive risk-taking and suicide attempts (108–110).

Perhaps we can best articulate what bodily sovereignty is by contrast to this, the far endpoint of its systematic violation. At this endpoint, the victim's internal organization and functioning has been profoundly undermined; indeed, she has been turned against herself, some parts of her body and spirit now continuing the work of the abuser. By contrast, then, perhaps the sovereignty of an embodied person is (at least in significant part) a state of right and functional relationship among her constituent parts or elements. The entitlements of sovereignty, then, are those necessary to protect and preserve that state of right relationship.

How can this (admittedly loose) characterization of persons' bodily sovereignty help us in thinking about national sovereignty? Let us first consider one initially plausible view of the relationship between the two forms of sovereignty, articulated by Noam Chomsky as follows:

> [national] sovereignty is . . . only a value insofar as it relates to freedom and rights, either enhancing them or diminishing them. . . . [I]n speaking of freedom and rights, we have in mind human beings—that is, persons of flesh and blood, not abstract political and legal constructions like corporations, or states, or capital. If these entities have any rights at all, which is questionable,

they should be derivative from the rights of people. That's the core essential liberal doctrine. It's also the guiding principle for popular struggles for centuries, but it's very strongly opposed . . . by sectors of wealth and privilege, and that's true both in the political and the socioeconomic realms. (2000, 200)

Chomsky's intuition about the moral and logical priority of individual persons' rights is widely shared; no doubt it grounds the reasonable view that a nation's internal sovereignty does not give its government the right to abuse (or to tolerate the abuse of) its citizens or any subset thereof.[33] In my view, however, Chomsky errs in implicitly restricting the natural home of "freedom and rights" to "human beings." His reference to "flesh and blood" is more promising. It points in the direction of the broader view I think we should endorse: that *biotic entities and communities* are the natural loci of sovereignty and the true holders of the entitlements associated therewith. As Jane Caputi has eloquently argued, if any territorial "body" needs protecting, it is the earth itself, which in its systematic exploitation and abuse is perhaps most closely analogous to women's bodies (1993, 2004). There are biotic entities and communities of many kinds and at many levels, however, from ponds and meadows to watersheds and bioregions.

Note, too, that while a nation is at least connected to a particular territorial region, a corporation is not so connected, nor is it oriented toward the protection or sustenance of a biotic community of any kind. As Derrick Jensen points out, invoking the etymological root *corporare*, corporations have gained for themselves the protections of personhood (and more) "by claiming, in essence, to be a living body," when in fact they are "the 'embodiment,' the reification, of a single idea—that of amassing wealth" (2002, 439–440). Not only are corporations not "living bodies" themselves, they lack even a nominal relationship to any such body or community of bodies—even the living human bodies who run them, who by design are released from responsibility for the actions of the collective and abstract "body" that is the corporation itself. It is thus appropriate that systematic corporate infringement on the sovereignty of nations, as well on that of persons and other biotic entities and communities, continues to be vigorously challenged by activists against neoliberal globalization.

All human beings and human communities are, of course, parts of larger biotic communities that encompass both land and other, nonhuman living beings. D.A. Clarke points out in this connection that

for indigenous people, their native land is not a "place" that they inhabit. It is a part of the self, it defines them as well as sustaining them. The land and the people are one thing and the coloniser/invader drives a wedge into that wholeness, forcibly alienating the people from the land. There is ample documentary evidence of indigenes committing suicide or going mad because of this forcible separation from the land which is the self. (personal communication, 2007)

One example of this phenomenon which received international attention in the late 1990s was the fight of Colombia's indigenous U'Wa people to keep Occidental Petroleum from drilling on their lands.[34] According to Shannon Wright, then director of the Rainforest Action Network's Beyond Oil campaign, the U'Wa explain their right to prevent the drilling by "say[-ing] that they adhere to a law that is older than the sun and moon and this is the divine law. And it is their right as a community to continue to exist and to protect their area" (Yeomans 1999). Non-indigenous peoples are less likely to fight such incursions, partly because our sense of membership in biotic communities has long since been blunted by our acculturation to extractive corporate cultures and economies. As Clarke puts it, this sense of place and belonging "has been stolen from us in a process rather similar to the 'seasoning' of girls and women . . . to be able to dissociate from the body in order to endure abuse and the violation of sovereignty" (personal communication, 2007).

CONCLUSION: A WOMAN'S BODY IS LIKE A FOREIGN COUNTRY

A classical tradition . . . personifies institutions, cities, and lands as goddesses—Europe and Europa, Athens and Athena, Ireland and Eire. . . . Th[is] archaic habit . . . [is] emblematic of an underlying principle of female *sovereignty*—a sacred concept embracing autonomy, self-rule, integrity, and radiance or resplendence. . . . No ruler is considered legitimate unless the Goddess, the ultimate guardian of the land, confers sovereignty upon him. (Caputi 2004, 359)

I have suggested that sovereignty should be understood most basically as a state of right relationship among diverse elements of biotic entities or communities, and derivatively as the entitlement of any such entity or community to protect those relationships and, through them, its own survival, integrity, and flourishing. So understood, the entitlements of sovereignty are morally basic and ineliminable. Violations of sovereignty disrupt those relationships (whether temporarily or permanently) in such a way as to make the entity or community no longer functionally self-preserving—in extreme cases, to turn the organism or community against itself by causing some of its parts to attack other parts.

Despite nations' artificiality and morally dubious provenance, national sovereignty has continuing moral importance primarily because, at this historical moment, it is among the only conceptual and political tools that can provide a brake on the interconnected threats to biotic communities posed by imperialism and corporatism. Any nation's right against infringements of its sovereignty is based, however, on its government's claim to provide a structure of authority among whose primary purposes is to preserve and protect the biotic entities and communities within its borders. Needless to say, actual national governments' levels of commitment to this aim, and their success even where the commitment is present, vary widely. Furthermore, it may well be that (as many suspect) the nation-state structure is not well suited to preserving biotic communities that can function democratically and sustainably over the long term.[35] According to Andrea Smith,

> just as we have to think beyond the state as the "answer" to violence, we need to think beyond the nation-state as the appropriate form of governance for the world. . . . Native women activists . . . have begun articulating notions of "nation" and "sovereignty" which are separate from nation-states. Whereas nation-states are governed through domination and coercion, indigenous sovereignty and nationhood is predicated on interrelatedness and responsibility. (184–185)

In riding to the defense of national sovereignty, then—in general, or in any particular case—we should remain aware of the artificial and likely temporary nature of the entities being defended and, concomitantly, of the provisional status of such entities' claims to sovereignty. This need not render our insistence on national sovereignty any less urgent and uncompromising in particular instances, as when activists around the world defended the right of Iraq as a sovereign nation not to be the target of U.S. aggression. It does mean, however, that such insistence should be embedded in a broader analysis that makes the preservation of biotic entities and communities morally, conceptually, and strategically central. Understood as a revolutionary claim on behalf of living beings and communities—and backed by effective resistance—the concept of sovereignty can pose an obstacle to corporate exploitation and extraction, to men's predation on women's bodies and lives, and to the expansion and entrenchment of empire.

NOTES

1. My title is taken from Marjorie Reiley Maguire's eloquent essay "Symbiosis, Biology, and Personalization," in which she contends (among other things) that even if human fetuses are full-blown persons with all the rights thereof, they are properly "beyond the protection of the law." This, she says, is because "a woman's body is like the borders of a foreign country. There is a sovereign immunity to a person's body that the law transgresses to the nation's detriment. The end cannot justify the means of such an invasion" (1989, 12–13).

2. Cohen herself contends that (as she puts it in a later article) "cosmopolitan liberalism undermines universalistic features of the international legal order that are meant to restrain aggression and block imperialist or great power predations in the name of an ethical vision of the world that is neither desirable nor feasible in the current context" (Cohen 2006).

3. Although the term "nation" is multiply ambiguous, I use it herein to refer to what Omar Dahbour (2006) calls "sovereign territorial states": that is, entities such as Canada, Mexico, Germany, and Nigeria.

4. For a useful discussion of these interconnections, see Jensen (2004b).

5. Comment in online forum. Quote used by permission. My thinking about the issues discussed herein has benefited enormously both from Clarke's previous writings (especially 2004) and from her generous comments on earlier drafts of this essay.

6. The slideshow referenced here is "Who Wants to Be a Porn Star?: Sex and Violence in Today's Pornography Industry," written and produced by Gail Dines, Robert Jensen, and Rebecca Whisnant.

7. "Gonzo" is one of the two types of films that make up the contemporary pornography industry. Unlike features, which have characters and some minimal plot, gonzo films are simply one sex scene after another ("wall to wall," as the industry puts it), often filmed in a private home or on some minimal set. Gonzo films tend to have more overtly harsh and aggressive content than do features, although, as gonzo increasingly shapes the mainstream of the industry, it pushes the boundaries of what is acceptable in features as well. Gonzo is the fastest growing sector of the pornography industry and is extremely profitable, thanks both to its popularity and to its low production costs.

8. D.A. Clarke: "It occurs to me that Nauru has been 'turned inside out,' the natural boundaries between what lies beneath the earth and what grows on top of it have been obliterated and the island's guts lie exposed to the eye like something slaughtered" (personal communication, 2007).

9. This point is perhaps most clearly seen by contrast. All human bodies are, of course, penetrable in that they have orifices which can be penetrated. Only in the case of females, however, is it thought to be both proper and necessary for these orifices to be penetrated. In contrast, a male who is penetrated is thought to have had his essential nature as a male violated; he has been "un-manned," even or perhaps especially if the penetration was consensual. So powerful is the association, in patriarchal ideology, between being penetrated and being feminized that the mere perceived suggestion of such penetration (as in a romantic or flirtatious overture from another man) often occasions violent retaliation.

10. See Roberts (1997) for a compelling account of how the bodies of Black women in the U.S., and especially their reproductive capacities, have been treated as especially manipulable, violable, and in need of rigid control.

11. In this connection, it is chilling to recall the email written by one of the Duke lacrosse players present at an event at which a young woman (whom they had brought there to strip for them) claimed to have been gang raped. Having indicated that he planned to invite some strippers over again the following night, this young man wrote: "I plan on killing the bitches as soon as the [sic] walk in and proceeding

to cut their skin off while cumming in my duke issue spandex." See http://www.the smokinggun.com/archive/0405061duke1.html.

12. For an analysis of trophy-taking as a ritual of domination, and of pornography as (among other things) a kind of trophy-taking, see Clarke (2004, 196–205).

13. I have in mind, as exceptions, conjoined twins and (more arguably) persons with dissociative identity disorder, or what is still sometimes colloquially called "multiple personalities."

14. This is a reference to pornography in which women are penetrated (or penetrate themselves) vaginally, orally, or anally with dramatically oversized and/or otherwise dangerous objects, such as bottles, lamps, knives, broomsticks, and baseball bats.

15. While feminist critics' claims about the prevalence of violence and aggression in mainstream pornography have sometimes been difficult to evaluate, a recent content analysis of fifty of the most widely rented adult DVDs and videos provides strong evidence in support of those claims (Wosnitzer et. al., 2007). This study found that the scenes in these films contained an average of 11.52 verbally and/or physically aggressive acts per scene, with 89.9 percent of scenes containing at least one such act. Women were the recipients of 94.4 percent of all aggressive acts, while men were the initiators of 72.7 percent of those acts. Unlike many previous researchers, Wosnitzer et. al. also coded for recipients' responses to aggression; these responses were neutral or positive in 95 percent of cases.

16. From an interview conducted by Chyng Sun on May 1, 2005, for the latter's film (forthcoming from Media Education Foundation, fall 2007) and book (forthcoming from Peter Lang, 2009), both titled *The Price of "Pleasure": Pornography, Sexualities and Relationships*.

17. Comment by contributor to online forum at http://stangoff.com. Quote used by permission.

18. The point here is analogous in some ways to Marilyn Frye's observation that "the slave who decides to exclude the master from her hut is declaring herself not a slave" (1983, 104).

19. Ensler's comments are from an interview in the video "Rape Is . . ." distributed by Cambridge Documentary Films (2002). For another woman's discussion of how early sexual abuse shaped her later life and her sexuality, see "The Making of a Whore: The Story of Lara Newman," available at http://www.dianarussell.com/lara .html.

20. Quoted in Jensen (2002, 150–151).

21. The same is arguably true of the right to decide whether and when one will conceive and gestate a child. It is worth reflecting here on the beliefs of some Christian-conservative women that contraception is an arrogation of the rightful power of God (and of their husbands as God's earthly representatives) to decide whether and when a fetus shall occupy their bodies. For an informative discussion of this set of beliefs as manifested in the Quiverfull movement, see Joyce (2006).

22. Thanks to D.A. Clarke for reminding me of this connection.

23. The reference here is to the idea, still too common in popular discourse and media, that a rape victim "asked for it" by transgressing the (unwritten and ever-shifting) rules that govern proper female behavior: "Of course rape is terrible, but you should have seen this girl . . . and what was she doing there, anyway?"

24. Relatedly, pornography frequently eroticizes the violation of incest taboos, as on sites called "Daddy's Whores" and "Use My Daughter."

25. Caputi explains that "pornography is no real alternative to systemic sex-negative morality; rather it is an intrinsic part of it. . . . For both, sex itself is the core taboo. Moralism systematically upholds the taboo and pornography systematically violates it. In the complex that evolves from this absurdity, taboo-violation itself becomes erotically charged. Evil becomes seductive and the good mostly boring" (2004, 75). This analysis also makes clear that she has in mind the violation not of repressive taboos (such as that against homosexuality) but rather of "life-preservative taboos, like those against incest, rape, murder, and related violations of the life force" (2004, 77).

26. I do not mean to minimize the role of feminists over many generations in pressing, often against enormous resistance, for the legal recognition of women's bodily sovereignty in its various manifestations. I mean only to suggest that, once grudgingly granted, such legal recognition—especially absent meaningful and reliable enforcement—can also play a paradoxically useful role for male supremacists.

27. Of course, the appeal of taboo-violation is not the only explanation for why sexual access to certain women and girls is prohibited to certain men. As many feminists have observed, such prohibitions also function to protect individual men's sexual ownership (whether formal or informal) of their own wives, daughters, and girlfriends.

28. Hence the obsession in pornography with virgins and with various subsequent "firsts": "Her First DP," "Her First Anal," and so on.

29. All three quotes from pornography directors are cited in Jensen (2004b). I owe a great deal to Jensen's analysis of pornography in this and other essays, an analysis brought together in Jensen (2007).

30. National borders do sometimes coincide with such natural boundaries; the most obvious examples would be island nations, such as Nauru.

31. Thanks to Marilyn Fischer for first emphasizing to me the importance of this fact.

32. D.A. Clarke drew the relevance of this phenomenon to my attention.

33. As Chomsky would be among the first to remind us, the occurrence of such governmental abuse does not automatically entail that military intervention to stop it is justified.

34. "From 1940 to 1970 . . . the U'wa had 85 percent of their ancestral territory stripped from them by the Colombian government. In the eyes of the U'wa leadership, Occidental posed the greatest danger to their people since the Spanish conquistadors threatened to enslave them more than 500 years ago. Then, according to tribal oral history, thousands of U'wa jumped to their death from a 1,400-foot cliff in an act of defiance. In April 1995, the Colombian press reported that the U'wa nation would commit mass suicide by jumping off the same cliff if Occidental was allowed to start oil exploration" (Yeomans 1999).

35. Thanks to Robert Jensen for bringing this point to my attention. For a useful discussion of the proper scale of sovereign communities, see Dahbour (2006), who defines the essential goods of sovereignty as "collectivity, locality, and democracy" (114) and contends that "the sovereignty principle is [not] necessarily tied to the scale of the [sovereign territorial state]" (113).

4

POLITICAL AND RELIGIOUS CONFLICT

10

Is Peacekeeping Care Work?

A Feminist Reflection on "The Responsibility to Protect"

Joan Tronto

Let us suppose that the great empire of China, with all its myriads of inhabitants, was suddenly swallowed up by an earthquake, and let us consider how a man of humanity in Europe, who had no sort of connection with that part of the world, would be affected upon receiving intelligence of this dreadful calamity. He would, I imagine, first of all, express very strongly his sorrow for the misfortune of that unhappy people, he would make many melancholy reflections upon the precariousness of human life, and the vanity of all the labours of man, which could thus be annihilated in a moment. And when all this fine philosophy was over, when all these humane sentiments had been once fairly expressed, he would pursue his business or his pleasure, take his repose or his diversion, with the same ease and tranquility, as if no such accident had happened. The most frivolous disaster which could befall himself would occasion a more real disturbance. If he was to lose his little finger tomorrow, he would not sleep tonight; but, provided he never saw them, he will snore with the most profound security over the ruin of a hundred millions of his brethren, and the destruction of that immense multitude seems plainly an object less interesting to him, than this paltry misfortune of his own (Smith 1981).

[I]f humanitarian intervention is, indeed, an unacceptable assault on sovereignty, how should we respond to a Rwanda, to a Srebrenica—to gross and

Joan Tronto

systematic violations of human rights that affect every precept of our common humanity? (UN Secretary General Kofi Annan, quoted in International Commission on Intervention and State Sovereignty 2001a, vii)

INTRODUCTION

The feminist ethics of care purports to be a valuable perspective with which to make moral judgments and thus from which to act in the social and political world. Although care is frequently associated with the intimate work of one person caring for another human body, many scholars have argued that in order for care genuinely to be a broad-based ethic, it needs to go beyond this understanding. It was to this end that Berenice Fisher and I originally formulated our general definition of care: "everything that we do to maintain, continue, and repair our world so that we may live in it as well as possible" (Fisher and Tronto 1990, 40).

Virtually no scholars or political actors would question the importance of care for discussing private, intimate life. But many scholars are not willing to permit care outside of these boundaries. In recent years, feminist scholars have begun to take up the feasibility of expanding the care ethic's scope to the international arena (see, e.g., Ruddick 1989; Gould 2004; Champagne 2006; Hankivsky 2006; Held 2006). In this essay I wish to discuss a hard case for care by trying to consider what care can say about responding to violence within states suffering from civil wars or other forms of internal violence. Reflecting back on one of the bloodiest centuries in human history, this is surely one of the critical tests for any ethical theory. In this paper I want to see if the care ethic can help us to understand the process of "peacekeeping."

Peacekeeping is a term of art in international discourse, and I will use the term somewhat more broadly and more imprecisely in this essay. "Peacekeeping" precisely refers to an intervention in which troops are inserted between or among warring parties who have reached an agreement about the desirability of ending violent conflict but who need some way to enforce or keep this peace. In this essay, I do not exclude that usage, but I will use the term "peacekeeping" to describe more broadly the insertion of troops to try to halt damage to citizens whose lives are threatened by warfare; thus, "peacekeeping" is broadened to include all forms of military humanitarian intervention in situations of conflict. This is different from humanitarian intervention in cases of natural disaster, and it is different from cases in which troops are introduced perhaps even to produce peace, but primarily for a partisan political purpose.

"Humanitarian intervention" is a relatively new phenomenon in world history;[1] since World War II nations have committed their military forces to try to protect civilian lives in myriad cases. Especially since the end of the Cold War and with the spread of internal wars in the 1990s, humanitarian intervention has become a pressing concern.[2] For some, the very idea is an oxymoron (Hayden 2003); how can one use military means to forge peace? For others, the logic of "just war" has been the framework within which to discern when intervention is appropriate; there is a "right to intervene" when the presumption of state sovereignty is overturned by the standards applied in making a "just war" argument (Walzer 2000).

Against these accounts of humanitarian intervention, a new one is emerging. It may not be too much of an exaggeration to say that a *paradigm shift* (Kuhn 1970) is occurring in the description of the conditions under which humanitarian intervention can be justified and carried out. The paradigm of "the right to intervene" is being displaced by an alternative paradigm, one described by the ICISS as "the responsibility to protect" and colloquially already called "R2P" (International Commission on Intervention and State Sovereignty 2001a). Exploring how R2P represents a paradigm shift is the task of this essay.

In the end, I will argue that while R2P represents a major change in the way in which the international community speaks about humanitarian intervention, the only way to make certain that R2P really is a different paradigm is if it goes further in the direction of a feminist practice of peacekeeping. I will begin by exploring the nature of "the responsibility to protect" and whether it constitutes a paradigm change; then I shall suggest some further feminist emendations that will make it genuinely caring and a truly transformative paradigm. For the shift from the "right to intervene" to the "responsibility to protect" is really a movement from one paradigm about morality to another, with concomitant shifts in the questions about power and responsibility that inhere in a moral framework.

THE PARADIGM SHIFT

From "Rights" to "Responsibilities"

The purpose of the ICISS was to provide a new framework within which to think about humanitarian intervention. Materially supported by the Canadian government and undertaken with UN support, the Commission's report is forthright in its attempt to move the international community toward a new way of thinking about humanitarian intervention (Evans and Sahnoun 2002). The report describes as follows some of the ways in which it shifts the focus of the discussion:

> The traditional language of the sovereignty-intervention debate—in terms of "the right of humanitarian intervention" or the "right to intervene"—is

unhelpful. . . . First, it necessarily focuses attention on the claims, rights, and prerogatives of the potentially intervening states much more so than on the urgent needs of the potential beneficiaries of action. . . . [B]y focusing narrowly on the act of intervention, the traditional language does not adequately take into account the need for either prior preventive effort or subsequent follow-up assistance, both of which have been too often neglected in practice.

The Commission is of the view that the debate about intervention for human protection purposes should focus not on "the right to intervene" but on "the responsibility to protect."

First, the responsibility to protect implies an evaluation of the issues from the point of view of those seeking or needing support, rather than those who may be considering intervention. Our preferred terminology refocuses the international searchlight back where it should always be: on the duty to protect communities from mass killing, women from systematic rape and children from starvation. (International Commission on Intervention and State Sovereignty 2001a)

Writing in the 1980s, Carol Gilligan discovered what she called a moral "different voice." Gilligan's different voice diverges from Kantian-derived moral theories in three ways: 1) the central concepts are responsibility and relationships rather than rights and rules; 2) the moral questions are concrete and narrative rather than formal and abstract; and 3) the moral theory is best described not as a principle, but as the "activity of care."[3] Although the ICISS still uses the language of "duty," they talk about the responsibility to protect in terms of the needs of the afflicted rather than the rights of the agents. Thus, they are some way along to making the paradigm shift to an ethic of care, though they do not use the "activity of care" language in their description.

Not only is there a paradigm shift, then, as the Commission argued, but it can best be characterized as one parallel to the shift from "justice" to "care." Of course, in the long ensuing feminist discussion of care, it is clear that the point is not to exclude the kinds of considerations that are taken to be fundamental to the justice perspective. Rather, as Larrabee puts it, "Gilligan did not want to overturn the Kohlberg theory, but rather to supplement it with a theory of moral concern grounded in responsiveness to others that dictates providing care, preventing harm, and maintaining relationships" (Larrabee 1993).

Upon reflection, perhaps the parallel between this new approach to humanitarian intervention and the revision of moral theory that arises out of the feminist ethic of care should not surprise us. In the first place, the contrast between Gilligan's moral "voice" and the standard moral framework of contemporary ethics parallels the contrast among moral theories in other historical eras, for example, the displacement of theories of moral sentiments by Kantian deontology after the eighteenth century (Tronto 1993).

In the second place, there is, after all, an interesting parallel between the assault on the logic of the "autonomous self" that motivated and supported many new directions in feminist philosophy in recent years, including the interest in care (see, e.g., Held 1993; Walker 1999; Mackenzie and Stoljar 2000, and the challenge to the notion of "sovereignty" in recent thinking in international relations. The "autonomous self" is presumed to be a moral actor endowed with disinterest and dispassion, prepossessed of his/her own self-interests, and making judgments based upon those interests. While this is something of a caricature (no moral philosopher thinks this image describes actual humans), this model of the "autonomous self" is congruent with a description of the task for moral theory as a self-generated declaration of the nature of rights and duties. So, too, the sovereign state is a mythical creature, one that shares many characteristics with the autonomous self. The sovereign state is seen as capable of complete independence, able to make decisions about its own interests based solely on its autonomous conception of those interests, and possessed of a right against outside interference in its internal affairs (since it is the only actor able to make judgments about its rights and duties). Indeed, the first feminist ethic of care work to address international relations was primarily devoted to showing some limitations of this notion of sovereignty (Robinson 1999).[4]

Sociologically, it should also not surprise us that, in the twenty-first century, the interconnections among states have become more salient in describing how sovereigns act. As our capacity to know about the world has increased, and as our capacities and power to respond to disasters elsewhere have increased, the fiction of the sovereign state becomes more difficult to maintain. As ICISS noted, "There is no longer such a thing as a humanitarian catastrophe occurring in a faraway country of which we know little" (International Commission on Intervention and State Sovereignty 2001a).

For sovereign states to react as if they have no duty to intervene in the face of humanitarian catastrophes presumes that, unless linked by specific and definable duties, humans, and the states they create, have no responsibility to others. Here is perhaps the most important aspect of the shift in moral theory in the last century: the shift from duty to responsibility is a profound one.

Feinberg (1980) argues that the difference between a duty and a responsibility is that duties are specified by the *rights* to which they are correlated, while responsibility is ambiguously bounded by the *relationship* to which it is a response.[5] Responsibility, Thomas Haskell reminds us, is a term that only entered the English language at the end of the eighteenth century. It is a remarkably complex idea. It requires that we see ourselves as capable of acting and as somehow implicated, causally, in the situation to be addressed (Haskell 1998). If "ought implies can," Haskell observes, then what follows is a very complicated understanding of what is necessary and what is transformable in human life, and hence, of what constitute the limits of responsibility. How should we think, then, about the converse; to what extent does "can imply ought"? Haskell glosses Bernard Williams' discussion of slavery in the ancient world, and observes that since ancient writers simply assumed that slavery was necessary, they did not imagine it could be immoral. Haskell then asks, "How do 'necessary evils' such as slavery come to seem remediable, thus shrinking the domain of necessity and expanding the realm within which the imperatives of responsibility can operate?"[6] (297)

The circumstance that has changed the world is our capacity to know about political violence and its effects everywhere in the world (Human Security Centre 2005). Thus, it becomes possible to speak not only of state security, defined, described and controlled by the state, but also of "human security." Human security begins not with the safety of states per se, but with that of the individuals who live within them. Scholars have been discussing human security for a decade, but with diplomatic understatement, the Commission introduced this idea as one to take seriously:

> The concept of human security . . . is now increasingly recognized to extend to people as well as to states. . . . Whether universally popular or not, there is a growing recognition worldwide that the protection of human security, including human rights and human dignity, must be one of the fundamental objectives of modern international institutions. (International Commission on Intervention and State Sovereignty 2001a, 6)

Clearly, insofar as horrific acts perpetrated against civilians (previously seen as "necessary evils") have come to seem remediable, there is a shift in the meaning of responsibility. Thus, the capacity to see the harms, the capacity to do something to remedy them, and a sense of greater global connection make it more difficult to answer Kofi Annan's question—"How should we respond to . . . gross and systematic violations of human rights that affect every precept of our common humanity?"—with a shrug of shoulders and a demurral that nothing can be done.

I have demonstrated that the paradigm shift from "the right to intervene" to "the responsibility to protect" reflects the parallel paradigm shift from "rights"-based morality to an "ethic of care." This intellectual fact, this striking coincidence, may be interesting in and of itself; surely there are reasons why more interconnected ways of thinking have become more prominent at this historical moment. But exploring these reasons, though interesting, does not yet address the question: is such a change a good one? In order to answer that question, we need to consider a major objection to this new way of thinking.

Nothing New Here: Is R2P a "Wolf in Sheep's Clothing"?

Perhaps the major objection[7] that has been raised to the "Responsibility to Protect" perspective is that it is nothing but a rationalization of ongoing liberal justifications of intervention (Chandler 2004; Richmond 2004). After all, no one expects that states will surrender the pursuit of their self-interest in the international arena. In reality, so-called peacekeeping missions are almost always about *Realpolitik*; humanitarian discussions are just a pretty gloss on the usual business of each state protecting its interests.[8] Even the UN's peacekeeping activities, which are an attempt to implement R2P, continue to provide each contributing sovereign state with control over when and how its forces will be deployed.[9] Political scientists call this approach "realism"; they assert that the anarchy among states in the world creates a dangerous environment within which each state must and does rely upon its own understanding of its interests and act accordingly.

How might one answer this objection that liberal and powerful states will use R2P as a rationalization to pursue their own interests without regard to the real principles that underpin it? On the one hand, it is always possible for ideas to be abused, and perhaps we need only say that. On the other hand, though, some theorists of international relations observe that even rational, realist states do sometimes expand their ideas about their own interests to include what others might have described as "idealistic" concerns. The end of the slave trade in the nineteenth century is one such example (Hochschild 2005); the leading theorist of this approach, Neta Crawford, points to decolonization and humanitarian intervention as two examples of ideas that have led to such profound change (Crawford 2002). If Crawford is correct, then the best way to demonstrate that R2P can be more than "a wolf in sheep's clothing," a rationalization to impose liberal order on states, is to demonstrate its power as an idea.

So: Are there ways to implement the "responsibility to protect" vulnerable people who would be harmed without humanitarian intervention in a way that does not simply enact the *Realpolitik* interests of more powerful states? Such implementation, I shall argue, requires developing and refining the idea of "responsibility to protect" in ways that take it in a more feminist direction. The parallel between the paradigm shifts sketched out above does not demonstrate that the responsibility to protect is necessarily an idea compatible with feminism. What I hope to show in the next section of this essay, though, is that applying the insights of feminist analyses of responsibility, through the feminist ethic of care, does help us to develop more clearly and effectively the argument for the responsibility to protect.

A FEMINIST CARE PRACTICE OF PEACEKEEPING: R2P ENLARGED

The problem with the ICISS is not that it is too radical, but that it did not go far enough. If we take the cues from a feminist ethic of care, it will become clear what the next steps are, both in planning and implementing interventions and in trying to get realist states to be more thoughtful about their self-interest. Because the ethic of care is what Margaret Walker calls an expressive-collaborative account of morality rather than a theoretical-juridical one, the main ethical questions that arise are different (Walker 1998). On the theoretical-juridical model, determining whether a particular action accords with principles is the key to the ethical discussion. As a result, the primary ethical question becomes "is this action just or right?" In this case, the key moral question is thus whether this intervention is justifiable. In contrast, expressive-collaborative accounts of morality arise out of an ongoing practice, and require that the questioning of the moral grounding for action continue as long as the action continues.

If this last argument is correct, then feminist scholars' explorations into applying care ethics may help us to discern some important aspects of how we might better think through questions of peacekeeping. In the next section of this paper, I propose to look more closely at what feminist scholars have realized about the paradigm of care in order to make recommendations for how scholars and practitioners, working through this paradigm shift, might better practice the responsibility to protect. We need also remember that the ICISS required a much more complex account of peacekeeping than just intervention, one that also includes a responsibility to prevent and to rebuild.

The Need for a Feminist Analysis

Before we turn to a care analysis, though, we need to address whether a gendered analysis is necessary. If we ignore the gendered nature of the discussion about intervention, we will miss an important way to reframe these activities. The language of "the responsibility to protect" is already a deeply gendered discourse, since "protection" implies a highly masculinized understanding of care (Young 2003). Recall the passage from the ICISS report: their concern was "the duty to protect communities from mass killing, women from systematic rape and children from starvation" (ICISS 2001, 17, Section 2.28). In emphasizing raped women and starving children, even as the Commission is making the paradigm shift towards care, they themselves are using a masculinized account of care in order to make it more convincing to their audience.[10] In fact, men, not women, die more frequently in wars and other forms of political violence (Human Security Centre 2005).

To understand the gender dimension of peacekeeping, we should first notice that, when people begin to talk about gender, they often begin to talk really about women, and to understand "women" in the most essentialist ways.[11] The United Nations follows this pattern, in that they often treat the gender dimension to peacekeeping as a question about *women*. In light of the slow progress toward gender equity elsewhere in the world, the commitment to gender equity in the UN security community is remarkable. The UN leadership is committed to trying to improve women's situations and to enhance peace. I worry, however, that their means for doing so often fall back into a kind of gender essentialism that is likely to have unintended consequences. For example, the UN has mandated through its Resolution 1325 that by 2015, UN peacekeeping forces should be 50 percent men and 50 percent women. This is an admirable goal. Nevertheless, when UN officials speak of the value of the 50-50 forces, do they presume that adding women will change the nature of the forces themselves? To think that this change will transform peacekeeping requires that we subscribe to a kind of essentialist thinking that is not borne out in reality (think of Abu Ghraib prison and its female participants and commander).[12]

A second and, I would argue, more positive approach is to recognize that "gender," understood in a less essentialist and more comprehensive and complex way, is always involved in matters of peacekeeping. As Dubravka Zarkov and Cynthia Cockburn warn, "a failure to understand the politics of masculinity and femininity in causing and sustaining violence, and in working to redress violence, has till now rendered such [international peacekeeping] operations less effective than they might have been. At worst, by playing into the existing gender order, some have reinforced aggressive and predatory forces, and entrenched violent and unstable environments" (Zarkov and Cockburn 2002). Nevertheless, Zarkov and Cockburn's message is not yet specific enough, for it does not make entirely clear what dimensions of gender have to be taken into account. Cynthia Enloe insists that one critical piece is to explore how gendered assumptions about the military, violence, and the proper roles of men and women contribute to the degree and specific nature of militarization in a given society (Enloe 2002a, 2004).

I would like to argue, though, that another way to integrate gender into our thinking about peacekeeping and peace building is to understand them as care practices. From this starting point, we focus on peacekeeping as a process, recognizing that gender issues are always implicated, deeply, whenever there is a discussion of care.

There are two advantages of moving this discussion forward to using the language of care rather than the language of gender (even of gender and its relationship to militarization). First, this approach does not essentialize gender or ignore its complex and differentiated reality. Shifting notions of both masculinity and femininity are deeply entrenched in questions of war and peace, and the usual presumptions that women are somehow more peace-loving than men can distort as well as further the cause of peace. This essentialized view may lead peacekeepers to misunderstand and presume that all women are victims of violence, and that all men are perpetrators of violence. While this is indeed a general pattern,[13] and one that needs to be considered in making policy, there can nonetheless be exceptions, and wise peacekeepers will use the exceptions to help transform gender relations as well as to achieve other goals.

Second, though, the concerns of peacekeepers and peace builders cannot stop with the gendered dimensions of the *militarized* sphere of society, but must extend their analysis further. In order to overcome the resort to violence that seemed reasonable to many in the society, peacekeepers need also to try to rebuild the society's economic and social institutions, to alter background conditions so that violence will no longer seem necessary or rational. Here, too, gender relations are critical. Since one of the intellectual advantages of the care approach is its holism, it would be a pity to lose this advantage here by restricting the discussion of gender to militarization. Other broad patterns of gendered care are also relevant, for example, in the division of labor in the economy and the household.[14] For example, in a society in which men's status is tied to their ability to provide for and to protect their families, if there are no jobs for men, it may well be more difficult to convince them to surrender their small arms, since they will see them as a way to protect and provide for their families.

But the goal of peace building cannot be implemented by paying attention only to gender. The hostilities that usually set off humanitarian crises involve deep divisions along racial, religious, ethnic, nationalistic, or class lines. If some still perceive themselves as the "winners" and others as the "losers" as peace is built, then obviously no lasting peace will emerge. Thus, the idea that the crisis is somehow over when there are elections and markets is dangerously naïve. As Neta Crawford observes, what is likely to result from such shortsighted humanitarian intervention is something that resembles an old-fashioned trusteeship. That current interventions produce "Authorities" rather than trusteeships may seem a sign of modernity, but as Crawford observes, it is likely to mean the continuation of political disenfranchisements, deepening economic inequalities, etc. (Farer et al. 2005). Peace building requires making clear the political, economic, and social stakes of the decisions made by peace builders and by parties to the original conflict.

The details of exactly how any society's deep gender structures will need to be involved in building peace will, of course, depend very much on the structure of gender relations within each culture.[15] What is important to realize, though, is that as with other dimensions of culture, gender relationships and attitudes can and do change. To encourage and facilitate such change is one creative way to demilitarize a culture and situation.

Yet emphasizing the gendered dimension of intervention is not enough to stop the appropriation of R2P by liberal states intent on pursuing their own interests and calling it something else. Indeed, the very importance of "gender" can be rightfully viewed with great suspicion when a focus on "gender" is used to advance some neoliberal economic policies (Bessis 2004). By broadening the discussion beyond gender to the concept of care (Tronto 1987), we can not only avoid relying on essentialized notions of gender, but also undercut any such self-serving and ultimately damaging appeals to "gender" on the part of liberal states.

Humanitarian Intervention: A Care Analysis

By now, a number of care theorists have described dimensions of a care analysis. When Berenice Fisher and I defined care as "a species activity that includes everything we do to maintain, continue, and repair our world so that we may live in it as well as possible," we also designated four phases of care, and I later described these four in terms of four moral dimensions. These dimensions help to explain the kinds of questions that should be asked both when a state or international coalition is considering an intervention and when they are thinking about how such an intervention should be conducted.

1. **Caring About—Attentiveness.** In the first instance, one must notice a need to care in order for any process of care to begin. In international relations, this amounts to recognizing the needs of others as the starting point, and the ICISS identified this as one of the key changes in R2P. There are many pitfalls here: needs may be invisible or misunderstood, either through sheer lack of attention or through deliberate ignorance. But for the most part, it is the capacity of people around the world to "care about" those who are victims of human rights abuses that fuels the prospects for humanitarian intervention.

Of course, this question is considerably more complex than it seems as first: which needs? Whose account of them matters? The idea is not to substitute a one-sided and self-serving account of the needs of others to justify intervention. There is no guarantee that trying to articulate the real needs in the situation will result in states acting to fulfil such needs, but doing so does help to clarify whether and how the situation might warrant intervention.

2. Taking Care Of—Responsibility. This is the point of contention for the current discussion of humanitarian intervention. Whose responsibility is it when some people's human rights and lives are threatened?

As I suggested earlier (following Feinberg and Young's non-liability model), responsibilities do not correspond precisely to duties. The questions of how responsibilities grow deeper, and of when and how to meet them, are complicated ones. I suggested earlier that two things seem to deepen responsibilities: capacities and connections. Being in relationship creates a deeper kind of responsibility (Young 2006). Being able to do something also opens the horizon to the possibility of a responsibility to do it, and we might posit that the degree of responsibility grows the more able one is, and the lower the cost of responsibility.

At the current historical moment, this seems to be the point where humanitarian responsibility breaks down. It is extremely difficult to get nation-states to take up the risks and costs of such responsibility. But it is crucial in this connection to address the nature of relationships that create responsibilities. Thomas Haskell's account of the Quaker opposition to slavery shows that such opposition grew out of their realization of connection to the slave trade: when they realized that the cloth they wore and the sugar they ate were produced by slave labor, they realized that they were implicated in the slave trade. Neta Crawford makes a somewhat similar point, as she demurs from the judgment that humanitarian intervention should be preceded by an "increase" in violations, a judgment that its proponent, Thomas Farer, calls a "spike test":

> In a world of global commerce, in arms trade, foreign aid and instant communications, we are all, whether as states, corporations, or individuals, already intervening in ways that are positive and negative for the promotion of human rights and democracy. Our interactions in a global and interdependent context are micro-interventions that set the stage for a possible military intervention in the world of the spike test. [Footnote omitted] (Crawford in Farer et al. 2005, 230).

In other words, Western governments, international organizations and individuals are always already implicated in the injustice and inequality that fuels violence; in the toleration of abusive systems, governments, and individuals; and in the provision of arms, equipment and money to abusers. Our wish is that it was not so; but this wish is father to a persistent denial of the real implications of our daily interactions.

Thus, there is a cosmopolitan order, but it is too often abusive, or, at least, it abets abusers. By the time a state or region gets to the point of meeting a spike test, there are few innocent or ignorant bystanders at the level of heads of states or in foreign offices. Humanitarian interventions may be necessary, but we must at least admit that they are Band-Aids over wounds that we have helped inflict or at least have not tried to staunch before. So, for example, as distasteful as it is to say it, when Milosevic tried to implicate the US in his war crimes against humanity, he was not entirely wrong to do so. This is why the International Commission on Intervention and State Sovereignty argued that there is a prior "responsibility to prevent" that accords with the responsibility to react to abuses. The Commission puts the onus of the responsibility to prevent on "sovereign states," who must certainly take action, but there are clearly other actors who bear some responsibility (Farer et al. 2005, 230). The key question to take up is how we might make discussion of such responsibilities a clearer priority.

3. **Care-Giving—Competence.** Although we don't often think of competence as a moral issue, but rather as a technical issue, the high stakes involved in military intervention make the question of competence clearly a moral one. In this frame, many of the questions often asked after an intervention become part of the intervention process. (Indeed, one common after-the-fact test of whether or not an intervention is a morally appropriate one is whether it has used excessive force and has not had a positive humanitarian outcome.)[16]

One of the insistent feminist realizations about the ethic of care is that it is embedded in daily practices that require a kind of reasoning different than that of technical rationality (Noddings 1984; Ruddick 1989; Waerness 1990; Held 1993; Tronto 1993, 1995; Sevenhuijsen 1998; White 2000). Feminist scholars have insisted that care is itself a kind of practice, one that requires taking the needs of the "other," the cared-for, as its fundamental starting point. It is by its nature relational, and it requires that the care giver be attentive to the care receiver, as well as to her or his own position vis-à-vis the charge (Kittay 1999). To care for someone or something is not the same process as applying a principle. It is in the nature of care that each individual action needs to be placed into the context of the whole situation. Having determined a particular goal to be desirable, all of the component pieces and steps taken become "nested ends," which should have as their goal to fit into a whole. Rather than being "rule" or "act" directed, the logic of the care ethic is more Aristotelian: action should be purposeful and oriented toward its ultimate end, and actions are moral insofar as they are in accordance with the higher end.

The combination of addressing needs, paying attention to context, and continually evaluating what to do on the basis of the whole endeavor and its purpose, requires a particular kind of thought process which is different from that of technical rationality. Sevenhuijsen labeled this process "judging with care" (Sevenhuijsen 1996).[17] Sevenhuijsen argues that judging with care requires not only attention to the internal values of caring itself, such as attentiveness, responsibility, competence, and responsiveness (Tronto 1993), but also requires that the process of caring be done in a context of trust, with a commitment to open and inclusive communication. White demonstrates along similar lines that caring practices are more effective when carried out democratically (White 2000).

While this may all seem very obvious, it has not necessarily informed the conduct of peacekeeping missions in the past. By its very nature, peacekeeping is difficult. Most peacekeeping occurs in a setting where there has been a civil war (there are some exceptions involving inter-state conflict), and such wars are almost always waged against civilians. It is also a kind of war in which the parties have thought, despite the enormous costs that humans incur when they go to war, that they had less to lose in going to war than by staying out of it (Anderson 1999). War at this point becomes self-perpetuating to a certain extent, in that those who have suffered atrocities cry out for retribution, and no party wants to be the one to admit that they will not avenge a harm done to them.

What the ethic of care suggests, then, is that the end—a stable and lasting peace—has to become the goal toward which all other activities are directed. Yet even here, it is possible to think in too technical, too scientifically rational, a manner. Indeed, the progress of technical, scientific rationality in the language of "peacekeeping" itself is interesting here. Peacekeeping refers only to the interjection of troops between hostile forces that have accepted a peace settlement. But the notion that there is a delimited purpose of "peacekeeping" separate from the larger question of how to restore and sustain peace is already problematic. As Margaret Anstee, a former UN official, puts it,

> There was a very prevalent theory during the nineties that there was a kind of continuum in these activities: you began with a military peacekeeping operation to ensure security and the maintenance of the cease fire; then you would go through reconstruction and rehabilitation and eventually come to a stage where you would return the country to normality. That has proved to be a total misconception. Peace building has to start as soon as possible. It has to be an integral part of the mission, an integral part of the mandate and indeed a very important element in the negotiations that precede all those activities. (Joint European Union–Latin American and the Caribbean Conference 2002)

From this standpoint, the ongoing social scientific discussion of what makes humanitarian intervention successful in post-conflict settings reads a bit differently than it does if we start from a supposedly more neutral or objective and "scientific" account of the situation. Political scientists who have looked at the causes of success or failure of peacekeeping and peace building operations have been willing to specify conditions under which success is likely or unlikely. For instance, in situations where the parties are far apart in negotiating positions, or where there are easily expropriated and highly marketable commodities (such as gems or timber), the likelihood of success is smaller (Stedman et al. 2002). Such findings, although scientifically valid, ignore the much more interesting and complex reality that the intervention itself (and the starting assumptions that direct its conduct) has an effect on the outcome. For example, imagine that the interveners take for granted the widespread idea that there are "spoilers" who are not really committed to the peace and who will defect from it as soon as possible. If the peacekeepers view the "spoilers" as waiting for the right moment to defect, rather than as people who can be persuaded to become more cooperative, then their idea is likely to become a self-fulfilling prophecy.[18]

This requirement that care, and peacekeeping as care, be genuinely engaged from multiple perspectives is a far-reaching and radical departure from many current aid and intervention practices. It is also a way to answer the objection frequently raised to the "responsibility to protect," that it is just another version of the Washington Consensus and another way for neoliberals to pretend to do good in the world when in fact they only benefit themselves. Indeed, though it is not usually highlighted, the Commission also insisted upon the more holistic approach stressed here, describing the need for prevention and peace building as important elements of R2P. As states intervene, they must be held to a standard of competence that makes it possible for humanitarian ends to be achieved.[19]

Because the care ethic stresses that among the outcomes of any care process is the creation and/or maintenance of, or harm to, relationship, it invites those who are providing "care" to be more systematic and self-reflective about what they might be doing. For example, peacekeeping forces might be able to lower the level of violent confrontation as soon as possible in a setting. Peacekeeping forces can be respectful of local customs and avoid conduct that will offend the people with whom they live.[20]

Similar arguments about improving intervention are made by Mary B. Anderson, who points out that aid agencies can provide aid in a way that, although perfectly reasonable from the standpoint of their goal, nevertheless undermines the peace. The solution is to think about the way providing aid fits into the overall goals of peace: reducing violence, increasing contact and building relationships of trust among formerly warring parties.[21]

The institutions that engage in humanitarian intervention more broadly understand these problems as well. As the Humanitarian Policy Group of the Overseas Development Institute (London) summarized in 2000, "the implication of many of these criticisms is that the humanitarian system is self-serving and is part of the problem and not the solution." Their solution is for "agencies to understand their political contexts better; this analysis should also cover the political economy of the aid system and the wider international political system of which it is a part" (20). From a care perspective, the proposal would be more concrete still: that one needs to think through the context of aid, the needs of the aid-receivers, their reaction to the aid, and their role in shaping the aid/care process. The Humanitarian Policy Group's call for better monitoring will not necessarily change this power dynamic.

4. **Care Receiving—Responsiveness.** In the end, though, the criterion by which we determine whether or not an intervention was successful is whether the abuses have ended. According to this criterion, there have been remarkably few successful humanitarian interventions, in part because the questions about responsibility and competence have not been able to overcome the interests of states in conducting humanitarian interventions in a self-serving manner. Care is about meeting the needs of those in need; in this respect, most of what has been called humanitarian intervention is not humanitarian.[22]

Furthermore, as Neta Crawford observes, if we want to be serious about the consequences of peacekeeping and humanitarian intervention, then we need also to consider the political situation of such states after peace is restored. Often, an administration or authority is established which has no checks, democratic or popular, on its way of governing. Even trustees in the League of Nations system, argues Crawford, had more protection (Richmond 2004; Farer et al. 2005).

Thus, being responsive requires that intervening powers continue to hold on to some responsibility, but proceed to think about it from the standpoint of the needs of the people. That these needs will come into conflict is obvious. Nevertheless, an ethic of care demands that the final account of needs be provided by and for the people affected themselves.

This position is easy to articulate and difficult to enact, though, because the temptation is always great in situations of care to make overly confident judgments about the needs of those being cared for. One of the most important ways in which a feminist ethic of care helps us to understand moral situations in their complexity is in the recognition that care relations are almost always between actors of unequal power. (For example, Uma Narayan (1995) observed that colonialism is a care discourse.) Especially when care recipients are truly needy, there is a real danger that the care givers will act paternalistically or even against the interests of those in need. Thus, any account of care forces us to ask constantly: who is caring for whom, what is the dimension of power in the care relations, and is that power distorting the nature of care?

In humanitarian interventions, there is a danger that the intervening powers will assume that their definition of the situation should prevail. Indeed, the only counterbalancing force to such a danger is the likelihood that this assumption will render their care incompetent. If the interveners have not really conceived of their activity in terms of care, in terms of the needs of the people affected, in the first place, then this danger becomes very great. The use of a care perspective does not prevent this subversion of purpose, but it does enable us to recognize it and to try to avoid it by integrating these concerns into the discussion about the mission's nature and purpose in the first place.

ASSESSING THE RESPONSIBILITY TO PROTECT

At the present moment, criticisms of the "responsibility to protect" come from two directions. The first suggests that the concept of R2P lacks any teeth to prevent states from pursuing their own self conceptions of self-interest. Thomas Weiss, one of the scholars most involved in preparing the ICISS's Report, seems to accept this account. He argues that the most powerful states, especially the US, seem to have lost the "political will" to make humanitarian concerns more central to their definitions of national interest. Describing his "disgust" (236) as events unfold in Darfur, Weiss concludes:

> The brief moment when individual rights appeared as important as sovereignty or perhaps more important on the international agenda now seems like ancient history. The notion that human beings matter more than states radiated brightly, albeit briefly, across the international political horizon until the wars on terrorism and Iraq. These current UN and US obsessions suggest that the political will for humanitarian intervention has evaporated. The US is the preponderant power, and its inclination to commit political and military resources for human protection has faded while other states complain but do little. (237)

On the other hand, other states view with great suspicion the claims made in favor of humanitarian intervention. Given how frequently those claims have been little more than justifications for pursuit of national self-interest, many may think it a good thing that the notion of a "responsibility to protect" has not gained more ground.

But feminist thinkers committed to peace and human security might want to support the "the responsibility to protect" for a number of reasons. First, the answer to the realist charge that the world is a dangerous place is simple: make the world a safer place. Then we need to argue for a changed notion of sovereignty such that the "responsibility to protect" becomes a part of sovereignty. On this account, in the face of anarchy, states should, understanding their own best interests, become more involved in the processes of making, keeping, and building peace. Clearly, one of the most important factors in the security of any given state is being surrounded by peaceable neighbors who are content with their place in the international system (Czempiel 2003). Second, it is important to remember that the "responsibility to protect" does not begin when armed conflict begins; rather, avoiding the outbreak of violence is another form of peace making or keeping. As the Human Security Centre reports, the number of violent internal wars declined after the mid-1990s, and they believe that one plausible explanation for this decline is that more states intervened to prevent the outbreak of violence.

Thus, it seems that the problem with the ICISS is not that it is too radical, but that it did not go far enough. If we take the cues from a feminist ethic of care, it will become clear what the next steps are, both in planning and implementing interventions and in trying to get realist states to be more thoughtful about their self-interest. Practices can then emerge that give substance to the kind of cosmopolitan civil society about which feminists have been writing for a century (Addams 1907/2003). Adam Smith's "man of humanity" in Europe believed that he had little in common with people in China. In today's world, while it is still possible for people to ignore the plight of others, it becomes more difficult for them to maintain this separation.

I began this essay by posing a hard question for an ethics of care: might care ever require violent intervention to protect the lives of civilians? I hope that I have made clear this answer: while such an intervention can be consistent with an ethic of care, the best care practices would prevent the need for such an intervention in the first place. The responsibility to protect makes clear what an ideal that feminists could endorse might look like, especially if we push the position's internal logic in a more feminist and care-based direction. Such an ideal cannot, by itself, prevent states from ignoring it. Nevertheless, with a clearer vision of a more humanly secure international system—one that includes the "responsibility to protect," properly understood—humans can act in ways consistent with a more peaceful future.

ACKNOWLEDGMENTS

I would like to express my thanks to Susan Woodward, to Torunn Lise Trygestad of the Norwegian Institute of International Affairs, and to panelists and audience members who heard earlier versions of the paper at panels of the American Sociological Association in 2004, the Canadian Political Science Association in 2006, and the American Political Science Association, 2006. Olena Hankivsky's comments were especially useful. The paper was also helped by comments received at a conference in the Politics Department, University of Goettingen in summer 2006, at a lecture at the University of San Martin in Buenos Aires, Argentina in fall 2006, and most

especially from the editors of this volume. I, however, remain fully responsible for the ideas and errors contained within this paper.

NOTES

1. Thomas Weiss and Don Hubert rehearse this history, which may originate as
early as the mid-nineteenth century, in International Commission on Intervention
and State Sovereignty (2001b), 16–19 and 47–77. [Hereafter, the Commission's
report will be cited as ICISS.]
2. "Since 1945, UN peacekeepers have undertaken 60 field missions and nego-
tiated 172 peaceful settlements that have ended regional conflicts, and enabled people in more than 45 countries to participate in free and fair elections." Currently
there are 18 UN peacekeeping missions deploying around 90,000 people. Source:
http://www.un.org/Depts/dpko/factsheet.pdf. Accessed 8 August 2006. On the
other hand, some argue that the moment for such humanitarian interventions may
have passed; see, e.g., Heinbecker (1995): "The question of the moment is . . .
whether any of us, Canada included, stands a reasonable chance of succeeding at
peacekeeping anymore" (9). For a serious critique of Canadian peacekeepers' practices, see Razack (2004).
3. "In this conception, the moral problem arises from conflicting responsibilities rather than from competing rights and requires for its resolution a mode of
thinking that is contextual and narrative rather than formal and abstract. This conception of morality as concerned with the activity of care centers' moral development around the understanding of responsibility and relationships, just as the
conception of morality as fairness ties moral development to the understanding of
rights and rules." Gilligan (1982).
4. For an important account of the ways in which sovereignty blocks global
democracy, see Goodhart (2005).
5. I am indebted to Iris Young for this reference. In writing this paper, I learned
a great deal from reading her papers on responsibility (2003, 2006).
6. See also Hochschild (2005).
7. Weiss (2004) surveyed the responses to R2P and identified four types of criticism of "the responsibility to protect" paradigm: that it was not sufficiently forward-
looking, that it might become a "blank check" used to justify far too many interventions, that it is only a way for states such as the US to impose their views on the
world, and finally, that it obscures the fact that the UN is not sufficiently democratic
and that the Security Council must be reformed. Of these arguments, the second
and third are related, and more central criticisms. They will be restated and considered at length here.
8. In the conclusion of the Danish Institute of International Affairs: "Judging
from the experience of more than 150 years of practice, in which humanitarian considerations have been invoked to justify intervention, it is obvious that the doctrine
gives room for abuse." Quoted in International Commission on Intervention and
State Sovereignty 2001b, 67. A sharper version of this point is made by Kimberly
Zisk Marten. She writes, "To get foreign countries to do what the international com-

munity wants them to do, namely develop along liberal, democratic, humanitarian lines, peacekeepers have to use force to stop those who try to undercut them. They have to pick political winners and losers according to their adherence to particular values, and they have to monitor political behavior so that those who support particular outcomes in target societies can be selectively rewarded. While their ultimate goals and many of the means they used were different, that is exactly what the imperial powers of a century ago did, too" (2004, 8).

9. Indeed, humanitarian intervention has high potential costs, and as a result, any state has to relate such a contribution to its own national interest. Following the Brahimi Report on intervention, the UN tried to address the limits of deploying its forces. The resulting post-2001 development of SHIRBRIG (a UN rapid deployment military force with a unified command, headquartered in Denmark), still permits member nations to decide on a case-by-case basis whether their troops will participate in a particular intervention (SHIRBRIG 2006).

10. An interesting earlier treatment of these metaphors of the dangers of war appeared in Virginia Woolf's *Three Guineas*. See Woolf (2006).

11. Ruddick had noted this danger already in *Maternal Thinking*, pointing out that "Maternal peace politics begins in a myth: . . . War is men's business; mothers are outsiders or victims; their business is life. The myth is shattered by history. Everywhere that men fight, mothers support them" (1989, 219).

12. Here is an example. This statement is from a speech by Josefa Benavente, a nurse in the Chilean Army, who has served in UN Peacekeeping operations:

The roles to be played by human genders have been pre-established since the beginning of humanity: man providing and protecting the home, and women caring and protecting the family. Over time, women gradually begin to venture into different areas that had previously been the exclusive domain of men. They do so with such efficiency and competency that they definitely become equal, and sometimes more important players, than men. Despite the fact that in peace operations men are still dominant, it has been shown that the role played by women in these missions can make a difference because women are capable of reducing the level of aggressiveness and lowering tension, as well as helping to create an environment of trust within conflict zones. (Joint European Union–Latin American and the Caribbean Conference, 2002)

Here is another example. The speaker is Francis Zachariae, from the Danish Ministry of Defense:

If women are equally important in the democratic process I would say that they are even more important in peacekeeping operations. The training of a conventional soldier will often concentrate on stereotypical male characteristics like strength and aggression and suppress stereotypical female characteristics like sensibility and compassion. In conventional war some of these stereotypical male characteristics could be useful and in peacekeeping the same characteristics could be fatal. As opposed to conventional thinking of equal rights between women and men it could be said that women are valuable to peacekeeping operations because they are different—less violent etc. The question is then— how do we get more women to participate in peacekeeping? (Joint European Union–Latin American and the Caribbean Conference 2002, 80)

Not all defenses of gender equity and Resolution 1325 are quite so essentialist. The Swedish Foundation Kvinna Till Kvinna puts the point differently:

> During war, men are typically involved in the fighting while women take care of the survival of the family. Women know what is needed to sustain society. The leaders who bring a country into conflict need to be involved in cease-fire agreements, but they are not well equipped to negotiate long-term peaceful solutions for their society. . . . By having the responsibility to keep everyday life going during the war, women develop unique experiences and know what is needed to build a functioning society. During conflict, women typically try to keep up contacts with women on the other side of ethnic divides. Also, they are often the first to reach out to meet with women from the other side when the cease-fire agreement is signed. They see alternatives and ways to solve the conflict. They have a vision of a society at peace. The leaders who started the war are not the ones best suited for peace building, as it is more than an end to the fighting; it is a totally new and different project. Women are a great asset in this respect, which ought to be utilized, as they have a different perspective on conflicts than the men in power have. (Kvinna 2006)

Another extremely valuable discussion of Resolution 1325, one which considers its basic importance to women in conflict situations as well as its radical potential to transform gender as a category in thinking about peacekeeping, is Cohn et al. (2004). See also Nakaya (2003).

13. A more sophisticated view is presented by R. W. Connell (2002): "So men predominate across the spectrum of violence. A strategy for demilitarization and peace must concern itself with this fact, with the reasons for it, and with its implications for work to reduce violence . . ." He continues, however, "we must not slide into the inference that therefore all men are violent. Almost all soldiers are men, but most men are not soldiers. Though most killers are men, most men never kill or even commit assault. Though an appalling number of men do rape, most men do not. It is a fact of great importance, both theoretically and practically, that there are many non-violent men in the world. This too needs explanation, and must be considered in a strategy for the reduction of violence and for peace."

14. Susan Woodward (2002) makes clear why and how economic matters have to be considered in peace building, and faults a technical approach often taken by international financial institutions in such settings. Although she does not address the gender dimension of her work in this essay, it is easy to see how her argument could be extended to address gender issues.

15. For one such argument about the need to understand the place of small arms in the process of demobilizing and demilitarizing combatants, see Spear (2002), 143.

16. As Tom Farer writes, "The third test asks whether the intervention is being or has been conducted in compliance with international humanitarian law and that such collateral damage as has occurred is minor in comparison to the damage to the subject population that would have occurred if the intervention had not proceeded and that its planners and executors have or had taken all reasonable measures to limit collateral damage.

The fourth test I take directly from Nick Wheeler's list: there must be a high probability that the use of force will achieve a positive humanitarian outcome. In order to meet this test, the interveners must from the outset set goals and choose means that can rationally achieve a humanitarian outcome markedly superior to the conditions that would have obtained in the absence of intervention. The one sure thing about force is that it destroys things. Under this test, to propose to invade a society, to thrash around breaking things, and then to leave without significantly ameliorating and possibly even aggravating the situation is unacceptable" (Farer et al. 2005, 219).

17. The English translation, unfortunately, did not keep this concept in the title, but the argument of the book is otherwise the same; see Sevenhuijsen (1998).

18. Susan Woodward suggested this important point to me.

19. A negative example is the US and NATO intervention in Kosovo, where aerial bombing inflicted great harm. For this reason, the head of Medecins Sans Frontieres demurred in her testimony before the UN about whether humanitarian groups should work more closely with intervening forces. See Dumait-Harper (2002).

20. Consider, e.g., prostitution. International forces only insisted that their personnel cease using prostitutes in Herzegovina in 2001, as they began to address the problem of trafficking in women. "[A] major problem we faced, and continue to face, was reluctance in the international community to accept that *we ourselves contribute significantly to the problem of trafficking*. There is a deep reluctance to acknowledge that international men are significant clients, users of the sexual services of foreign women who do not provide those services freely but are coerced. An approximate calculation by human rights officers in the IPTF is that the international community constitutes 30 per cent of the customers of the foreign women, numerically, but accounts for 80 per cent of the revenue accruing to the men who manage them" (Rees 2002, 63). IPTF is International Police Task Force.

21. Anderson (1999) gave this example: an aid agency cut the blankets they gave to people in half. While the women could resew the blankets, they had no commercial value once they were cut, and robbers were thus foiled.

22. Some critics of the NATO/US intervention in Kosovo make such arguments. See, inter alia, Jovic (2003), especially the essays by George Meggle, Richard Falk, Robert M. Hayden, and Marjorie Cohn.

11

From Hegelian Terror to Everyday Courage

Bat-Ami Bar On

Relatively early in *The Phenomenology of Mind*, Hegel creates a connection between terror, freedom, and truth[1] that I find both provocative and disturbing (Hegel 1807/1967). He first introduces the connection to terror by talking about the risking of one's own life, claiming, for example, that "it is solely by risking life that freedom is obtained; only thus it is tried and proved that the essential nature of self-consciousness is not bare existence, is not the merely immediate form in which it at first makes its appearance, is not the mere absorption in the expanse of life" (233). He states in a similar vein that "the individual who has not staked his life, may no doubt be recognized as a Person; but he has not attained the truth of this recognition as an independent self-consciousness" (233).

I tend to want to dismiss the Hegelian connection of life-risking (and the sense of freedom that accompanies it) to the uncovering of a personal truth worthy of recognition by others, and of both to the feeling of terror. For Hegel, a certain kind of terror is central to the development of ethico-epistemological identity and grounded subjectivity. I find especially suspect his romantic assignment of primacy of place to the feeling of terror in the process of self-discovery and identity formation.[2] Such romanticism seems to me quite misguided when we consider the evidence that, in general, persistent and continuous terror has grave consequences. Studies of Palestinians and Israelis, for example, have shown that, as a result of an always-present war and its awful risks, a majority of the two populations now exhibit at least one (and usually more than one) of the symptoms of Post Traumatic

Stress Syndrome. Moreover, such psychological trauma seems itself to contribute to the cycle of Israeli-Palestinian violence (Bleich et. al. 2003, De
Jong et. al. 2003). Assuming that I can generalize from this and similar
examples, it seems to me that the self as constituted by terror and trauma
is typically characterized by ethical and epistemological deficits, including
an inability to extend oneself as needed toward the difference of others,
rather than by the robust, hospitable, and relationally comfortable kind of
independence that Hegel suggests emerges from terror (Bar On 1991).[3]

Although I am troubled by Hegel's romanticism, by his emphasis on the
emotions as the wellspring of ethico-epistemological subjectivity, and especially by his centering of terror, I am also very reluctant to adopt accounts
of the development of ethico-epistemological subjectivity that marginalize
or understate the emotions, or that attempt to tie the emotions down and
channel them productively. These accounts strike me as painting in dull
pastels the formation of identity, and especially as undervaluing one's subjective sense of oneself as an ethical and knowing being with the strength
needed to be in an adult relation to others and to the world.[4] My suspicion
of such overly sanitized approaches to the emotions leads me to worry that,
in dismissing Hegel's remarks about terror, I will be overlooking something
important.[5]

In what follows, therefore, I try to make sense of the emphasis on terror
in the Hegelian picture of self-discovery and identity formation and to see
where such emphasis leads. I pursue my explorations of Hegel in a circu-
itous manner. After describing Hegel's position in more detail, I outline a
criticism of his ideas first offered by Sartre, who suspected Hegel of being
over-optimistic about the consequences of feelings of terror. Since Frantz
Fanon explains terror's less auspicious consequences in a more situated way
than does Sartre, I turn to Fanon to make better sense of those consequences, while arguing that Fanon's recommendations for how to recover
from them are importantly mistaken.

To understand the inadequacies in both Hegel's and Fanon's treatments
of terror, I then turn to Cynthia Willett's readings of Hegel and Frederick
Douglass, readings that she offers in contrast to Fanon, whose account she
rejects due to his advocacy of violence. I question this rejection, calling on
Simone de Beauvoir's insights regarding violence in relation to gender.
Beauvoir's insights return me to Hegel and an existential construction of
the freedom that is inaugurated by terror. Since I remain unenamored of
the kinds of terror that concerned Hegel and Fanon, as well as Sartre and
Beauvoir—of terrors, that is, that are closely interwoven with violence—I
end the essay by exploring everyday terrors, everyday freedoms, and the
existential courage that they require.

I

Hegel, in the *Phenomenology*, initially discusses the risking of life, and what he sees as its transformative power, in the context of a duel-like life-and-death struggle between what seem to be two equals. A bit later, however, he shifts his metaphors and resituates the risk in a way that allows him to emphasize the experience of fear, now associated with the awareness of being in an extremely unequal dyadic relation—specifically, of being ruled or dominated as much as a slave is by a master. The slave-master relationship is, for Hegel, the paradigmatic case that best exemplifies the formation of an independent ethico-epistemological subject.[6] The Hegelian slave experiences "absolute fear" or terror, because the slave is aware that, by definition, a master has the power of life and death over a slave. The terror that the slave experiences initiates an internal process. It "melts (the slave) to (the) inmost soul," causes a "trembling throughout every fiber" or a "complete perturbation of (the slave's) entire substance," and is felt as "the absolute dissolution of all stability into fluent continuity" (237).

Hegel declares that this feeling of terror is "the beginning of wisdom" (238). He does so because he conceives of it, in virtue of these destabilizing consequences, as denaturalizing. Hegel believes that denaturalization, which he sees as a kind of defamiliarization of all that was taken for granted prior to the experience of terror, frees one's consciousness, a freeing perhaps similar to that which feminists have described as the result of "consciousness raising."[7] According to Hegel, although achieving a mature form of wisdom requires more than the freedom of one's consciousness that is born out of terror—a freedom found in the rupture that releases one from the sense of givenness[8]—without such freedom, no matter how clever one is, one is not an ethical subject and has no chance at a truth of one's own that can be recognized by others as worthy of their consideration.

Hegel does not believe, however, that the recognition of another's truths, and therefore of the other as an ethico-epistemological subject, is bestowed easily. The recognition by one person (say X) of another person (Y) and of Y's truth presupposes X's understanding of her- or himself both as independent from others (such as Y) and as existing in a web of relations with others (including Y) on whom s/he is dependent. So, according to Sartre, Hegel's optimism about recognition may be excessive (Sartre 1943/1966, especially 321–329). It is possible for Y's experience of terror to have limited effects because others (like X) do not necessarily see themselves as members of the same community as Y and thus as having to grant Y ethical standing, or Y's truth the proper epistemic status.[9] In such situations, one can ignore the other person and their truth. While doing so may indicate epistemic and ethical shortcomings, as suggested by both feminists and critical race theorists (Harding 1991, Mills 1997),[10] such shortcomings are less obvious when people's interdependencies appear to them remote and obscure, as they must in late- and post-modernity.[11]

Without recognition, the truth that springs out of the freedom that results from terror is muted. Fanon is among the few who have described the muteness of truth born of terror where recognition is lacking. In *The Wretched of the Earth*, he depicts the colonial situation in almost Hegelian terms, but Fanon's account gives greater concreteness to the experience of rule and domination. Whereas for Hegel, everyone in a domination-subjection relation is still a member of the same community, for Fanon, the colonized and colonizers live in a Manichean world whose logic is one of "reciprocal exclusivity" (1961/1968, 39). This logic, Fanon believes, makes reconciliation impossible: the colonizer remains a colonizer, keeping "alive in the colonized an anger which he deprives of outlet" (1961/1968 54), while the colonized, having learned to "stay in his place . . . dreams . . . of muscular prowess . . . of action and aggression," of becoming "the persecutor" (1961/1968 52). Eventually, the colonized strike, first at their own, and later for their own freedom and against the colonizers.

The Hegelian slave, even when not yet recognized, does not turn to violence. The slave is the productive partner in the master-slave dyad and, in the wake of terror and its effects, remains productive and disciplined, which for Hegel is a necessary condition for the slave's continued development of an independent perspective. For Fanon, in contrast, it is precisely the violence that the colonized unleash against the colonizers that is productive, since for the colonized "life springs up again out of the rotting corpse of the [colonizer]" (1961/1968 93). The colonized's violence is, according to Fanon, very much like Hegelian terror, a "cleansing force" that frees the colonized from their "inferiority complex," their "despair," and their fear and that "restores [the colonized's] self-respect" (1961/1968 94). It releases creativity and leads to mutual recognition among the colonized who, by acting violently together, establish themselves as ethical subjects with truths of their own.

It now appears as if the conditions for a truth born out of terror have been instituted by the colonized for themselves. But the world as Fanon sees it is still Manichean, since the colonizers are not changed by their experiences[12] and the colonized's recognition of each other is only a limited, in-group version of recognition.[13] In addition, it is not clear whether any individual can actually be recognized in the proper way within the colonized group since, according to Fanon, the colonized's violent uprising breeds unity, binding them "together as a whole" to form a "great organism of violence" and throwing them "in one way and one direction" (1961/1968 93). This leaves no space for particularity or individual perspective,[14] and as a result, recognition, which presupposes difference, is emptied of its deeper meanings.[15]

Fanon, like Hegel before him, is not successful in his attempt to connect terror (or, even more directly, violence) and truth, because he too is unable to secure mutual recognition of others as ethical subjects and of their worthwhile truth. Thus, the connection between terror, violence, and truth, which initially appeared to be an insight, now seems misleading. For many feminists, this conclusion will not be surprising, as both Hegel and Fanon can be read as offering nothing more than a masculinist fantasy.[16]

II

Cynthia Willett (1995), aware of the feminist criticisms of Hegel, nonetheless believes that Hegel is insightful and therefore she attempts to purge his account of its more fantastic elements—elements that she sees as not merely masculinist but also Eurocentric. To work out her reframing of the insights in question, she turns to a variety of sources, including Frederick Douglass. According to Willett, although Douglass intially appears to replicate the Euromasculinist fantasy of Hegel and Fanon, this appearance dissipates on closer inspection; in fact, she contends, Douglass better articulates the Hegelian insights.[17] Of great importance to Willett is Douglass's report about his fight with Covey, because the fight represents a pivotal moment of change.

Covey, Douglass's master, was intent on breaking him into docile slavery. Writing of the aftermath of his fight with Covey, Douglass claims that "[t]his battle . . . was the turning point in my career as a slave," since it "rekindled the few expiring embers of freedom, and revived within me a sense of my own manhood" (1845/1986, 113). Relatedly, he claims elsewhere that "[a] man without force is without the essential dignity of humanity" (1855/1987, 151). Douglass thus seems to emphasize a masculinity that is anchored in violence, not unlike Fanon. However, Willett asserts that in fact Douglass "reclaims an essential element of the self—the tactile self" formed in the physical interaction of mother (or loving care giver) and fetus/infant/child—indeed, surprisingly, that he does so "by resisting the social humiliations of slavery in physical combat" (1855/ 1987, 171).

Willett, who sees Fanon as offering an "ethics of regenerative violence" (1995, 133) that she finds objectionable, interprets Douglass quite differently and in very positive terms. She can do so in part due to her psychoanalytic framework, which allows her to read Douglass's textual references to his childhood[18] as cohering with her view of the self as always already social, formed relationally from the very beginning, and recognized from the very beginning as interdependent.[19] For Willett, all relations of subjugation and domination basically pervert the self as formed in the early stages of human development, which she calls the tactile self. But she seems to understand that perversion not as formative through and through, but rather merely as a layer that can and often does obscure the tactile self. The tactile self remains untouched and recoverable. I am not sure about this, and I am less sure about how little Willett thinks such recovery requires: in Douglass's case, one act of defiance and violence.[20]

I think that, in addition to endowing one act of defiance and violence with too much power to recover the tactile self, Willett can distinguish between Douglass and Fanon only by shying away from the language of violence when it comes to Douglass. Douglass vividly describes seizing Covey "hard by the throat," "causing the blood to run," kicking someone who helps Covey "under the ribs" (1845/1986, 112–113) so hard that he vomits, throwing Covey to the ground, and fighting with him for almost two hours. Though she is often critical of abstraction, Willett does not mention any of these particulars of Douglass's struggle with Covey, nor does she use the term "violence" to refer to Douglass's actions.

Thus, Willett basically sanitizes Douglass's experience. She replaces the violence and terror of that experience with a relatively benign struggle for relational independence—a struggle that she sees as key to remembering a submerged and elapsed sense of self that is developed extremely early in one's life. Like terror for Hegel and violence for Fanon, this struggle shakes the givenness of the present and leads toward a truth. But, just as with Hegel's possibly unrecognized slave and Fanon's colonized, the shaking of the givenness of the present happens only for Douglass and does not change Covey at all. At no point does Covey recognize Douglass as anything other than a slave. In addition, the motivation to struggle and fight, which Fanon explains as the surfacing of suppressed emotions like anger and the desire for revenge, remains mysterious for Douglass. As he says, "from whence came the spirit I don't know" (1845/1986, 112).

Because Willett is not successful in her attempted postcolonial, anti-racist, and pro-feminist revision of Hegel, saving the Hegelian connection between terror and truth does not seem feasible. Indeed, at this point one may want to seek alternatives to the Hegelian model (including to Hegelian-like models such as Fanon's) to further understand relational independence and its significance for truth in the context of a mutual recognition of others as ethico-epistemological subjects. Feminist work on autonomy is suggestive here (Meyers 1987, Friedman 1997). Diana Meyers, for example, has proposed that autonomy (or independence) can exist in a heteronomous environment (or web of interdependent relations) if it is understood as a learned competence to, among other things, choose for and by oneself, reason responsibly, and judge thoughtfully. In Meyers's view, deficits of autonomy are not a function of sociality and relationality as such, but rather of their organization and structuring and of what, specifically, one is taught. Meyers suggests, as a result, that one can envisage a reorganization and restructuring of social relations that would yield a more robust form of autonomy qua competence (Meyers 2003).

Among the tempting aspects of feminist accounts of autonomy such as Meyers's is that they build on women's experiences. This feature, however, is not an entirely unmixed blessing. While feminists have rightly centered and revalued women's experiences in our theorizing, we have sometimes forgotten or marginalized concerns about the lack involved in gendered experience—that is, about the experiences that, as gendered, one is prevented from having. Feminists have attempted both to expose received conceptions of autonomy as resting on a gendered male experience and to rework the concept of autonomy in such a way that it refers to women's experiences. This reworking construes women's experience positively, but sometimes neglects a critical engagement with the lack of certain experiences that is a function of gender exclusion.

III

In a gendered world, the gendered experience is shaped by lack.[21] Women are positioned socially in such a way that among the experiences they usually lack are positive experiences of violence. Women and men are differently situated with respect to violence, and ample feminist literature continues to be devoted to women's victimization by violence: to rape and incest, domestic abuse, and the specificities of women's suffering in war (Brownmiller 1975; Card 1996b, 2002; Enloe 2002b). Such feminist work on the negative experience of violence is extremely important. Because the formation of female gender usually excludes positive experiences of violence of the kind that Fanon and Douglass value, however, there are consequences to women's gendered experiences of violence to which feminists usually do not attend.

I think that one can glimpse these consequences by looking at some comparisons between women and men with respect to violence. Such a comparison is evident in Sartre's preface to *The Wretched of the Earth*, where he portrays women as solely the victims of violence. The choice of violent action belongs to men, who, with their weapons, prove their humanity, and who by killing their European oppressors become free, create themselves, and come to know themselves. Women are depicted by Sartre only as the fatalities of massacres. Unlike the dead women, the colonized man is, Sartre claims, only "potentially dead" (23), and for colonized men this is a source of courage. Sartre, however, is committing a factual error in his description of colonized women's experience; in particular, he should have paid better attention to the decolonizing struggle that inspired him most, that of Algeria (Lazreg 1994).

Sartre writes of decolonization as if women did not participate in the fight against colonialism and especially in the Algerian War of Independence. In fact, close to eleven thousand women registered with the Algerian Ministry of War Veterans, forming about three percent of all fighters. Most of these were not combatants, but a few were. When Fanon writes about decolonizing Algeria in "Algeria Unveiled," he cannot but acknowledge women's contributions to the Algerian War of Independence. At the same time, however, his description of women and their contributions is quite different from his description of men. According to Fanon, the fighting was initiated by men in 1954 and the men began to recruit women a year later, after a decision that "was not reached lightly" (1959/1965a, 48). He adds that, even when the women's proximity to violence was great (and for some it became so beginning in 1956, with the turn to terrorism by the insurgents), they were usually accessories to the violence, carrying the "grenades and the revolvers that the *fidaï* would take . . . at the last moment" (1959/1965a 57). The *fidaï* were, of course, men. Finally, Fanon notes, the women's bodily experiences were of bodies that were unveiled. Although the loss of the veil freed them, this newly felt bodily freedom was awkward; each woman changed and "relearn[ed] her body," but without overcoming a lived conflictual relation to it" (1959/1965a 59–60). For men, in contrast, the conflicted body is experienced only before they begin to fight, and the conflict is resolved when their bodies act violently.

Being denied access to violent action has high costs. Simone de Beauvoir testifies to these when, using the Hegelian framework, she points at women's inability to transcend their givenness: "woman is basically an existent who gives Life and does not risk *her* life" (1949/1961, 59). Here Beauvoir ignores the fact that, historically, "giving life" has been risky and women have been well aware of the risk.[22] She does, however, make strong claims about women's negative experiences of violence, and specifically about rape as "an act of violence that changes a girl into a woman" (348). She also offers an analysis of women's fears as a function of women's "lack of physical power"[23]—a lack which might have not mattered but for the fact that women live their lives in a heterosexist gender system that, Beauvoir believes, "leads to more general timidity" in women (310).

IV

While Beauvoir seems to unintentionally reformulate certain Hobbesian assertions, Hegel reformulates these assertions intentionally (Honneth 1992). In the *Leviathan*, Hobbes alleges that "[n]ature hath made men so equal" (183) in physical and mental ability and that "[f]rom this equality of ability ariseth equality of hope in attaining our Ends," resulting in antagonism and the "endeavour to destroy or subdue one another" (184) whenever there is perceived scarcity. Whereas Hobbes turns to force as a means to establish peace in this situation, Hegel sees this move as making ethics impossible and thus attempts instead to rework people's struggles with each other in ways that can lead to their mutual recognition as ethico-epistemological subjects.

Even though Hobbes is almost tempted to generalize his claims beyond gender, writing that "there is not always that difference of strength or prudence between the man and the woman," he nevertheless takes it for granted that in general men tend to excel. He accepts as a fact that "for the most part Common-wealths have been erected by the Fathers and not by the Mothers of families," and a posited "natural inclination of the sexes, one to another" (253) basically smoothes out any questions of competition or enmity between women and men. Hegel too believes that women and men are drawn to each other naturally, which for him also implies a kind of peace due to their "reciprocal recognition" of each other; yet this recognition is "natural" and this means that the relation between women and men is not exactly ethical (474). Moreover, Hegelian men (like Hobbesian men) are capable of ethics, but not so Hegelian women, who are natural particularists, remain forever immature, and are thus a danger to the community that must be suppressed.[24] According to Hegel, men are capable of ethics because they are capable of war, "the spirit and form in which the essential moment of ethical substance, the absolute freedom of ethical self-consciousness from all and every kind of existence, is manifestly confirmed and realized" (497).

Hegel strikes me as nostalgic for a kind of war that I am hard pressed to believe has ever existed.[25] Even if it did, war changed dramatically during Hegel's lifetime, due to its nationalization and democratization during and following the French Revolution and to the development of strategies that instrumentalize soldiers.[26] In 1806, while Hegel was in Jena, 122,000 French troops defeated a large contingent (about 114,000 troops) of the professional but outmoded Prussian army at the Battle of Jena-Auerstädt. The defeat was costly for the Prussians, who suffered 25,000 casualties (a casualty rate of 21 percent) as compared with 10,000 French casualties (a casualty rate of 8 percent). It led to the collapse of Prussia and its coming under the control of France, and as a result to the spread of French revolutionary ideas. Hegel, who was working on the *Phenomenology*, welcomed the juridico-political changes that Prussia underwent as a result of its loss to France.[27] Though he conveys a sense that war is a negative force, Hegel did not comment on the devastation left behind in Jena.

It may take different sensibilities than Hegel's to attend first to the "calamities of war."[28] What I think takes priority for Hegel, most probably due to Jena as well as to other battles and successes of the French military, is the momentary opening of a space for a heroism from below, a heroism of the people.[29] As a result Hegel, almost accidentally, points at something new to consider when thinking of the relation between terror (or violence) and truth. Recall that in the Hegelian schema, the slave's experience of terror frees the slave insofar as it undermines the sense of givenness in which the slave is immersed. For Hegel, this freedom is the beginning of an ethico-epistemological subjectivity. Hegel cannot and does not claim that women are incapable of feeling terror, so the Hegelian slave's chance at freedom appears to be gender-neutral.[30] But this is so only if the freedom can emerge from passively undergoing terror—that is, by suffering a rupture caused by terror rather than by being rupturing agents as well.

Hegel would have written the master-slave metaphor differently if he had a slave like Douglass as an example. Similarly, if Susan Buck-Morris (2000) is right and Hegel's master-slave metaphor abstracts from the Haitian Revolution of 1791–1803, he would have written it differently if he had stayed truer to that example rather than domesticating the slave. The domesticated slave, man or woman, does not contribute to the rupture of the given. To contribute to the rupture requires action. This is what Fanon, Sartre, and Beauvoir gesture at when they center violent action, rather than the experience of terror per se, as key to independence. Tellingly, however, what Hegel's depiction of war truly emphasizes is courage, specifically the courage to risk one's life. Hegel believes that men but not women are capable of war, simply because more men than women have access to acting violently. But what is ultimately freeing and truth-enabling about war, for Hegel, is its reliance on a capacity common to both men and women: the capacity for embodied courage.[31]

V

Courage, especially bodily courage, can be learned. And yet, Douglass is right to wonder what moved him to act courageously when Covey turned to discipline him. His choice was existential (Boxill 1997), and his courage was existential as well. Situations that call for courage are frightening, even terrifying, and Hegel is quite right to assert that under conditions of terror a sense of normalcy cannot be maintained. Instead of the given of before, one faces a terrible existential freedom,[32] and one cannot predict one's actions. Hegel, however, is interested in predictability. He is moved in this direction by the political experience of terror in the French Revolution (Comay 2004), and he gets predictability out of the passivity of the domesticated slave, who experiences but does not contribute to the rupturing of the given. He would probably have liked predictability in the case of the citizen soldier as well, but he cannot make it work: the citizen soldier's choices and conduct remain unpredictable.[33] For the passive and domesticated slave, wisdom begins simply with the denaturalization of the given. In the unpredictable case of the citizen soldier, however, wisdom cannot begin before an existential choice is made. The citizen soldier has a chance at ethico-epistemological subjectivity, but its achievement requires acting courageously when facing an existential choice in a condition of existential freedom. The courageous act is, to use a phrase borrowed from Beauvoir, "the authentic proof of each one's loyalty to himself, to his passions, to his own will" (309).

There are contexts other than war (and war-like encounters) that open a space within which one might or might not act in an existentially courageous way. Given how problematic war actually is as a space for courage—and especially for popular courage, a courage of ordinary people[34]—these other contexts are extremely important. For Cornel West (1999), situations that offer opportunities for existential courage are constitutive of the human condition.[35] According to West, one such situation is death. He explains encounters with death as opportunities for existential courage via a critical discussion of W. E. B. DuBois's failings in this regard. By "refus-[ing] to linger with the sheer tragedy of his son's death," West writes, DuBois sidestepped the challenge "to wrestle in a sustained way with the irreducible fact of an innocent child's death" (92). According to West, though DuBois is courageous in many ways, at the time of his son's death he is not existentially courageous in that, in this moment of terrible freedom, he attempts to ward off despair with semi-empty formulas.

I think, though, that West moves too quickly to judge DuBois. West does not contemplate the moment of terror that DuBois must have felt as he grasped the fact of his son's imminent death. This terror is very different from that in the Hegelian model where terror is a response to one's own personal vulnerability, the slave's or the soldier's. What DuBois was facing was his child's vulnerability. For a parent, it is terrifying to witness one's own vulnerability and that of one's child. The parental experience of this double vulnerability accentuates the poignancy of relationality. I believe that a deeply problematic aspect of the Hegelian model is that it does not begin with a consciousness whose experience of terror is like DuBois's: the consciousness of a soldier who is a mother, perhaps, or that of a parent (or lover, or friend) in the face of unpredictable terrorism.

The Hegelian slave, Fanon's (and Sartre's) colonized peoples, and Beauvoir's women are all conceived as starting in primary relations of domination and subjection—relations with a master, colonizers, and men respectively—from which they must become free if they are to be ethico-epistemological subjects. Hegel seems to construe the soldier as occupying a similar position, though without specifying what relations the soldier has that are severed when the soldier risks his life in battle. While for Hegel, Fanon (and Sartre), and Beauvoir relations remain important, they seem to think of relations as taking place between individuals who first and foremost conceive of themselves as such. Their identity is always one of separateness from others even while with them.[36] But the identity of a parent (and actually also of a child, who of course must separate and individuate in order to flourish), a lover, or a friend is always a connected identity, and the relation to one's child (parent), lover, or friend is not merely experienced as having an effect on one's sense of personal identity, but as significantly constituting one's identity. Assuming the relation is not itself oppressive, one wants (or ought to want) to be liberated not from it, but for it.

I do not mean to suggest that individuality and freedom are not of great value; I believe they are. But to be disconnected from others, to have an identity that is not imprinted by and reconfigured through connectedness with others, is to be individuated and free in a manner that places one outside of mooring webs of relations, a manner that Arendt (1958/1976, 1958/1998) describes as contributing to people's "superfluity." With Marx (and Engels) (1848), she argues that the West's superfluous people are a product of modern capitalism, which destroys traditional relations, empties relations of meaning, and creates two classes of people, the capitalists and the lumpenproletariat, both of which are basically unproductive (hence superfluous). According to Arendt, modern racism and nationalism serve to compensate people psychologically for their superfluity; thus superfluity is a necessary condition for modern imperialism. Totalitarianism, according to Arendt a uniquely modern phenomenon, intentionally aims to intensify superfluity, since the latter is a condition of its possibility.

There is a sense in which the Hegelian slave and soldier, Fanon's (and Sartre's) colonized, and even Beauvoir's women are superfluous people even before their possibly freeing existential moments. Modern enslavement and modern colonization were practiced with a profound disregard of enslaved and conquered people's humanity and of their rooting relations, producing their superfluity in multiple ways.[37] The nationalization of soldiering produced the superfluous soldier: the new French Army, the model of the nationalized army, had one million conscripted unmarried young men eighteen to twenty-five years old serving in a military that expanded French rule in and outside of Europe. Women were made superfluous in capitalist modernity through the refashioning of their privatization, which took place at the same time that industrialization removed production from the home.[38] Realizing all this, I am even more convinced that the Hegelian model is problematic, and I wonder even more about existential freedom, choices, and courage in the everyday lives of people lucky enough to be related and connected to others.

Still, I want to acknowledge that there is something special about existential freedom, choice, and courage in special conditions like those faced by soldiers, police officers, and fire fighters, for example. As distinguished from most of us in most of the ordinary (and not so ordinary) situations of our lives, soldiers, fire fighters, and police officers, many of them indeed connected to particular others in significant ways, are expected to be courageous and heroic in an impartial way toward those they serve. In contrast, partiality marks most everyday courage and heroism.

NOTES

I presented this paper at FEAST in January 2006 and am grateful for the comments I received from many of the participants at the conference. I am also grateful to Lisa Tessman who read and commented on this paper several times.

1. For Hegel, truth is first and foremost ontological and therefore can be a property of a person. As such, it is closest to what we might call a sense of authenticity. Insofar as truth is a relation for Hegel, even between a person and her- or himself, he can be construed as having something like an identity theory of truth.

2. Lukacs (1933) reads Hegel differently. Lukacs distinguishes the romantic understanding of history from Hegel's, claiming that Hegel already turned to political economy. But that does not necessarily make Hegel anything but a romantic (Connell 2001).

3. In this regard see also Susan Brison's powerful account of rape trauma (1997). Trauma as Brison describes it is destructive rather than constructive, and one's identity needs repair post-trauma.

4. I like Martha Nussbaum's similar complaint about the Stoics (2001a), but I am not sure about her neo-stoicism, since I have not been convinced by her claim that she retains the sense of the emotions as conveying "urgency and heat" (27).

5. I am suspicious of my motivations, since I may want to maintain the kind of picture that Hegel paints as an exercise in self-redemption. Given my own experiences of terror, I might be too afraid of looking around—especially now as terrorism (and therefore also a kind of terror that I am very familiar with) is being globalized—and seeing just damage and nothing else as individual lives and social relations are changed in alarming ways. So, one way or another, I am determined to explore Hegel because maybe there is something in the assignment of a primacy to terror that otherwise I tend to fail to notice.

6. Jürgen Habermas (2003) notes that, prior to the *Phenomenology*, Hegel used romantic love as the model for thinking through mutual recognition and the achievement of independence. For Habermas this suggests that an initial equality can be the stage of recognition. What Habermas does not note is that Hegel's love model is heteronormative and thus not egalitarian. Habermas joins many in commenting on the master-slave metaphor. See the very influential 1930s lectures of Alexander Kojev and the similarly influential 1940s and 1950s commentary of Jean

Hyppolite. See also Cole (2004) who, in addition to arguing for reading the master-slave dialectic historically as referring to the Medieval period, discusses a contradiction within Marxism regarding Hegel's master-slave dialectics. For a critique of the assumption of the importance of the master-slave dialectic for Karl Marx, see Arthur (1983).

7. Sandra Bartky's work on consciousness-raising and its ruptures remains unique. See "The Phenomenology of Feminist Consciousness," in Bartky (1990).

8. This is an important emphasis of post-positivist realists such as Satya Mohanty (1993, 2001) and Linda Alcoff (2000).

9. As feminist epistemologists have noted, this is a typical experience of women (Code 1981). Feminist jurisprudence has a version of this assertion in discussions of reasonability. A classical expression of this can be found in Williams (1991), who also brings forth an anti-racist perspective on the subject.

10. This is also an implication of Axel Honneth's work (e.g., 2001) because of his multifaceted concept of recognition, which brings together epistemic and ethical aspects.

11. Barber (2003) offers an interesting reflection on this happening in and for the United States.

12. Fanon is more nuanced elsewhere (*AE* 1959).

13. Note the growing awareness of a need for a reconciliation that bridges the parts of the Manichean world. See, for example, Minow (1998, 2002) who is just one of the authors treating this problem.

14. Fanon exemplifies this with his critical remarks about French intellectuals who did not support the colonized's violent uprising (1957). In *The Wretched of the Earth* one can see the same attitude, as in Fanon's criticisms of the colonized bourgeoisie (61–69).

15. Hannah Arendt (1958a, 1958b) is perhaps one of the theorists most acutely aware of this.

16. For feminist critical readings of Hegel, see Hartsock (1983) and many of the articles in Mills (1996). For some feminist critical readings of Fanon, see Bergner (1995), Chow (1995), and Sharpley-Whiting (1997). Feminist critical readings of both Hegel and Fanon have become more nuanced over time.

17. Douglass's fight with Covey is also commented on from non-feminist perspectives. See most recently Kohn (2005).

18. Lisa Tessman called my attention to differences between women's and men's slave narratives, and it seems to me that Willett might have not found as good a fit had she used women's slave narratives. See Prince (1831) and Jacobs (1857).

19. There is enough evidence to support Willett's view that something quite important happens, if not in the case of the pregnant woman-fetus, then from birth on between loving care givers and children. Axel Honneth, who seems unaware of feminist work like that of Willett, also turns to this stage to think through aspects of his theory of recognition (1992/1995, 4).

20. As critical as I am of Willett here, I do think that her work contributes to what Diana Tietjens Meyers (2002) calls new or revised figurations of the self. Meyers's formulation of the idea of figurations starts earlier (1994).

21. It is complex to acknowledge this lack and the possibility that it is significant.

In US academic feminism, there is a tension between gender equality (which recognizes lack because it requires some measure of comparison but, as most critics point out, tends to remain oriented toward men's experiences) and difference (which equalizes by leveling and giving equal worth to all experiences). These may represent, as Nancy Fraser (2005) suggests, not merely two different positions, but positions that are time-sensitive and form two phases of feminism which might, as she suggests, be replaced by a third position because we are in a new phase.

22. According to the United Nations Population Fund, even now somewhere a woman dies in pregnancy or childbirth every minute.

23. Iris Marion Young (1980) contends that Beauvoir does not attend to the orientation of the female body, missing, I think, just this point.

24. Benhabib (1992) reads Hegel in a manner that brings some of these points out, but she does not look at the relations between gender and violence.

25. Under certain readings (e.g., Shay 1994, Tatum 2004), even heroic poetry exposes the dark sides of war.

26. Among the first to reflect on the changes of war during this time is Clausewitz (1832), who was a Prussian officer and was captured in Jena. He reworked strategic thinking in accordance with his experiences. Van Creveld (1991) develops a historically situated discussion of changes in war and strategic thinking that centers Clausewitz.

27. Avineri (1972), in his classical study of Hegel, comments on this theme.

28. One need not be a feminist to have such sensibilities. I borrow the phrase "calamities of war" from Kant, who uses it in "On Perpetual Peace" (1795), so perhaps one needs Kantian or more liberal sensibilities than Hegel's. Benjamin Constant, a contemporary of Hegel, noted in 1806 that European modernity has commercial interests and the sensibilities they engender at its center. Howard (1978) offers a general overview of liberalism's complex relation to war. But see also Avineri (1969) and his reading of Hegel on war as displaying just the kind of liberal sensibilities that Constant alludes to and Howard describes.

29. In Europe prior to the French revolution, courage as a trait and the heroic acts that embodied it were seen as aristocratic. Machiavelli (1521) incorporates the idea of a popular heroism into his arguments for a militia.

30. Changfoot (2004) claims that this is and is critical of Hartsock. I think that Changfoot is overly generous to Hegel.

31. Hegel's position is contradicted by Van Creveld (2002), who argues that, although women are mentally as capable as men, nonetheless women should not be integrated into fighting forces because of the physical differences between women and men and the changing nature of war with its growing reliance on special forces and the like.

32. Hegel, of course, was not an existentialist since he clearly put "essence" before "existence." However, Sinnerbrink's (2004) suggestion that Hegel has an "ontological" sense of freedom which is a precondition for his "normative" sense of freedom, points at what existentialists might have found in Hegel's idea of freedom.

33. There are various memoirs and analyses of soldiers' behavior on the battlefield. Gray (1959), Bourke (1999), and Shepard (2001) provide some excellent examples.

34. Coker (2002, 2004) addresses the loss of a space for courage and heroism in modern/postmodern wars due to the coming together of certain kinds of technological developments and strategies that minimize human engagement. This is changing, but at the same time soldiering is professionalized, so either way the opportunity for heroism from below of the kind Hegel envisaged does not exist in modern/postmodern wars.

35. I thank Lisa Tessman for this reference.

36. This is exemplified by Beauvoir's and Sartre's relation with each other and with others.

37. One can get a glimpse of the conjunction of the two in Las Casas (1552).

38. Few books capture women's sense of superfluity better than Friedan (1963).

12

Praying for a Godly Fumigation

Disgust and the New Christian Right

Lynne S. Arnault

It is interesting that termites don't build things, and the great builders of our nation almost to a man have been Christians, because Christians have the desire to build something. The people who have come into (our) institutions (today) are primarily termites. They have destroyed institutions that have been built by Christians, whether it is universities, governments, our own traditions, that we have. . . . The termites are in charge now, and that is not the way it ought to be, *and the time has arrived for a godly fumigation.*

> —Pat Robertson in *New York Magazine* cover article by Michael Kramer (August 18, 1986; italics added)

Not just politically correct, these women are brutally correct. They are the hard of the hard, the most militant of a militant and hostile generation. Spawned during the '60s in the age of the Beatles, gurus, LSD, and hippies, they are the misfits of American society. But now the misfits are in charge. The lunatics are running the insane asylum, and they're out to make us into the pathetic creatures they have become. They are the feminist vultures who flew over the cuckoo's nest.

> —Texe Marrs, *Big Sister Is Watching You*

[Homosexuality] is perversion of the highest order. It is against God, against God's word, against society, against nature. It is almost too repulsive to imagine and describe. It is filth.

> —James Robison, *Thank God, I'm Free*

INTRODUCTION

Despite its name, the New Christian Right (NCR) is not a "new" phenomenon:[1] it is a direct descendant of two waves of conservative Christian political activism—one that took place in the 1920s as "a series of loosely connected campaigns against alcohol, Catholicism, and the teaching of evolution in the public schools"; the other in the 1950s that "crested with the campaign against international communism."[2] Still, the staying power and clout of this latest resurgence has been remarkable. An unabashed born-again Christian is the sitting President, and well-funded, media-savvy, and highly influential right-wing Christian organizations are thriving, thanks in large measure to the grassroots organizing and activism of women.[3] To be sure, the focus of the NCR has shifted with the times; it has had to weather scandals, political setbacks, and divisiveness within its own ranks; and there is tension for many of its members between political activism and a longstanding tradition of separatism that views the political world as a corrupting influence and a distraction from the quest for salvation. Nonetheless, this latest incarnation of politicized conservative Christianity is one of the most powerful, if not *the* most powerful, political movements in the current American political arena.

Because exposing contradictions in the NCR's conceptual framework and pressing for evidence-based explanations and justifications are not liable to affect its members' thinking, it is tempting to characterize the NCR as a movement that relies on emotionality and faith—where emotionality is understood as being antithetical to rationality, and faith means never needing to engage in "judicious study of discernible reality" (Suskind 2004, 51). Nevertheless, feminists would do well to resist this characterization of the NCR. It reinscribes traditional Western dualistic understandings of emotions and spirituality as irrational and feminized—an undesirable irony, not only because most feminists want to see such hierarchical binaries dismantled, but also because this reinscription dovetails perfectly both with the NCR's explicit association of the head with men and the heart with women and with its agenda to restore what it considers to be traditional manliness to the center of culture.[4]

If we resist opposing reason to emotion and if, therefore, we understand emotions not as raw unattached happenings within us, but as having identificatory cognitive states,[5] the emotions that matter or that are useful to members of the NCR become philosophically interesting and revelatory. A case in point, I hope to establish, is the NCR's deployment of moralized disgust.[6] Many Americans, I dare say, were surprised by George Bush's undisguised grimaces and smirks of disgust during the 2004 Presidential debates. For feminists used to being, or seeing others, denigrated by the NCR as objects of disgust—as, for example, moral perverts and misfits, vul-

tures that flew over the cuckoo's nest,[7] failed human beings,[8] swamp dwell-
ers,[9] and vermin[10]—Bush's displays of disgust may not have been especially
surprising. Nonetheless, because right-wing Christian America has appropriated moralized disgust so skillfully, the political economy of this emotion bears critical scrutiny. Why does moralized disgust work so well for the
NCR in terms of helping to produce, not only a strong affective anchor for
the movement's ideology, but also a politically dedicated membership? Is
what works for right-wing Christians also useful for feminists? Can moralized disgust provide feminists with a valuable means of resisting oppression
and advocating emancipatory change?

My argument will be that although disgust can generate some of our
strongest sentiments of moral condemnation and thus may seem to provide
a potent form of progressive political action, it cannot take us very far in
liberatory directions because it is animated by the linked desires for purity,
domination, and univocality. What makes moralized disgust a congenial
form of political action for the NCR, I argue, is precisely what makes it
unsuitable as a means of working against the grain of oppressive power.

THE NEW CHRISTIAN RIGHT:
PIETY AND POLITICS

As a first step in understanding the political economy of moralized disgust,
it is useful to have a brief characterization of the New Christian Right, for it
is a movement that is quite diverse and often divided. Contrary to common
impressions held in some quarters, factionalism is an ever-present threat to
the cohesion of the NCR. Most of its members agree on basic theological
doctrines such as biblical inerrancy, the supernatural reality of miracles, the
virgin birth, the atonement, the bodily resurrection of Christ, and the second coming, but there are fundamental disagreements, for example, about
the significance of spiritual gifts such as faith healing and the ability to
speak in tongues, about the character and timing of the approaching end
of the world, about the importance of social and missionary outreach, and
about the United States' role in the world.[11]

As Michael Lienesch notes with respect to the latter two points, members
of the NCR are divided on the question of whether "America's role in the
world should be that of providing a moral model eschewing intervention
in favor of morally resplendent isolation" or that of taking on the mantle of
leadership "to save other nations from religious backwardness and political
corruption" (Lienesch 1993, 195). There tends to be agreement, however,
that the United States is, or should be, an internally homogenous, radically
separate world that protects itself against the growing permeability of social
and national boundaries characteristic of increasing globalization. One

need only look at the titles of two of Pat Buchanan's recent books, *State of Emergency: The Third World Invasion and Conquest of America* and *The Death of the West: How Dying Populations and Immigrant Invasions Imperil Our Country and Civilization* to get a sense of the NCR's essentialist outlook and negative understandings of the meaning and viability of "multicultural" societies.

For the purposes of this paper, the term "New Christian Right" refers to a loosely knit, politicized cadre of morally and socially conservative fundamentalist, evangelical, and pentecostal Christians in the United States. It is a mostly but not exclusively Protestant coalition that emerged on the national stage during the late 1970s and that sees itself, on the one hand, as engaged in a divinely ordained campaign to restore the "Christian" character of American culture, to provide a "Christian" solution for the social problems of society, and to reinstate laissez-faire capitalism, which it sees as inherently "Christian,"[12] and, on the other hand, as having a God-given mission to save and redeem the rest of the world, either by example or by intervention.

For members of the NCR, contemporary political conflict is an all-out, age-old struggle between the forces of good and evil. On their view, the 1960s in the United States was an era of unbridled permissiveness and anomie in which "traditional manliness" and the "traditional family" were disastrously dislodged from the center of American culture. Typically drawing on Puritan, Victorian, and postwar images of the family as "church," "haven," and "corporation," Christian conservative thinkers differ on the meaning of what they take to be the "traditional family," but they share the beliefs that patriarchy is authorized by both the Bible and biology and that the family is (or should be) a unit in which men rule, women submit, and children obey (Lienesch 1993, 52–53).

One striking illustration of this overtly patriarchal conception of the family is found in "purity balls," the 1998 brainchild of the Rev. Randy Wilson and his wife, Lisa, who run the Generations of Light ministry in Colorado Springs. Envisioned by Wilson as events where girls as young as ten could dwell on "everything that their femininity is about, their beauty, their dress, their makeup" (Emery 2002), purity balls are gala affairs where girls get dressed up in floor-length gowns for a formal night out with their fathers as their dates. These events—which are alleged to be soaring in popularity[13]—have virtually all the hallmarks of a wedding: the "proud, tuxedo-clad father, the frosted white cake, the limousines, and an exchange of vows. But there is no groom and the girl in the long gown is no bride. She's daddy's little girl" (Zablit 2007). She pledges to stay pure or sexually abstinent until marriage, and her father vows to protect that purity and to be a living example of integrity and purity.[14] Noticeably absent, as Mary Zeiss Stange (2007) points out, is the mother.

The NCR's cosmology is comprehensive and totalizing: it is "built on a narrow interpretation of natural law, in which the only natural form of sexual activity occurs within the monogamous traditional family, where gender differences and heterosexuality are absolute. These are fundamental elements of a universal moral order, its truths are absolute, not relative or situational, with ethical behavior based at the deepest level on the Ten Commandments, God's 'driver's manual' for human behavior" (Kintz 1997, 5–6).

Because the NCR sees the "traditional family" as "the fundamental building block and basic unit of society and its continued health as a prerequisite for a healthy and prosperous nation" (Falwell 1981, 205), it embraces the "traditional family" as the primary focus of public policy and visualizes the family, the community, the church, the economy, the polity, and the world as a "closed set of concentric circles stacked on top of the other and ascending heavenward" (Kintz 1997, 6). In its marriage of religion and politics, the NCR sees the state's primary role as guarding and enforcing moral virtue. Thus, members of the NCR embrace anti-statist libertarianism and an intensely normative conservatism: they want, on the one hand, the opportunity for material success unhampered by governmental controls and, on the other hand, a government that will halt social change in the United States and return society to an imagined past (White 1991). In this moral universe, the "traditional family takes precedence over both the individual right to privacy and the individual freewheeling capitalist" (Kintz 1997, 6). The inherent tensions between cultural traditionalism and unregulated free enterprise, therefore, are resolved in a "systemically gendered view of the world . . . The organic unity of the family resolves male egoism and female selflessness into a smoothly functioning expression of divine intent" (Hunter 1987, 2–8).

The quest to return to an (alleged) earlier homogeneity and orthodoxy contributes to making the NCR ripe for what many observers identify as its social intolerance, its rejection of civil liberties in the name of social values and political agendas, its trivialization of systemic oppressions, its reduction of equality to the possibilities of economic competition, and its insensitivity to the problem of poverty, which it tends to see as "the natural condition of things" because of Adam and Eve's expulsion from the Garden of Eden.[15] Needless to say, feminist claims that women and men are equal, that women (like men) are self-possessed individuals, that gendered divisions of labor should be dismantled both in and outside the home,[16] that women are potential leaders in their own right, and that first-world hegemony should be eliminated are anathema to most of the NCR membership. They represent a clear sign that the United States is on the verge of, if not already in, a decline of cosmic significance.

This point cannot be overemphasized. For leaders of the NCR, feminism

is the handmaiden of the modern era's greatest evils—secularism, liberalism, humanism, socialism, and communism—and as such, it is an enemy
of the family, of the American nation, and of God and religion. According
to Beverly LaHaye, the founder of Concerned Women for America, feminism is one of the greatest dangers facing American civilization and the
Christian church today: "It is a philosophy of death. At its core in modern
times there is a stridently anti-life motivation. Radical feminists are self-
destructive and are trying to bring about the death of an entire civilization
as well . . . A philosophy based on selfishness, rebellion, and anger should
have absolutely no place in our churches" (LaHaye 1984, 54, 121). Not
surprisingly, LaHaye urges women to have "a consistently quiet spirit"
(LaHaye 1980, 76) and to make the happiness of their husbands their primary goal (LaHaye 1976, 74). To live fully, the wife must die to herself and
submit to her husband (LaHaye 1976, 73). In most circles of the NCR, even
submission to an unsaved or abusive husband is required. Through her
submission, the wife can become an agent of God, putting her unsaved or
abusive partner on the road to salvation. Paradoxically, then, the exercise
of self-sacrifice, dependency, and submission serves as a way for women
(unlike men, who are by nature self-interested) to find agency, liberation,
self-identity, and a sense of self-worth.

The fervor with which the NCR has attacked feminism is a testament to
the threat that gender equality poses to its values and agendas. On the other
hand, since the NCR is a movement that came of age during what Rudnick
and Andersen (1989, 35) have dubbed "the irony epidemic," its successes
and influence beg for explanation. One wonders what accounts for the
NCR's extraordinary success in moving American politics to the right, given
its appearance during an era of conspicuous indifference.

As many have commented, American society has become saturated with
technologically fabricated and doctored images, body-doubles and plastic
surgery, incessant spin doctoring, virtual realities, fictional documentaries,
"reality shows" whose realities are transparently contrived, and politicians
and other authority figures who routinely lie. The effect of this—a growing
cynicism about the possibility or value of investing in any structures of
meaning—changes the possibilities of experience and everyday life. As
Lawrence Grossberg notes, when all images, realities, and truths are equally
deserving and undeserving of being allowed to matter, then nothing really
matters or can be anchored to impassioned commitment. In postmodern
America, the world is reduced to a facetious insignificance in which passion
is patently manufactured and manipulated: everything "can be taken seriously and simultaneously, made into a joke."[17] The popularity and longev-
ity of the Jerry Springer talk show illustrates this point perfectly: guests
defend their own versions of reality with mud- and chair-slinging antics, all
the while conveying, not only that everyone has his or her own version of

things and that passion has become performance, but also that no version
is better than any other and, therefore, that nothing warrants genuine
affective investment.

According to Grossberg, because of the conditions of postmodernity in
the American context, large numbers of Americans find themselves living as
though little has a good chance of mattering, at least for long. Being actively
indifferent and exhibiting an ironic posture toward intense affective mattering have become common modes of being. Lacking a center against which
to make meaning and measure their efforts and, therefore, experiencing
fragmentation, uncertainty and unease, many people are unable or unwilling to become actively invested in political issues and struggles (Grossberg
1992, 222):

> Postmodernity, then, points to a crisis in our ability to locate any meaning
> as a possible and appropriate source for an empassioned commitment. It is a
> dissolution of the "anchoring effect" that articulates [links] meaning and
> desire to affect. . . . [It involves] an inability to anchor our will in something
> else. It is not that nothing matters—for something has to matter—but that
> there is no way of choosing, or of finding something to warrant the invest-
> ment. (Grossberg 1992, 222)

Given a society increasingly emptied of deep commitments, one has to be
impressed by the NCR's success in building a coalition of members who are
intensely invested in and committed to its ideologies, values, and political
agendas, including anti-feminism.[18] In his study of the NCR, Clyde Wilcox
proposes that the "simplest and most straightforward explanation for the
support of the Christian Right is that it stems from a set of religious and
political beliefs and values" (Wilcox 1992, 40). This thesis is seconded by
Michael Lienesch, who suggests that to understand the success of the NCR,
one must ultimately look to the complex and sometimes contradictory
worldview of this movement, just as one would for any social movement
(Lienesch 1993, 20–21).

But is the success of the NCR (or any other social movement) explained
so simply? If Grossberg is correct in saying that one of the hallmarks of
postmodernity in the United States is that "Meaning and affect—
historically so closely intertwined—have broken apart, each going in its
own direction" (Grossberg 1992, 223), then we are still left wondering
what the affective anchors for the NCR's ideology are. Taking note of the
specific religious beliefs held by members in the NCR—including the belief
that what makes their core views and values matter so deeply to them and
that what draws them into political action is a process of divine sanctifica-
tion and revelation—does not, in and of itself, explain what links the ideology of members in the NCR to political desire and will. Nor does it settle

one way or another whether divine intervention plays a role in the production of their faith or in the actions initiated by their faith. In other words, describing the specific religious beliefs of the faithful does not, by itself, explain why—amidst an epidemic of irony—members in the NCR do not wear their religion more lightly. The thesis shared by Wilcox and Lienesch fails to recognize the need to explain why the core beliefs and values of the NCR have come not only to matter and to have great value to its constituents, but to draw them into political action and struggle.

In her interesting study of the emotions that matter in contemporary Christian conservatism, Linda Kintz argues, among other things, that "by linking the passions for what matters in the family to national identity," intimate familiarity or familiarization—the amorphous, powerful feelings one has, or wishes one had, for one's family—has played an important role in generating affective mattering and in mobilizing conservative Christians politically (Kintz 1997, 7–8). Noting that the NCR emerged on the heels of the 1960s and early 1970s—a time of tremendous civic unrest and social change, as well as increasing economic uncertainty—Richard White has suggested that the ability of Christian conservatism to cultivate a "coalition of resentments" (White 1991, 576) has done much to build a politically dedicated membership.[19] I hope to contribute to the discussion by showing that one of our least decorous emotions—disgust—has also contributed to the NCR's success in attracting people who are intensely and actively committed to its project of redeeming America and the nation's destiny as a "redeemer nation." By providing an affective anchor for its ideology, the NCR's deployment of moralized disgust, I want to argue, has played an important role in the movement's ability to produce members who become actively involved in its campaigns against progressive, liberatory causes.

A PROFILE OF DISGUST

Explaining what makes moralized disgust a powerful political tool for the NCR requires, as a first step, providing a brief profile of disgust. It is noteworthy, for example, that disgust has a unique aversive style. As William Miller points out, disgust "uses images of sensation or suggests the sensory merely by describing the disgusting thing so as to capture what makes it disgusting" (Miller 1997, 9). Disgust is arguably the most visceral and the least decorous of the emotions that figure in our everyday moral discourse. When we are disgusted, we "talk of how our senses are offended, of stenches that make us retch, of tactile sensations of slime, ooze, and wriggly, slithering, creepy things that make us cringe and recoil. No other emotion, not even hatred, paints its object so unflatteringly, because no other emotion forces such concrete sensual descriptions of its object" (Miller 1997, 9).

By characteristically using a vivid sensory idiom, then, disgust proclaims the baseness and inferiority of its object. This emotion depends upon the belief that its elicitors present or constitute a particular kind of threat, namely, the danger inherent in pollution and contamination. According to Miller, disgust conveys "a strong sense of aversion to something perceived as dangerous because of its power to contaminate, infect, or pollute by proximity, contact, or ingestion" (Miller 1997, 2). Disgust embodies the appraisal, then, that its source is base and defiling and that we must shield ourselves from it lest it compromise our status, our purity, or our proper placement in the social order (Miller 1997, 8–9).

Finding a hair in one's food at a restaurant is a perfect example of a trivial (but usually strong) disgust-reaction.[20] Despite the fact that we will remove the offending object immediately, we Americans are apt to experience difficulty returning to the dish in which it was found, and we may lose our appetite altogether. It seems clear that our disgust in this situation rests upon the somewhat magical belief that a single hair, especially one that belongs to a stranger, has the power to debase or defile our being if ingested.

Because disgust concerns bodily products and the borders of the body— always dicey issues in our dualist culture—we should not be surprised that our reasons for feeling disgust in one or another circumstance are often inarticulable, obscure, or question-begging. I would note, however, that being marked by explanatory opaqueness does not mean that disgust-reactions are not "reason-based": our beliefs can go wrong for many reasons, by operating beneath the level of consciousness or by being false, contradictory, unexamined, disorderly, or atavistic. In order to maintain that a type of emotion is suffused with cognition, one is not committed to saying that any given instance of the emotion must rest on beliefs that are intelligible or reasonable in the normative sense.

Having said this, we should note, of course, that the beliefs that underlie disgust are not necessarily irrational in the normative sense: finding a dead mouse in a box of cereal would elicit disgust from most of us, and the belief underlying this disgust—that dead rodents can contaminate food—is not an unreasonable one, although I suspect that we would be appealing to a medicalized conception of contamination. It bears emphasizing that while the capacity to feel disgust is probably universal, as individuals we do not experience disgust at the same things. Like other emotions, disgust is a richly social and cultural phenomenon, one whose content is open to wide variations across cultures and time. Indeed, the disgust that grips us on any given occasion is always a particular historical formation. Thus, for example, in some parts of the world, belching loudly and deliberately is a socially acceptable means of conveying appreciation for a good meal; in others, it is simply a disgusting practice. Furthermore, because cultures are far from being homogeneous "spaces" whose inhabitants all share a uniform and consistent understanding of the world, the events and situations that trigger disgust will vary, not only cross-culturally, but also among people in any given cultural context. Hence, while most of the people I know are repulsed by finding hair in their food at restaurants and by the thought of finding a dead rodent in a cereal box, I would not want to presume that this is true for all Americans. Similarly, for some Americans, purity balls are a badly needed antidote to the disgusting by-products of evils such as feminism.[21] For feminists and others, they are creepy, disgusting affairs because of their sexual, even incestuous, overtones, their infantilization of young women, and their message that female sexuality is male property, to be guarded and protected by men.

Whatever its object, lurking behind disgust's claim to superiority is the desire for purity and the fear that the high is vulnerable to the defiling powers of the low: the "world is [seen as] a dangerous place in which the polluting powers of the low are usually stronger than the purifying powers of the high" (Miller 1997, 9). This point is put succinctly and rather graphically by Paul Rozin when he states, "A teaspoon of sewage will spoil a barrel of wine, but a teaspoon of wine will do nothing for a barrel of sewage" (Rozin 1987, 32). As the "one-drop" rule[22] and laws that forbade African Americans to touch the water fountains, bathrooms, bus seats, and restaurant spaces used by whites illustrate, disgust's appraisal that its source is base and polluting can be so strong that it activates the demand for social control, if not also for legal protection. Thus, a person with one drop of Black blood was classified as being "Black," and Jim Crow laws were created, establishing the right for white people to be free of the defilement and impurity that close contact with Black people would purportedly bring.[23]

By seeing its objects as threatening to contaminate or damage one's being and by painting its objects as base by using a characteristically vivid sensory idiom, disgust has deep roots in our ambivalence about embodiment and its connections with imperfection, vulnerability to decay, and finitude. By being bound to metaphors of sensation, disgust obviously tends to do much of its moral work on matters concerning the body. Thus, in the United States, for example, incest, cannibalism, and necrophilia are widely regarded with revulsion. We should note, however, that this work is selective: not all violations of the human body are equal. Disgust operates more readily in mainstream U.S. American culture when what takes place are violations of (white, middle-class, heterosexual) male bodies rather than violations of female bodies, especially those of women of color, poor women, or lesbians. Moreover, disgust is not always constant. For example, in those rare cases of male-on-female domestic battery that elicit public recognition and disgust, all too often the object of disgust becomes a moving target: though initially disgusted by what the victimizer has done, many people end by becoming disgusted with the victim, for ostensibly allowing herself to become so degraded. Instead of serving a progressive agenda in such cases, disgust becomes a means of blaming the victim for her situation and of tagging her as psychologically flawed, if not also morally defective.

Although disgust tends to do much of its moral work on matters concerning the body, it is also liable to involve judgments about members of groups and persons who are stigmatized either because they do not meet our cultural standards of being "civilly disattendable,"[24] as is the case in the United States with the extremely obese, the deformed, the mentally ill, and the grotesquely ugly (Miller 1997, 197–205), or because they have become emblematic in our culture of physicality or animality. Because disgust is animated by the desire for purity, that is, by the aspiration to be free of the imperfections and the vulnerabilities of finitude and embodiment, it has helped to produce and maintain pernicious social hierarchies. As Martha Nussbaum has noted:

> So powerful [in the West] is the desire to cordon ourselves off from our animality that we often don't stop at feces, cockroaches, and slimy animals. We need a group of humans to bound ourselves against, who will come to exemplify the boundary line between the truly human and the basely animal. . . . Thus, throughout history, certain disgust properties—sliminess, bad smell, stickiness, decay, foulness—have repeatedly and monotonously been associated with, indeed projected onto, groups by reference to whom privileged groups seek to define their superior human status. Jews, women, homosexuals, untouchables, lower-class people—all these are imagined as tainted by the dirt of the body. (Nussbaum 2004b, 107–108)

Of course, disgust is not the only type of emotion that has reflected and reinforced deleterious social relations. But I would argue that moralized disgust is particularly problematic because, unlike negative emotions such as contempt, indignation, and outrage—which have done their fair share of maintaining injurious social hierarchies—it rests on the core idea of contamination. Moralized disgust's policing of the body politic is based, in other words, not on substantive harms or wrongs, but on the symbolic relationship its objects bear to anxieties about our animality, embodiment, finitude, and capacities for harmdoing (Nussbaum 1999, 32). This means that avowals of disgust are conversation-stoppers: either you agree with them or you don't. To adapt one of Nussbaum's illustrations (Nussbaum 1999, 27), if I don't think homosexuality is morally disgusting, what could you possibly say to make me change my mind? You could shift from the ground of disgust to some other ground, say, indignation (they are being given "special rights") or fear (they will molest your children), but then it is no longer homosexuality's disgust-properties that purportedly make it morally objectionable. Or you could dwell on the properties that you attribute to homosexuality and that you think make it disgusting—for example, a man fellating or anally penetrating another man—but what could you offer as non-question-begging reasons for saying that these properties make homosexuality disgusting?

Appeals to revulsion fail, therefore, to countenance the possibility of ongoing discussion, deliberation, and debate. An aura of indisputability surrounds expressions of disgust. As Miller notes, the "avowal of disgust expects concurrence. It carries with it the notion of its own indisputability. . . . It argues for the visibility, the palpability, the concreteness, the sheer obviousness of the claim" (Miller 1997, 201). Thus, when we express disgust, we are *not* inviting others to seek evidence, shift through facts, connect ideas, entertain doubts, countenance alternate points of view, or seek out justifications. We are simply asking for condemnation: the moral defectiveness that has been revealed seemingly requires no reflection, critical analysis, or demonstration (Miller 1997, 201). Challenges are apt to be met, as a result, in any number of conversation-stopping ways—with an assertion of helplessness ("I can't help it, that's just the way I feel"); with a declaration of defiant partiality, if not entitlement ("I have a right to my opinion"); with a question-begging statement ("I don't know; it just *is* disgusting"); with a belittling remonstration for the other's obtuseness ("Don't be stupid"); or with a further expression of disgust ("You're sick!")

We need to recognize, of course, that with any emotion we will eventually come to the end of explanation, at least in a straightforward cognitive sense.[25] Take outrage, for example. If you do not feel outrage about the Nazis' mass murder of Jews, and I think you are apprised of all the relevant considerations and have been given every opportunity I can think of to understand what it must have been like for the victims, that's that. There is really nothing more that I can say to convince you or to make you feel outrage. This should not surprise us, for changes in a person's emotional economy do not always involve simply the acquisition of more or better information with which to deliberate. What is often required is the *willingness* to travel to other people's "worlds," that is, to seek to understand what it is to be them and what it is to be oneself in their eyes (Lugones 2003, 97). In other words, instead of additional propositional information or a better process of deliberation, what may be needed to elicit outrage from you about the Holocaust are new forms of social and political engagement that make you become "aware of the same things differently" (Bartky 1990, 14). To be sure, I can express outrage or disgust at what I take to be your obtuseness or lack of concern about a past social evil, but this form of expression is not liable, at least in a straightforward cognitive sense, to influence your thinking and, therefore, to make you feel outrage.

Having noted the limits of propositional information, I would nonetheless argue that the wrongs and harms that I can reference to explain or defend my outrage bear much more extended debate and discussion than is the case with disgust. Moreover, we should note that, in addition to having the air of being argument-proof in the sense that any and all possible arguments against it are seen as being simply unworthy of consideration, moralized disgust is an epistemological resource that often casts suspicion on the epistemological, and even moral, fitness of anyone who speaks against it. For the disgusted subject, the facts speak for themselves: if you are not disgusted by the objects of her disgust—for example, homosexuality and cross-dressing—then you probably lack epistemic worthiness, and you may yourself be deviant or aberrant in some significant way. Thus, it is little wonder that disgust is all too liable to be a party to social subordination, exclusion, and oppression. By assuming that if you are not with us, you have no claim on respectability, the disgusted subject not only declares the baseness and inferiority of the objects of her disgust, but also consigns those with conflicting viewpoints to epistemic limbo, if not also to a place on the garbage heap.[26]

To say, then, that disgust does not aim to ground social action on the public exchange of reasons is an understatement. This emotion is an epistemological resource that welcomes impermeability, instant certitude, and imperviousness to considerations that might make its judgment doubtful. Using the term loosely, we might say that the epistemic dynamics of disgust are "Manichean" in nature:[27] disgust depoliticizes moral and political life by encouraging us to believe that the good is ready-made—that it is not in question, not contestable, and not something that must be continually shaped, proved in action, and verified by its consequences (Sartre 1966, 281). For the disgusted Manichean, we need not constantly struggle with one another to shape a decent society; we need only purify the one that exists (Sartre 1966, 281). In the words of Pat Robertson, a right-wing, Christian evangelist, we need only summon the exterminator "for a godly fumigation." Thus, moralized disgust is an epistemological resource that typically operates by peremptorily dismissing or excising "unacceptable" points of view and social arrangements as categorically defective and condemnable. It is animated by the desire for purity, which is linked with the desires for domination, homogeneity, and univocality.

This is not to say that as a moralized emotion, disgust is utterly impervious to challenges and change. Though its natural tendency as a mode of disapprobation is to paint its objects as unquestionably morally defective, in fact a person's particular disgust-reaction can cease to be an avowal of *moral* condemnation without necessarily losing its negative normativity. For example, given cultural shifts in people's understandings of such things as gender, sexuality, and sources of moral authority, as well as more familiarity with people who are homosexuals, more acceptance of diversity, and new forms of social and political engagement, an individual might begin to endorse a sexual pluralism that morally countenances homosexuality, despite continuing to find homosexuality itself viscerally repulsive.

Nonetheless, while this instance demonstrates that the aura of indisputability that surrounds avowals of moralized disgust can be dispelled, we should note that non-moralized disgust is not likely—especially in the context of increasingly distant and precarious relations between affect, on the one hand, and ideology and desire, on the other hand—to prompt a person to become actively invested in, and committed to, the political struggles of sexual minorities. This is borne out by that fact that, despite increasing popular tolerance for sexual minorities and, presumably, lower levels of disgust (whether moralized or non-moralized), activists have had only modest and often short-lived successes in opposing oppression and inequality based on sexual orientation. Activists in the NCR have met with far more success.

THE APPROPRIATION OF DISGUST

Having established that moralized disgust is tied to the linked desires for purity, social control, and univocality, we are now in a position to understand, on the one hand, what makes this emotion a congenial form of political action for the NCR and, on the other hand, why—in a society increasingly emptied of deep commitments and passions—this emotion helps to produce a strong affective anchor for the NCR's ideology, as well as a politically dedicated membership. As I discussed above, cultural analysts have contended that meaning and affect have broken apart in postmodern America and that, as a result, the world for many Americans has been reduced to a facetious insignificance. Lacking a center against which to make meaning and to measure their efforts, experiencing fragmentation, uncertainty and unease, many people are unable or unwilling to become actively invested in political issues and struggles (Grossberg 1992, Ch.8). Given this, the successes and influence enjoyed by the NCR seem particularly remarkable.

Though it makes the NCR no less a formidable opponent, recognizing that moralized disgust is tied to the desires for purity, social control, and univocality helps to demystify the difference that exploiting this emotion makes for politicized conservative Christianity. As I pointed out above, the NCR's cosmology is comprehensive and totalizing; it is built on a narrow interpretation of natural law. The movement holds its truths to be self-evident and absolute, and it embraces a logic based on absolute binaries. Because it sees itself engaged in a life-and-death fight for the nation's soul and providential role as a "redeemer nation," the NCR's outlook is apocalyptic and its leaders see themselves as playing a prophetic role, that is, as "being in but not entirely of their world" (Lienesch 1993, 43). Moreover, as a comment that was made to the journalist Ron Suskind by a senior adviser to George W. Bush aptly illustrates, the NCR is imbued with an aura of indisputability and certainty. Suskind was told that people like him are "in what we call the reality-based community . . . [people who] believe that solutions emerge from your judicious study of discernible reality. . . . [But that's] not the way the world really works anymore. . . . We're an empire now, and when we act, we create our own reality. And while you're studying that reality—judiciously, as you will—we'll act again, creating other new realities, which you can study too, and that's how things will sort out. We're history's actors . . . and you, all of you, will be left to just study what we do" (Suskind 2004, 64).[28]

Now, if one's worldview unapologetically includes, as does the NCR's, the presumption that some people, ideas, practices, and values are monstrous aberrations that threaten God's natural law and also possibly the Second Coming of Christ, and if one welcomes impermeability, certitude, and imperviousness to considerations that might make one's judgment doubtful, as do most members of the NCR, moralized disgust is a highly compatible political resource. But what makes this emotion not only congenial to politicized conservative Christians, but also helpful in linking passion to meaning? According to Grossberg, ours is a culture in which large numbers of people think that it is "all right to invest yourself in something as long as you realize that there is really nothing to invest. You play the game for whatever the stakes, without taking either the game or the stakes too seriously (although seriousness is a perfectly acceptable game to play as well)" (Grossberg 1992, 217). How, then, does moralized disgust help members of the NCR become, or remain, intensely invested in and committed to the movement's beliefs, values, and political agendas?

Ironically, as befits "the irony epidemic," the NCR is counter-cultural: its members do not play at seriousness; they take their religious and political beliefs, as well as the stakes of these beliefs, to have great import. It is thus not by accident that the NCR is perhaps *the* most powerful and influential American political movement, playing quite seriously for the ultimate stakes: "salvation" for self, family, nation, and world. Ironically, again, moralized disgust helps enable the NCR to make its ideology and agendas matter by exploiting and reconfiguring the conditions of American postmodernity, in particular, fragmentation, uncertainty, and unease. By deploying moralized disgust to "trash" opposing views and values as dangerous contaminants—the filthy work of Satan—the NCR offers its members a center against which to make meaning and to measure their beliefs and efforts. Of course, by raising the specter of pollution—by implying, for example, that gender equality or shared global leadership defiles God's plan for creation—the NCR's use of disgust is also helping to generate fear, unease, and a sense of vulnerability to the defiling powers of the "low." Nonetheless, given the epistemic dynamics of moralized disgust, the NCR is able to capitalize on these conditions: the more the "low," for example, feminists and homosexuals, make arguments to defend their "abominable" beliefs and push for social change, the more they cast suspicion on their own epistemological and moral fitness, and the more the NCR's absolutist certainties must matter and its call for political action must be heeded. The moral absolutes offered by the NCR exhibit the will to purity, sameness, and domination. As such, they provide those who embrace them with an indispensable inoculation against possible contamination and, simultaneously, with a call to action—a summons to become ever vigilant, loyal, committed, and tireless agents of purification and righteousness. Thus when leaders of the NCR employ moralized disgust, they provide their followers with an antidote for the conditions of postmodernity, and in so doing, they help produce a strong affective anchor for their ideology, as well as a politically dedicated membership.

In disgust's defense, one must acknowledge that this emotion does not always or necessarily target inappropriate objects. From a feminist point of view, the widespread disgust that, for example, the murders of James Byrd,[29] Matthew Shepard,[30] and Laci Peterson[31] elicited in the United States was well placed. These examples bring us back to the question of feminist appropriations of disgust: is what is good for right-wing Christian activists also good for feminists? Can moralized disgust provide feminists with a valuable means of resistance to oppression and a form of progressive political action?

The proposal to appropriate moralized disgust as a form of progressive political action is not without some merit.[32] For example, if I express disgust to people about the cruelties perpetrated by American soldiers at Abu Ghraib prison in Iraq and get communicative "uptake," to use Marilyn Frye's term (1983), I can know that my moral disapprobation is shared by others—and *this* has the value that comes from knowing that there is a world, among all the multiple and conflicting worlds I inhabit, that decries and opposes certain cruel practices. If my avowal of disgust does not get any communicative uptake, it will seem senseless to my audience, if not also ridiculous, crazy, disgusting, or dismissible in some other way. Nonetheless, it contains recognition or reaffirmation that there is more than one world of sense—and *this* has the value that comes from not accepting official interpretations of reality and from being self-possessed.

There is yet another way in which using moralized disgust to condemn oppressive social practices and structures is valuable: while not getting communicative uptake in any straightforward cognitive sense, my expression of disgust may nonetheless echo or reverberate emotionally in the people I am addressing. To adapt Claudia Card's characterization of emotional echoing, my audience may pick up and feel my disgust without any perception of its basis or, perhaps, without even any awareness that what they are doing is reproducing my feeling (Card 1990, 152–166). Despite lacking intelligibility in any straightforward cognitive sense, if my disgust echoes or reverberates emotionally in the people I am addressing, it will have the value of communicating an indictment of their interpretations of reality.

But here is the rub. Will my using moralized disgust to *indict* oppressive structures of meaning also be capable of generating the *desire* for understanding in those to whom I am communicating my disgust and in whom this expression of disgust is reverberating emotionally? Will my using moralized disgust to indict oppressive worlds of sense even be capable of communicating to them that we *need* understanding across worlds of sense? Moreover, at what point does the self-possession that is powered by moralized disgust risk becoming arrogant perception, that is, the failure to see another and to see oneself in the eyes of the other (Lugones 2003, Ch. 4)? While not conceptually linked with arrogant perception, is moralized disgust nonetheless liable to encourage us to see others by consulting only *our* will, intent, fears, and imagination (Frye 1983, 75)? And finally, is moralized disgust the sort of mechanism that may help us find common ground with one another, but also lure us into thinking that we can shape resistance together only if we embrace a politics that assumes or values homogeneity?

The well-known cruelties perpetrated on detainees by American soldiers at Abu Ghraib prison in Iraq and the widespread practices of female genital cutting are pertinent cases to explore with these questions in mind, especially since they force us to consider the political economy of moralized disgust in an increasingly globalized world, that is, in contexts that recognize the growing permeability of national and social boundaries. With respect to the Abu Ghraib prison abuse case, it is noteworthy that, whatever their views about the invasion and occupation of Iraq, most Americans were disgusted by the images of abuse and torture that they saw: disgust not only reverberated emotionally, but also generated communicative uptake. As David Levi Strauss observes, "Unlike the Brits, who immediately questioned the veracity of the *Daily Mirror* images of prisoner abuse, we believed the Abu Ghraib images without question, because they only confirmed what we already knew but didn't want to accept: that behind all the pretty talk about wanting freedom for the good people of Iraq lurked naked aggression, deep-seated cultural contempt, and the arrogant smirk of unilateralism, and the realization that we are now mired in a hellish conflict with no end in sight. . . . The most striking thing about the images from Abu Ghraib, and what marks them as unmistakably American, is that peculiar mixture of cold-blooded brutality and adolescent frivolity; of hazing or fooling around, and actual deadly torture—reality and fantasy conjoined" (Strauss 2004, 93–94).[33]

By producing waves of revulsion throughout the world, the Abu Ghraib images put a face on the U.S. occupation of Iraq that may never be forgotten, especially by the Muslim world. It seems sensible to posit that, by forcing a willfully ignorant and indifferent American public to confront the brutal, callous, and degrading treatment of alleged insurgents and "enemy combatants"[34] that was taking place in its name, the moralized disgust generated by these images provided progressive activists in the United States with a valuable mechanism for indicting and challenging official interpretations of reality, in this case that there was nothing untoward or unethical about the Bush administration's disregard for international humanitarian law as it applies to the treatment of prisoners in any one of the facilities that make up the network of U.S. detention camps around the world. We need to recognize, of course, that when the Abu Ghraib photographs were first released, other powerful emotions besides disgust were elicited, for example, indignation, horror, contempt, and outrage. We cannot know exactly what share of the resulting moral disapprobation should be attributed to disgust rather than other negative emotions, but we can be sure, I think, that the role that disgust played in generating moral condemnation helped give heart, legitimacy, and renewed impetus to those struggling against the oppressive actions, practices, and policies of the United States in Iraq and elsewhere.

Still, we should question how much, in the end, disgust really worked against, rather than with, the grain of power. It is significant, in my opinion, that just as the torture of Abu Ghraib prisoners yielded almost no new information and just as few of the detainees subjected to torture at Abu Ghraib turned out to be linked to the insurgency (Strauss 2004, 100), for many Americans, experiencing disgust at the Abu Ghraib images produced uninformed and relatively fleeting moral condemnation. If ever glimpsed, it did not take long for many Americans to distance themselves from the deeper realities that the photographs carried and that carried them, including, for example, contempt for other cultures, vainglory, and "the pornography, sadism, hyper-sexualization, hazing, incarceration, recreational racism, and ritual violence of everyday patriotic life" in the United States (Grossinger 2004, 127). In place of sustained interrogations of their self-understandings and of attempts to understand the perspectives and experiences of Arabs and Muslims, for example, many Americans rather quickly accepted official assurances that the meaning of Abu Ghraib was transparent, bounded, and univocal—that what had taken place was the result of the unsanctioned conduct of a few aberrant, dishonorable, low-ranking American soldiers.

Given the nature of disgust, how surprising was this outcome? As I argued above, disgust is an emotion that causes us to recoil from that which seems to defile, pollute, or pose a danger to the supposed purity and superiority of our persons or of the body politic. This emotion is animated by the desire for purity, univocality, and sameness. Because disgust works by discouraging us from developing a reflective understanding of those who are objects of our disgust, we are all too likely, when we experience disgust, to demonize its source, if not also eventually to despise those whom we first viewed as victims.

Given the epistemic dynamics of disgust, the "bad apples" construction of the Abu Ghraib abuse scandal was an explanation waiting to happen. By declaring a few low-ranking soldiers to be base and inferior, this rationalization allowed Americans to express strong moral condemnation of the treatment some prisoners at Abu Ghraib had endured without really indicting themselves, their government, or the predatory character of American will. It enabled Americans to avoid seriously attempting, on the one hand, to untangle exactly which practices of ill-treatment were formally or informally approved and at what levels of the U.S. government, and on the other hand, to discern the complex and perhaps conflicted motivational structures from which the indicted soldiers' actions issued. By the same token, the "bad apples" explanation let Americans willfully ignore, if not also remain utterly oblivious to, the multifaceted meanings that the images of the soldiers' behavior carried for Muslims and Arabs in general and for the particular victims whose images had been made into highly public war trophies. With the "bad apples" rationalization, Americans were conveniently able to avoid asking the difficult question of whether there might be something rotten at the core rather than just a few rotten apples. *This,* as I argued above, is how moralized disgust typically operates. When we express this emotion, we are often simply asking for condemnation: the moral defectiveness that we have discerned presumably requires no critical analysis, dialogue with those who occupy different social locations, ongoing investigation for deeper understandings, or search for restorative justice. Because the good is assumed to be ready-made, purification is all that is needed.

Of course, there are many reasons besides disgust-reactions that account for the fact that, after the abuses and cruelties at Abu Ghraib prison were exposed, many Americans failed to appreciate the need for understanding across worlds of sense. Nonetheless, moralized disgust is implicated in this case because it animated so many people's reactions to the photographs and because it is often laced with arrogant perception, binary constructions of good and evil, and disregard for the multiplicity of social realities and the difficulties of communicating across worlds of sense. While failing to gain greater understanding, or even appreciation for the *need* for greater understanding, of other worlds of sense is of little consequence to members of a movement such as the New Christian Right, for feminists and others committed to emancipatory ideals, this missed opportunity suggests that moralized disgust is actually a means of political action that tends to work with, rather than against, the grain of power.

Another example of the limits of moralized disgust as a form of progressive political action is provided by the controversy surrounding opposition to the cutting of women's genitalia in parts of Africa, the Middle East, and Asia, as well as, to a lesser extent, in North America and Europe where there are growing numbers of immigrants, refugees, and visitors who seek, or who are acquainted with, female genital cutting (hereafter, FGC). For feminists who come from societies that traditionally practice some form of FGC[35]—and for those they consider to be their allies—the controversy surrounding these practices is centered as much on Western polemics as on meaningful actions to reduce their incidence. Few of these feminists consider themselves to be in favor of FGC, especially in its severe forms, "any more than they would consider themselves in favor of female infanticide, foot-binding, rape, slavery, or genocide" (James and Robertson 2005, 1). What they take issue with, then, is not the desirability of eliminating harmful genital cutting, but Western discursive practices surrounding FGC.

Western representations of FGC often treat cultures where practices of FGC exist as bounded, discrete social groups assumed to have historically unvarying, homogeneous interests, needs, beliefs, and power bases. By discussing FGC without taking into account the specific spatial, socioeconomic, political, and historical contexts in which these practices take place and which shape the motivational structures of those who participate in them, "Culture and traditions are often coded as harmful, coercive and [ironically] superfluous":

> Much of the Western-oriented literature opposing female genital operations also constructs culture and tradition in problematic ways. Rather than focusing on "culture" as historically changeable and broadly encompassing beliefs and practices characteristic of a social group, the discourse on genital operations understands culture as ahistorical "customs" or "traditions." Such traditions are simultaneously depicted as the meaningless hangovers of a pre-modern era and as the defining characteristic of the third world. In this scenario, traditions in the third world are hardened essences that can only be shed by modernization, whereas in the West, "backward" cultural traditions are conceived of as being steadily replaced by "rational" ways of life. (Walley 2005, 35)

Ignoring the "detailed, complicated, and complex meanings and tensions that embed and surround . . . [female genital] surgeries" (Gunning 2005, 114) is not benign, for it results in representations of women that deny their agency or their humanity or both. Women who have undergone genital cutting are often depicted by Westerners as hapless victims of "unreasoned adherence to tradition and/or malicious ignorance" (James and

Robertson 2005, 5). Women who perform genital cutting, on the other hand, are typically characterized as pitiless torturers. Or, because genital cutting is usually performed at the request of parents and relatives and because the female family members as well as those who perform genital cutting were themselves once subject to practices of genital cutting, women who participate in genital cutting are sometimes represented as pawns of a patriarchal culture so uncivilized that even family members "are callous or barbaric enough to torture their own" (Walley 2005, 38).

Feminists who come from countries where FGC is practiced are aware, of course, of being perceived as members of "uncivilized" cultures, and this places them in the position of needing to challenge the ahistorical, decontextualized, ethnocentric, and arrogant representations of practices they may nonetheless oppose. For example, in defense of the societies they come from, some feminists have criticized Western feminists' failure to link FGC with gender-related problems that are prevalent in their own societies, such as violence against women, child prostitution, breast enlargement surgery, and rape (Lane and Rubinstein 1996, 38). Members of the Women's Caucus of the African Studies Association have likewise noted that Westerners would do well to remember that many of their cultures "do not regard the sexuality of women as a benign or positive force . . . [and that] clitoridectomy and infibulation should not be addressed as phenomena isolated from the larger context of women's general needs. Many African women need food for themselves and their children, greater control over the means of food production, access to clean water, a secure fuel supply, access to health care, including family planning, and ways to acquire cash income. Concern about clitoridectomy and infibulation as the sole issue affecting the status of women may be a luxury that only the West can afford" (quoted in James and Robertson 2005, 2).

What Westerners also need to recognize is that their efforts, if "unguided by detailed cultural knowledge, may . . . inspire a backlash in which the custom is viewed as intrinsic to the group's now threatened identity" (Lane and Rubinstein 1996, 38). At the very least, sensationalizing FGC and "treating African and Asian women in a condescending manner . . . [create] a defensive reaction among people involved with the practice, who might otherwise be allies in the fight for eradication" (Toubia 1995, 7). This observation is similar to one made by Françoise Kaudjhis-Offoumou, who comments that "Controversies over the question of female genital mutilation have aroused impulsive and emotional reactions among Western women; African and other victims of excision have the impression that some of these women are trying to give us lessons, to accomplish a civilizing mission and are therefore shocked, even *revolted*. . . . [Such conflicts] *halt frank discussion of the problems* and do not further the cause of getting rid of FGC" (Kaudjhis-Offoumou 1994, 159; italics added).

As I have argued, "halting frank discussion of problems" is just what avowals of disgust (or revulsion) tend to do, both because they embody the appraisal that their source is base and because an aura of indisputability and certainty surrounds them. Of course, once we take account of historical and contemporary relationships of power and privilege, we must recognize that it is the moralized disgust that _Westerners_ almost invariably express when they learn of the existence of FGC that is most responsible for halting frank discussions. The main culprit is _not_ the disgust-reactions of African or Asian women when they realize that most Western women, because of the disgust they experience when they think about the existence of FGC, are trying "to accomplish a civilizing mission."[36]

Western polemics about FGC, therefore, unfortunately provide an almost perfect illustration of how the political liabilities of moralized disgust outweigh its potential benefits. In the context of controversies over FGC, moralized disgust has empowered arrogant perception and binary constructions of good ("civilized") and bad ("uncivilized'). It has encouraged Western feminists to ignore the multiplicity of social realities, the existence of enmeshed oppressions, and the complex motivational structures from which the actions of women who participate in some form of FGC originate. Finally, it has lured many of us into ignoring the difficulties of communicating across worlds of sense and into thinking that we can shape resistance to FGC with members from the involved communities only if we all embrace a politics that assumes or values homogeneity.

In my opinion, then, while appropriating moralized disgust as a means of resisting oppression and of advocating emancipatory change is not without value, the political potential is modest. By their very nature, oppressive practices and social structures are animated by the desires for purity, univocality, and domination. How successfully can we expect to dismantle these practices and structures with an instrument of social control that is itself tied to purity, univocality, and domination? To borrow from Audre Lorde, how can we dismantle the master's house using the master's tools—in this case, a tool that, on the one hand, requires us to disown physicality, plurality and finitude because they make purity transient and vulnerable and that, on the other hand, encourages us to embrace arrogant perception, instant certitude, and imperviousness to considerations that might cast doubt on our judgment?

The proposal to appropriate moralized disgust to help with the work of opposing injustice and oppression presumes that capitalizing on progressive disgusts is a relatively innocent praxis. But this assumption ignores the content and epistemic dynamics of this emotion. Because it involves claims about contamination and danger to the purity of the body politic, moralized disgust can too easily steer us away from the hard work that opposing multiple oppressions entails, including that of trying to discern "how much and what sort of 'agency' . . . we need to move with others without falling into a politics . . . that values or assumes sameness or homogeneity" (Lugones 2003, 5). As I argued above, disgust is liable to encourage us to pray for a "godly fumigation" or, barring this, to look for shelter upwind. Assuming that a society that resists hegemonic constructions of the social is not ready-made but must be continually shaped and proved in action, we need the power of emotions that recognize the deep multiplicity of social realities and that support creative, pluralistic means of interpretation and communication. What we do not need is the power of an emotion that encourages us to construct those we find disgusting as monstrous aberrations whose dispositions, inclinations, and weaknesses are radically other and that fails, therefore, to countenance the existence of enmeshed oppressions and the fact that a person's behavior may issue "from [both] a resistant and an oppressed motivational structure" (Lugones 2003, 13).

Disgust's aura of indisputability may smell sweeter to us when it emanates from our own disgusts, but indisputability by any other name is still impervious and imperial. As an epistemological resource that works by seeing oppression in terms of simple binaries, by precluding recognition of irreducible multiplicity, and by obviating the need for ongoing reflection and analysis, progressive disgust, no less than conservative disgust, tends to undercut what is essential to good political praxis. With the exception of the caveats already noted, then, moralized disgust is largely a self-defeating means of progressive political action. In fact, if our goal is really to work against the grain of oppressive power, attempting to capitalize on moralized disgust may mean that we end up viewing one another with disgust and embracing the kind of logic and epistemological imperialism employed by the New Christian Right.

NOTES

Research for this paper was undertaken with the support of the Faculty Committee on Research and Development at Le Moyne College. Earlier versions of this paper were presented at the Midwest SWIP (Society for Women in Philosophy) Spring 2005 conference and at the 2006 FEAST (Association for Feminist Ethics and Social Theory) conference. I am very grateful for the feedback I received at both forums and would like particularly to thank Sarah Hoagland for her thoughtful suggestions and constructive criticisms.

1. Although it enjoys the greatest word recognition, the term "New Christian Right" is unfortunate, not only because it erroneously implies that right-wing Christian activism is "new," but also because it reflects and reinforces the linguistic hijacking of "Christian" for a particular sectarian brand of Christianity. I am indebted to Kathleen Nash for the term "politicized conservative Christianity."

2. Lienesch (1993, 4–5). See also Bendroth (1993); Hunter (1987, 116–154); and Wilcox (1992, 1–20).

3. See Hardisty (1999, Ch.3); Kintz (1997, Ch.3); Diamond (1998, Ch.6); and Diamond (1989, 104–110).

4. See Kintz (1997, Ch.1) and Lienesch (1993, Ch.2).

5. Elizabeth V. Spelman's characterization of a cognitive theory of emotion is useful here. As she writes: "The central tenet of what is currently known as the cognitive theory of emotions [vs. the dumb theory of emotions] is that our emotions are not a clue to or sign of internal poppings and firings and other gyrations— mental or physical—within us, but rather indicate how we see the world. Typically emotions have identificatory cognitive states: what identifies my emotion as anger is, among other things, a belief that some unjust harm has been done; what makes my emotion a matter of fear is, among other things, my belief that danger is imminent . . . we could not regard our emotions as very interesting facts about us—in particular, as deeply connected to ourselves as moral agents—if emotions were simply internal events, things happening in us like headaches or bleeding gums" (Spelman 1997, 102–103).

6. All avowals of disgust are normative in character: they convey negative evaluations of their objects. However, not all avowals of disgust are moralized. For example, most people who think that raw oysters are a disgusting food source for humans are making a nonmoral normative judgment. But when people characterize necrophilia or incest as disgusting, they are usually making a normative judgment that is moral in character.

7. See Texe Marrs epigraph.

8. "If you are not a born-again Christian, you're a failure as a human being." (Attributed to Jerry Falwell. Source unknown.)

9. This expression comes from a speech Pat Buchanan gave at Harvard University: "Friends, neither Beltway party is going to drain this swamp, because to them it is not a swamp at all, but a protected wetland and their natural habitat. They swim in it, feed in it, spawn in it" (Buchanan, "A Plague on Both Your Houses," in a speech at Harvard University on March 16, 2000). Although Buchanan is not targeting feminists directly, it is not difficult to imagine that, in other contexts, he would have been referring to feminists.

10. See Pat Robertson epigraph.

11. For additional information, see, for example: Bendroth (1993); Diamond (1989, 1998); Falwell (1981); Griffith (1997); Hardisty (1999); Kintz (1997); LaHaye (1976, 1980, 1984); Lienesch (1993); McGirr (2001); White (1991); and Wilcox (1992).

12. As Kintz explains, for members of the NCR, laissez-faire capitalism is inherently Christian because the essence of unregulated capitalism—the creation of wealth—is seen as being homologous to the essence of God, which is his identity as Creator (Kintz 1997, 223).

13. Leslee Unruh, founder of Abstinence Clearinghouse, claims that "some 1,400 Purity Balls were held across the United States in 2006, mainly in the south and midwest, and that double that number were expected to take place this year" (Zablit 2007).

14. The following pledge is taken by fathers at a Generations of Light purity ball: "I, (daughter's name)'s father, choose before God to cover my daughter as her authority and protection in the area of purity. I will be pure in my own life as a man, husband and father. I will be a man of integrity and accountability as I lead, guide and pray over my daughter and as the high priest in my house. This covering will be used by God to influence generations to come." Retrieved 28 March 2007 from the World Wide Web: www.generationsoflight.com/generationsoflight/html/index.html. I would like to thank Peggy DesAutels for bringing the existence of purity balls to my attention.

15. For a more nuanced discussion of the NCR's views on poverty and the economy, see Lienesch (1993, Ch. 3), and Kintz (1997, Chs. 6 and 7).

16. In a small sector of the modern evangelical movement, gendered divisions of labor concerning women's roles in the home and in the church have been challenged, especially at the level of operative as opposed to professed beliefs. See Bendroth (1993).

17. Grossberg (1992, 217). See Ch. 8.

18. Clearly the NCR's influence and achievements are overdetermined. The focus of the following discussion centers on just one explanatory factor. For a comprehensive explanation and interpretation of the NCR's successes, a wide variety of cultural, organizational, historical, psychological, political, sociological, and theological factors would obviously have to be taken into account.

19. Along these lines, see also Hardisty (1999).

20. Because the objects of disgust can be trivial as well as very important, this emotion provides an exception to Martha Nussbaum's general claim that emotions "insist on the real importance of their object," that is, embody the subject's sense of what objects and events possess a very high importance in her own scheme of goals and projects. Nussbaum (Nussbaum 2001a, 33.)

21. See Greg Charles, "Let fathers be the judge." Charles (2007).

22. According to F. James Davis, "The nation's answer to the question 'Who is black?' has long been that a black is any person with *any* known African black ancestry. This definition reflects the long experience with slavery and later with Jim Crow segregation. In the South it became known as the 'one-drop rule,' meaning that a single drop of 'black blood' makes a person a black." Davis (1991).

23. Of course, racism has a stunning illogic: while whites were disgusted by the prospect of having to share bathroom facilities and dining counters with Blacks, they were not repulsed when Black servants prepared and served them food or wet-nursed their babies, surely one of the most intimate of human activities.

24. Borrowing from Erving Goffman's work on stigma (1963), Miller notes that we are liable to experience moralized disgust when another's self-presentation causes undue concern or attention—that is, when it violates social anticipations that have become transformed into "moral claims on others not to upset the smooth-running routine we feel entitled to count on" (198).

25. For an articulation and discussion of angers that do not communicate in a straightforward cognitive sense but that have communicative "uptake" by "echoing" or "reverberating" across worlds of sense, see Lugones (2003, Ch. 5).

26. This phrase is borrowed from Nussbaum's assertion that we should "cast dis-

gust on the garbage heap where it would like to cast so many of us" (Nussbaum 1999, 22).

27. By "Manicheanism," I mean a view of the world in which all of human history is the product of the struggle between two great, independent warring realms, absolute good and total evil. The following discussion adapts and borrows from Sartre's analysis of anti-semitism in "Portrait of the Antisemite." Sartre (1966, 270–287).

28. See also Kintz (1997) and McGirr (2001).

29. In 1998, James Byrd, Jr., a middle-aged African-American man, was killed by three white men. Byrd was chained by his feet to a pick-up truck and dragged to pieces along two and a half miles of road outside of Jaspers, Texas.

30. Matthew Shepard was a gay college student who was lured from a bar by two straight men on a cold October night in 1998, driven to the outskirts of Laramie, Wyoming, tied to a fence, savagely pistol-whipped and left to die.

31. On December 24, 2002, Laci Peterson, age twenty-seven and eight months pregnant, was reported missing from her home in Modesto, California. Her headless, badly decomposed body and the remains of the fetus she had been carrying were found one day apart in April 2003 on the east shore of the San Francisco Bay. In November 2004, her husband, Scott Peterson, was convicted of first-degree murder for the death of Laci and second-degree murder for the death of their unborn child.

32. In what follows shortly, I use Lugones' discussion about the communicative "uptakes" or "intents" of different forms of anger to probe the political potential of moralized disgust. See Lugones (2003).

33. The images were so American that some Americans were disgusted, not by what they saw in the images, but by the fact that others were disgusted by the images. For Rush Limbaugh, for example, the behavior caught on film was just "a pure media-generated story." Stacking up naked, hooded men, making prisoners strip and wear women's underwear on their heads, forcing prisoners to masturbate while looking at a female guard: according to Limbaugh, these were just the pranks of good ol' boys and "babes" behaving badly—engaging in tomfoolery and hazing "no different from what happens at the Skull and Bones initiation" or at a Madonna or Britney Spears concert. For Limbaugh, then, our disgust should have been reserved, not for the American MP's caught on film "blowing off steam," but for those who became disgusted by the photos or who had not been properly disgusted by photos of the atrocities Americans have suffered at the hands of extremists. *Rush Limbaugh Show* (May 3–4, 2004).

34. See Olshansky (2005) for the Bush administration's singular and confusing rubric of "enemy combatant."

35. For a description of both the diverse procedures that come under the label of FGC and the controversies surrounding these procedures, see, for example, Lane and Rubinstein (1996) and James and Robertson (2005).

36. Nor is the main culprit in halting frank discussions the moralized disgust that some groups of (mostly rural) Africans or Asians experience when they first learn that there are societies that do not practice FGC (Lane and Rubinstein 1996, 35). The fact that it rarely occurs to Americans that some women are disgusted by the thought of unaltered adult female genitalia is a prime example of arrogant perception.

Bibliography

Açar, Feride. 2004. "Recent Key Trends and Issues in the Implementation of CEDAW." In *Gender and Human Rights in the Commonwealth*. London: The Commonwealth Secretariat.

Adams, Carol J. 1990/2000. *The Sexual Politics of Meat*. New York: Continuum.

Addams, Jane. 1899/2003. "Democracy or Militarism." In *Addams's Essays and Speeches on Peace (1899–1935)*, edited by Marilyn Fischer and Judy D. Whipps. Bristol, England: Thoemmes Press.

———. 1900/2003. "Commercialism Disguised as Patriotism and Duty." In *Addams's Essays and Speeches on Peace (1899–1935)*, edited by Marilyn Fischer and Judy D. Whipps. Bristol, England: Thoemmes Press.

———. 1902/2002. *Democracy and Social Ethics*. Urbana, Ill.: University of Illinois Press.

———. 1907/2003. *Newer Ideals of Peace*, edited by Marilyn Fischer and Judy D. Whipps. Bristol, England: Thoemmes Press.

———. 1915/2003. "The Revolt Against War." In *Addams's Essays and Speeches on Peace (1899–1935)*, edited by Marilyn Fischer and Judy D. Whipps. Bristol, England: Thoemmes Press.

———. (June 16) 1917a/2003. "Patriotism and Pacifists in War Time." In *Addams's Essays and Speeches on Peace (1899–1935)*, edited by Marilyn Fischer and Judy D. Whipps. Bristol, England: Thoemmes Press.

———. (July) 1917b/2003. "Labor as a Factor in the Newer Conception of International Relationships." In *Addams's Essays and Speeches on Peace (1899–1935)*, edited by Marilyn Fischer and Judy D. Whipps. Bristol, England: Thoemmes Press.

———. (October 16) 1917c/1984. "Food Conservation." TM carbon. In JAPM 47: 1567–1585. [Note: Materials by Jane Addams marked as "JAPM" are in the microfilm collection of Jane Addams papers. The first number is the reel; the number following the colon is the frame number. In *The Jane Addams Papers, 1860–1960*, edited by Mary Lynn McCree Bryan. Ann Arbor, Mich.: University Microfilms International, 1984.]

———. (post November) 1917d/1984. "Conservation of the World's Food Supply." TM carbon. In JAPM 47: 1586–1606.

———. (December 26) 1917e/1984. "Letter to Judge Lindsey." In JAPM 11:554.

———. 1918a/1984. "World's Food Supply and Woman's Obligations." General Federation of Women's Clubs, *Biennial Convention Official Report.* 251–263. In JAPM 47: 1657–1670.

———. 1918b/1984. "World's Food and World's Politics." In *Addams's Essays and Speeches on Peace (1899–1935),* edited by Marilyn Fischer and Judy D. Whipps. Bristol, England: Thoemmes Press.

———. (January 20) 1919a/1984. "The Next Step." In JAPM 47: 1832–1840.

———. (February 11) 1919b/1984. "Address by Miss Jane Addams [on the League of Nations]." Stenographic transcription. In JAPM 47: 1850–1868.

———. (February 13)1919c/1984. "How to Feed the World." Stenographic transcription. In JAPM 48: 0001–0015.

———. 1920/2003. "Feed the World and Save the League." In *Addams's Essays and Speeches on Peace (1899–1935),* edited by Marilyn Fischer and Judy D. Whipps. Bristol, England: Thoemmes Press.

———. 1922/2002. *Peace and Bread in Time of War.* Urbana, Ill.: University of Illinois Press.

———. 1924/2003. "Presidential Address." In *Addams's Essays and Speeches on Peace (1899–1935),* edited by Marilyn Fischer and Judy D. Whipps. Bristol, England: Thoemmes Press.

Addams, Jane, and Alice Hamilton. 1919/2003. "After the Lean Years." In *Addams's Essays and Speeches on Peace (1899–1935),* edited by Marilyn Fischer and Judy D. Whipps. Bristol, England: Thoemmes Press.

Alcoff, Linda. 2000. "Who Is Afraid of Identity Politics?" In *Reclaiming Identity: Realist Theory and the Predicament of Postmodernism,* edited by Paula M.L. Moya and Michael Roy Hames-García. Berkeley: University of California Press.

Alcoff, Linda, and Elizabeth Potter. 1993. *Feminism and Epistemology.* New York: Routledge.

American College of Obstetrics and Gynecology Committee on Ethics. 2004. *Ethics in Obstetrics and Gynecology.* Published by ACOG.

Anderson, Bridget. 2000. *Doing the Dirty Work? The Global Politics of Domestic Labor.* London: Zed Books.

Anderson, Mary B. 1999. *Do No Harm: How Aid Can Support Peace or War.* Boulder, Colorado: Lynne Rienner.

Anderson, R.E., and D.A. Anderson. 1999. "The Cost-Effectiveness of Home Birth." *Journal of Nurse Midwifery* 44:30–35.

Anderson, Scott A. 2002. "Prostitution and Sexual Autonomy: Making Sense of the Prohibition of Prostitution." *Ethics* 112:748–780.

Arendt, Hannah. 1958/1976. *Origins of Totalitarianism.* 2nd ed. New York: Harcourt Brace Jovanovich.

———. 1958/1998. *The Human Condition.* 2nd ed. Chicago: University of Chicago Press.

———. 1974. *Rahel Varnhagen: The Life of a Jewish Woman.* Translated by Richard and Clara Winston. New York: Harcourt Brace Jovanovich.

Arras, John, ed. 1995. *Bringing the Hospital Home: Ethical and Social Implications of High-Tech Home Care.* Baltimore, Md.: Johns Hopkins University Press.

Arthur, Chris. 1983. "Hegel's Master-Slave Dialectic and a Myth of Marxology." *New Left Review* 142:67–75.

Avineri, Shlomo. 1969. "The Problem of War in Hegel's Thought." *Journal of the History of Ideas* 22:463–474.

———. 1972. *Hegel's Theory of the Modern State*. Cambridge: Cambridge University Press.

Baber, Harriet. 1987. "How Bad is Rape?" *Hypatia* 2:125–38.

Bailey, Ronald. 2002. "Dr. Strangelunch: Why We Should Learn to Love Genetically Modified Food." In *The Ethics of Food*, edited by Gregory E. Pence. Lanham, Md.: Rowman and Littlefield.

Bakan, Abigail B., and Daiva Stasiulis. 1997. *Not One of the Family: Foreign Domestic Workers in Canada*. Toronto: University of Toronto Press.

Bale, Judith R., et al. 2004. *Improving Birth Outcomes: Meeting the Challenge in the Developing World*. Washington, D.C.: National Academies Press.

Barber, Benjamin R. 2003. *Fear's Empire: War, Terrorism, and Democracy*. New York: W. W. Norton.

Bar On, Bat-Ami. 1991. "Why Terrorism is Problematic." In *Feminist Ethics*, edited by Claudia Card. Lawrence: University Press of Kansas.

Bartky, Sandra. 1990. *Femininity and Domination: Studies in the Phenomenology of Oppression*. New York: Routledge.

Beauvoir, Simone de. 1949/1961. *The Second Sex*. Translated and edited by H. M. Parshley. New York: Bantam.

Bendroth, Margaret Lamberts. 1993. *Fundamentalism and Gender: 1875 to the Present*. New Haven, Conn.: Yale University Press.

Benhabib, Seyla. 1992. "On Hegel, Women, and Irony." In *Situating the Self: Gender, Community and Postmodernism in Contemporary Ethics*, by Seyla Benhabib. New York: Routledge.

———. "Feminism and Postmodernism: An Uneasy Alliance." In *Feminist Contentions: A Philosophical Exchange*, edited by Seyla Benhabib, Judith Butler, Drucilla Cornell, and Nancy Fraser. New York: Routledge.

———. 2003. *The Reluctant Modernism of Hannah Arendt*. Lanham, Md.: Rowman and Littlefield.

Berger, Peter. 1963. *Invitation to Sociology: A Humanistic Perspective*. Garden City, New York: Doubleday.

Bergner, Gwen. 1995. "Who Is that Masked Woman? or, The Role of Gender in Fanon's Black Skin, White Masks." *PLMA* 110:75–88.

Bernstein, Alyssa. 2004. "Democratization as an Aim of Intervention: Rawls's Law of Peoples on Just War, Human Rights, and Toleration." In *Archiv für Rechts und Sozialphilosophie*, Beiheft Nr. 95. Franz Steiner Verlag.

———. 2006. "A Human Right to Democracy? Legitimacy and Intervention." In *Rawls's Law of Peoples: A Realistic Utopia?*, edited by Rex Martin and David Reidy. Malden, Mass.: Blackwell Publishing.

———. 2007a. "Human Rights, Global Justice, and Disaggregated States: John Rawls, Onora O'Neill, and Anne-Marie Slaughter." In *The Challenges of Globalization: Rethinking Nature, Culture, and Freedom*, edited by Steven Hicks and Daniel Shannon. Malden, Mass.: Blackwell Publishing.

————. 2007b "Justifying Universal Human Rights via Rawlsian Public Reason." In *Archiv für Rechts und Sozialphilosophie*, Beiheft Nr. 108. Franz Steiner Verlag.

Bessis, Sophie. 2004. "International Organizations and Gender: New Paradigms and Old Habits." *Signs* 29: 633–647.

Bleich, Avraham, Marc Gelkopf and Zahava Solomon. 2003. "Exposure to Terrorism, Stress Related Mental Health Symptoms, and Coping Behavior Among a Nationally Representative Sample in Israel." *Journal of the American Medical Association* 290:612–620.

Bogdan-Lovis, Elizabeth. 1995. *The Death of Birth: A Critical Interpretive Analysis of Second Wave Liberal Feminist Efforts to Influence Women's Childbirth Experiences in the United States During the Last Third of the Twentieth Century*. Master's Thesis, Michigan State University.

————. 1996-97. "Misreading the Power Structure: Liberal Feminists' Inability to Influence Childbirth." *Michigan Feminist Studies* 11:59–79.

————. 2001. Review of Caton 1999. *Victorian Studies* 43:686–88.

Borlaug, Norman. 2002. "Are We Going Mad?" In *The Ethics of Food*, edited by Gregory E. Pence. Lanham, Md.: Rowman and Littlefield.

Bourke, Joanna. 1999. *An Intimate History of Killing: Face-to-Face Killing in Twentieth-Century Warfare*. New York: Basic Books.

Boxill, Bernard. 1997. "The Fight with Covey." In *Existence in Black: An Anthology of Black Existential Philosophy*, edited by Lewis R. Gordon. New York: Routledge.

Brison, Susan J. 1997. "Outliving Oneself: Trauma, Memory, and Personal Identity." In *Feminists Rethink the Self*, edited by Diana Tietjens Meyers. Boulder, Colo.: Westview Press.

Brownmiller, Susan. 1975. *Against Our Will: Men, Women and Rape*. New York: Simon and Schuster.

Buchanan, Patrick J. 2002. *The Death of the West: How Dying Populations and Immigrant Invasions Imperil Our Country and Civilization*. New York: St. Martin's Press.

————. 2006. *State of Emergency: The Third World Invasion and Conquest of America*. New York: St. Martin's Press.

Buck-Morris, Susan. 2000. "Hegel and Haiti." *Critical Inquiry* 26:821–65.

Bunch, Charlotte. 1990. "Women's Rights as Human Rights: Toward a Re-Vision of Human Rights." *Human Rights Quarterly* 12:486–498.

————. 1995. "Transforming Human Rights from a Feminist Perspective." In *Women's Rights, Human Rights: International Feminist Perspectives*, edited by Julie Peters and Andrea Wolper. New York: Routledge.

Butler, Judith. 1990/2006. *Gender Trouble: Feminism and the Subversion of Identity*. New York: Routledge.

————. 1995. "Contingent Foundations: Feminism and the Question of 'Postmodernism'." In *Feminist Contentions: A Philosophical Exchange*, edited by Seyla Benhabib, Judith Butler, Drucilla Cornell, and Nancy Fraser. New York: Routledge.

Butler, Nicholas Murray. 1912/1972. *The International Mind*. New York: Garland Publishing, Inc.

Calhoun, Cheshire. 1994. "Separating Lesbian Theory from Feminist Theory." *Ethics* 104:558–581.

Calkins, Mary Whiton. 1917. "Militant Pacifism." *International Journal of Ethics* 28:70–79.

Callahan, Daniel, and Angela Wasunna. 2005. *Medicine and the Market: Equity vs. Choice*. Baltimore, Md.: Johns Hopkins University Press.

Caputi, Jane. 1993. *Gossips, Gorgons, and Crones: The Fates of the Earth*. Santa Fe, N.Mex.: Bear and Company.

———. 1998. Interview for documentary "No Safe Place: Violence Against Women." Transcript online at http://www.pbs.org/kued/nosafeplace/interv/caputi.html.

———. 2004. *Goddesses and Monsters: Women, Myth, Power, and Popular Culture*. Madison: University of Wisconsin Press.

Card, Claudia. 1990. "Homophobia and Lesbian/Gay Pride." Unpublished manuscript, cited in Lugones 2003.

———. 1991. "Rape as a Terrorist Institution." In *Violence, Terrorism and Justice*, edited by R.G. Frey and Christopher W. Morris. Cambridge: Cambridge University Press.

———. 1996a. "Against Marriage and Motherhood." *Hypatia* 11:1–23.

———. 1996b. *The Unnatural Lottery: Character and Moral Luck*. Philadelphia: Temple University Press.

———. 2002. *The Atrocity Paradigm*. New York: Oxford University Press.

Caton, Donald. 1999. *What a Blessing She Had Chloroform: The Medical and Social Response to the Pain of Childbirth from 1800 to the Present*. New Haven, Conn.: Yale University Press.

Champagne, Helene. 2006. *Peacebuilding: Toward a Global Ethic of Responsibility?* http://www.peacestudiesjournal.org.England/docs/Ethic%20of%20Peace building%20final%20version%20edited.pdf.

Chandler, David. 2004. *"The Responsibility to Protect?* Imposing the 'Liberal Peace.'" *International Peacekeeping* 11:59–81.

Changfoot, Nadine. 2004. "Feminist Standpoint Theory, Hegel and the Dialectical Self: Shifting the Foundations." *Philosophy and Social Criticism* 30:477–502.

Charles, Greg. 2007. "Let Fathers Be the Judge." Retrieved 28 March from the World Wide Web: www.blogs.usatoday.com/oped/2007/03/purity_view_is_.html.

Chatterjee, Deen, ed. 2004. *The Ethics of Assistance: Morality and the Distant Needy*. New York: Cambridge University Press.

Chicago Women's Liberation Union. 1971. "How to Start Your Own Consciousness Raising Group." Available at http://www.cwluherstory.com/CWLUArchive/crcwlu.html. Accessed October 2005.

Chomsky, Noam. 1999. "Sovereignty and World Order." Speech delivered at Kansas State University, 20 September. Available at http://www.zmag.org/chomsky/talks/9909-sovereignty.htm.

———. 2000. *Rogue States: The Rule of Force in World Affairs*. Cambridge, Mass.: South End Press.

Chow, Rey. 1995. "The Politics of Admittance: Female Sexual Agency, Miscegenation and the Formation of Community in Frantz Fanon." *The UTS Review* 1:5–29.

Clarke, D.A. 2004. "Prostitution for Everyone: Feminism, Globalisation and the 'Sex' Industry." In *Not for Sale: Feminists Resisting Prostitution and Pornography*, edited by Christine Stark and Rebecca Whisnant. Melbourne, Australia: Spinifex Press.

Clausewitz, Carl von. 1832/1968. *On War*. Edited by Anatol Rapoport. New York: Penguin.

Code, Lorraine. 1981. "Is the Sex of the Knower Epistemologically Significant?" *Metaphilosophy* 12:267–276.

———. 1991. *What Can She Know? Feminist Theory and the Construction of Knowledge*. Ithaca, N.Y.: Cornell University Press.

Cohen, Jean L. 2004. "Whose Sovereignty? Empire Versus International Law." *Ethics and International Affairs* 18:1–24.

———. 2006. "Sovereign Equality vs. Imperial Right: The Battle over the 'New World Order.'" *Constellations* 13:485–505.

Cohn, Carol, Helen Kinsella, and Sheri Gibbings. 2004. "Women, Peace and Security." *International Feminist Journal of Politics* 6:130–140.

Coker, Christopher. 2002. *Waging War Without Warriors: The Changing Culture of Military Conflict*. Boulder, Colo.: Lynne Rienner.

———. 2004. *The Future of War: The Re-Enchantment of War in the Twenty-First Century*. Malden, Mass.: Blackwell Publishing.

Cole, Andrew. 2004. "What Hegel's Master/Slave Dialectic Really Means." *Journal of Medieval and Early Modern Studies* 34:577–610.

Comay, Roberta. 2004. "Dead Right: Hegel and the Terror." *South Atlantic Quarterly* 103:375–395.

Connell, Phillip. 2001. *Romanticism, Economics and the Question of Culture*. New York: Oxford University Press.

Connell, R. W. 2002. "Masculinities, the Reduction of Violence and the Pursuit of Peace." In *The Postwar Moment: Militaries, Masculinities and International Peacekeeping, Bosnia and the Netherlands*, edited by Cynthia Cockburn and Dubravka Zarkov. London: Lawrence and Wishart.

Constant, Benjamin. 1806/1988. "The Spirit of Conquest." In *Political Writings*. Translated and edited by Bianca Fontana. New York: Cambridge University Press.

Cornell, Drucilla. 2002. *Between Women and Generations*. New York: Palgrave Press.

Crawford, Neta. 2002. *Argument and Change in World Politics: Ethics, Decolonization, and Humanitarian Intervention*. Cambridge: Cambridge University Press.

Crocker, David. 1992. "Functioning and Capability: The Foundations of Sen's and Nussbaum's Development Ethic, Part I." *Political Theory* 20:582–612.

———. 1995. "Functioning and Capability: The Foundations of Sen's and Nussbaum's Development Ethic, Part II." In *Women, Culture, and Development: A Study of Human Capabilities*, edited by Martha C. Nussbaum and Jonathan Glover. Oxford: Clarendon Press; New York: Oxford University Press.

Cuomo, Chris J. 1998. *Feminism and Ecological Communities: An Ethic of Flourishing*. London: Routledge.

Cuomo, Chris J., Claudia Card, Ann Ferguson, and Cheshire Calhoun. 1998. "Author Meets Critics Panel: APA Eastern Division Meeting, 1996." *Hypatia* 13:198–231.

Czempiel, Ernst-Otto. 2003. "Interdependence and Intervention." In *The Lessons of Kosovo: The Dangers of Humanitarian Intervention*, edited by Aleksandar Jovic. Peterborough, Ontario: Broadview Press.

Dahbour, Omar. 2006. "Advocating Sovereignty in an Age of Globalization." *Journal of Social Philosophy* 37:108–126.

Dairiam, Shanthi. 2004. "Progress, Achievements, Constraints and Key Priorities." In *Gender and Human Rights in the Commonwealth*. London: The Commonwealth Secretariat.

Davion, Victoria. 1994. "Is Ecofeminism Feminist?" In *Ecological Feminism*, edited by Karen J. Warren. London and New York: Routledge.

————. 2006. "Coming Down to Earth on Cloning: An Ecofeminist Analysis of Homophobia in the Current Debate." *Hypatia* 16:58–76.

Davis, Allen F. 1973/2000. *American Heroine: The Life and Legend of Jane Addams*. Chicago: Ivan Dee.

Davis, Angela Y. 1998. "The Approaching Obsolescence of Housework: A Working-Class Perspective." In *The Angela Y. Davis Reader*, edited by Joy James. Oxford: Blackwell Publishing.

Davis, F. James. 1991. "Who is Black? One Nation's Definition." Retrieved 31 December from the World Wide Web: www.pbs.org/wgbh/pages/frontline/shows/jefferson/mixed/onedrop.html.

De Jong, Joop T., Ivan H Komproe, and Marc Van Ommeren. 2003. "Common Mental Disorders in Postconflict Settings." *The Lancet* 361:2128–2130.

De Vries, Raymond. 2004a. *A Pleasing Birth: Midwives and Maternity Care in the Netherlands*. Philadelphia: Temple University Press.

————. 2004b. "Businesses are Buying the Ethics They Want." *Washington Post*, 8 February.

————. 2006. "Our Unhealthy Health Care System" *New York Times*, 25 September.

Dewey, John. 1917/1980. "The Future of Pacifism." In *The Middle Works. Vol. 10. 1916–1917*, edited by J. Boydston. Carbondale, Ill.: Southern Illinois University Press.

————. 1945/2003. "Foreword" to the 1945 edition of Jane Addams, *Peace and Bread in Time of War*, edited by Marilyn Fischer and Judy D. Whipps. Bristol, England: Thoemmes Press.

Diamond, Sara. 1989. *Spiritual Warfare: The Politics of the Christian Right*. Boston: South End Press.

————. 1998. *Not by Politics Alone: The Enduring Influence of the Christian Right*. New York: The Guilford Press.

Dill, Bonnie Thornton. 1994. *Across the Boundaries of Race and Class: An Exploration of Work and Family among Black Female Domestic Servants*. New York: Garland.

Dines, Gail. 1998. "King Kong and the White Woman: Hustler Magazine and the Demonization of Black Masculinity." *Violence Against Women* 4:291–307.

————. 2006. "The White Man's Burden: Gonzo Pornography and the Construction of Black Masculinity." *Yale Journal of Law and Feminism* 18:283–297.

Donnelly, Jack. 2003. *Universal Human Rights in Theory and Practice*. 2nd ed. Ithaca, N.Y.: Cornell University Press.

Douglass, Frederick. 1845/1986. *Narrative of the Life of Frederick Douglass*. (1845) New York: Penguin.

————. 1855/1987. *My Bondage and My Freedom*. Edited by William Andrew. Chicago: University of Chicago Press, 1987.

Dumait-Harper, Catherine. 2002. *Regarding "The Responsibility to Protect"* [webpage]. Global Policy Forum 2002 [viewed 25 July 2006]. Available from http://www.globalpolicy.org/empire/humanint/2002/0215msfspeech.htm.

Dworkin, Andrea. 1983. *Right Wing Women.* New York: Perigee Books.
————. 1987. *Intercourse.* New York: Free Press.
————. 1993. "Feminism: An Agenda." In *Letters from a War Zone,* by Andrea Dworkin. Brooklyn, N.Y.: Lawrence Hill Books.
"Eight Million Americans Rescued from Poverty with Redefinition of Term." 1999. *The Onion,* 10 November.
Elshtain, Jean Bethke. 1997. "Moral Woman and Immoral Man: A Consideration of the Public Private Split and Its Political Ramifications." In *Contemporary Political Philosophy: An Anthology,* edited by Robert E. Goodin and Phillip Pettit. Malden, Mass.: Blackwell Publishing.
Emery, Erin. 2002. "'Purity Ball' in Colorado Springs Focuses on Healthy Relationships and Abstinence." *Denver Post,* 7 March.
Enloe, Cynthia. 2002a. "Demilitarization—Or More of the Same? Feminist Questions to Ask in the Postwar Moment." In *The Postwar Moment: Militaries, Masculinities and International Peacekeeping, Bosnia and the Netherlands,* edited by Cynthia Cockburn and Dubravka Zarkov. London: Lawrence and Wishart.
————. 2002b. *Maneuvers: The International Politics of Militarizing Women's Lives.* Berkeley: University of California Press.
————. 2004. "'Gender' is Not Enough: The Need for a Feminist Consciousness." *International Affairs* 80:95–98.
Evans, Gareth, and Mohamed Sahnoun. 2002. "The Responsibility to Protect." *Foreign Affairs* 81:99–110.
Falwell, Jerry. 1981. "An Agenda for the Eighties." In *The Fundamentalist Phenomenon: The Resurgence of Conservative Christianity,* edited by Jerry Falwell (with Ed Dobson and Ed Hindson). Garden City, N.Y.: Doubleday and Company.
————. 1987. *Strength for the Journey: An Autobiography.* New York: Simon and Schuster.
Fanon, Frantz. 1957/1969. "French Intellectuals and Democrats, and the Algerian Revolution." In *Toward the African Revolution: Political Essays.* Translated by Haakon Chavelier. New York: Grove.
————. 1959/1965a. "Algeria Unveiled." In *A Dying Colonialism.* Translated by Haakon Chavelier. New York: Grove.
————. 1959/1965b. "Algeria's European Minority." In *A Dying Colonialism.* Translated by Haakon Chavelier. New York: Grove.
————. 1961/1968. *The Wretched of the Earth.* Translated by Constance Farrington. New York: Grove.
Farer, Tom J., Daniele Archibugi, Chris Brown, Neta C. Crawford, Thomas G. Weiss, and Nicholas J. Wheeler. 2005. "Roundtable: Humanitarian Intervention After 9/11." *International Relations* 19:211–250.
Fausto-Sterling, Anne. 2000. *Sexing the Body: Gender Politics and the Construction of Sexuality.* New York: Basic Books.
Feinberg, Joel. 1980. "Duties, Rights, and Claims." In *Rights, Justice and the Bounds of Liberty,* edited by Joel Feinberg. Princeton, N.J.: Princeton University Press.
Ferguson, Ann. 2005. "Butler, Sex/Gender, and a Postmodern Gender Theory." In *Feminist Interventions in Ethics and Politics,* edited by Barbara S. Andrew, Jean Keller, and Lisa H. Schwartzman. Lanham, Md.: Rowman and Littlefield.

Firestone, Shulamith. 1980. "From *The Dialectic of Sex.*" In *Politics of Housework,* edited by Ellen Malos. London: Allison and Busby.

Fischer, Marilyn. 2000. "Jane Addams's Pragmatist Pacifism." In *Peacemaking: Lessons from the Past, Visions for the Future,* edited by Judith Presler and Sally J. Scholz. Atlanta: Rodopi Press.

———. 2003a. "Introduction." to Jane Addams, 1907. *Newer Ideals of Peace.* Edited by Marilyn Fischer and Judy D. Whipps. Bristol, England: Thoemmes Press.

———. 2003b. "Introduction." to Jane Addams. *Addams's Essays and Speeches on Peace.* Edited by Marilyn Fischer and Judy D. Whipps. Bristol, England: Thoemmes Press.

Fisher, Berenice, and Joan C. Tronto. 1990. "Toward a Feminist Theory of Caring." In *Circles of Care,* edited by Emily Abel and Margaret Nelson. Albany, N.Y.: SUNY Press.

Fraser, Nancy. 2005. "Mapping the Feminist Imagination: From Redistribution to Recognition to Representation." *Constellations* 12:295–307.

Frazer, James George. 1890/1991. *The Golden Bough: A Study in Magic and Religion.* New York: Oxford University Press.

Freeman, Samuel. 2006. "Frontiers of Justice: The Capabilities Approach vs. Contractarianism." *Texas Law Review* 85:385–430.

Friedan, Betty. 1963. *The Feminine Mystique.* New York: W.W. Norton.

Friedman, Marilyn. 1997. "Autonomy and Social Relationships: Rethinking the Feminist Critique." In *Feminists Rethink the Self,* edited by Diana Tietjens Meyers. Boulder, Colo.: Westview Press.

Frye, Marilyn. 1983. *The Politics of Reality: Essays in Feminist Theory.* Freedom, Calif.: Crossing Press.

Frye, Marilyn, and Carolyn Shafer. 1977. "Rape and Respect." In *Feminism and Philosophy,* edited by Mary Vetterling-Braggin, Frederick Elliston, et al. Totowa, N.J.: Littlefield, Adams and Company.

Gilligan, Carol. 1982. *In a Different Voice: Psychological Theory and Women's Development.* Cambridge, Mass.: Harvard University Press.

Goffman, Erving. 1963. *Stigma: Notes on the Management of Spoiled Identity.* New York: Simon and Schuster.

Goodhart, Michael. 2005. *Democracy as Human Rights: Freedom and Equality in the Age of Globalization.* New York: Routledge.

Gould, Carol C. 2004. *Globalizing Democracy and Human Rights.* New York: Cambridge University Press.

Gray, J. Glenn. 1959/1967. *The Warriors.* New York: Harper and Row.

Griffith, R. Marie. 1997. *God's Daughters: Evangelical Women and the Power of Submission.* Berkeley: University of California Press.

Grossberg, Lawrence. 1992. *We Gotta Get Out of This Place: Popular Conservatism and Postmodern Culture.* New York: Routledge.

Grossinger, Richard. 2004. "Abu Ghraib: A Howl." In *Abu Ghraib: The Politics of Torture,* sponsored by the Society for the Study of Native Arts and Sciences. Berkeley: North Atlantic Books.

Gunning, Isabelle R. 2005. "Female Genital Surgeries: Eradication Measures at the Western Local Level—A Cautionary Tale." In *Genital Cutting and Transnational Sis-*

terhood: Disputing U.S. Polemics, edited by Stanlie M. James and Claire C. Robertson. Urbana, Ill.: University of Illinois Press.

Haberman, Clyde. 2006. "Two Protests. One Study in Contrasts." *New York Times,* 27 June.

Habermas, Jürgen. 2003. "From Kant to Hegel and Back Again." In *Truth and Justification,* translated by Barbara Fultner. Cambridge, Mass.: MIT Press.

Hamilton, Alice. 1943/1985. *Exploring the Dangerous Trades.* New York: Little, Brown and Company.

Hankivsky, Olena. 2006. "Imagining Ethical Globalization: The Contributions of a Care Ethic." *Journal of Global Ethics* 2:91–110.

Haraway, Donna J. 1991. "A Manifesto for Cyborgs: Science, Technology, and Socialist Feminism in the 1980s." In *Simians, Cyborgs, and Women: The Reinvention of Nature,* by Donna Haraway. New York: Routledge.

———. 2004. "A Manifesto for Cyborgs: Science, Technology, and Socialist Feminism in the 1980s." In *The Haraway Reader.* New York: Routledge.

Harding, Sandra. 1986. *The Science Question in Feminism.* Ithaca, N.Y.: Cornell University Press.

———. 1991. *Whose Science? Whose Knowledge? Thinking from Women's Lives.* Ithaca, N.Y.: Cornell University Press.

Hardisty, Jean. 1999. *Mobilizing Resentment: Conservative Resurgence from the John Birch Society to the Promise Keepers.* Boston: Beacon Press.

Harris, Adrienne and Ynestra King, eds. 1989. *Rocking the Ship of State: Toward a Feminist Peace Politics.* Boulder, Colo.: Westview Press.

Harris, Angela. 1990. "Race and Essentialism in Feminist Legal Theory." *Stanford Law Review* 42:581–616.

Harris, John F. 2001. "God Gave U.S. 'What We Deserve,' Falwell Says." *Washington Post,* 14 September.

Hart, H.L.A. 1966. *Law, Liberty, and Morality.* New York: Vintage.

Hartsock, Nancy C. M. 1983. *Money, Sex, and Power: Toward a Feminist Historical Materialism.* Boston: Northeastern University Press.

———. 2006. "Experience, Embodiment, and Epistemologies." *Hypatia* 21:178–183.

Haskell, Thomas L. 1998. *Objectivity is Not Neutrality: Explanatory Schemes in History.* Baltimore: Johns Hopkins University Press.

Hayden, Robert M. 2003. "Biased 'Justice': Humanrightsism and the International Criminal Tribunal for the Former Yugoslavia." In *The Lessons of Kosovo: The Dangers of Humanitarian Intervention,* edited by Aleksandar Jovic. Peterborough, Ontario: Broadview Press.

Hegel, G.W.F. 1807/1967. *The Phenomenology of Mind.* Translated by J.B. Baillie. New York: Harper and Row.

Heinbecker, Paul. 1995. "Foreword." In *The "New Peacekeeping" and European Security: German and Canadian Interests and Issues,* edited by Hans-Georg Ehrhart and David G. Haglund. Baden Baden: Verlagsgesellschaft.

Held, Virginia. 1993. *Feminist Morality: Transforming Culture, Society, and Politics.* Chicago: University of Chicago Press.

———. 2002. "Moral Subjects: The Natural and The Normative." Presidential

Address. *Proceedings and Addresses of the American Philosophical Association.* Newark, Del. November.

———. 2006. *The Ethics of Care: Personal, Political, and Global.* New York: Oxford University Press.

Herman, Judith. 1992/1997. *Trauma and Recovery.* New York: Basic Books.

Herman, Sondra R. 1969. *Eleven Against War.* Stanford, Calif.: Hoover Institution Press.

Heyes, Cressida J. 2006. "Changing Race, Changing Sex: The Ethics of Self-Transformation." *Journal of Social Philosophy* 37:266–282.

Hitt, Jack. 2004. "Island of the Damned." In *Naked: Writers Uncover the Way We Live on Earth,* edited by Susan Zakin. New York: Four Walls Eight Windows.

Hobbes, Thomas. 1651/1968. *Leviathan.* Edited by C. B. McPherson. New York: Pelican.

Hochschild, Adam. 2005. *Bury the Chains: Prophets and Rebels in the Fight to Free an Empire's Slaves.* New York: Houghton Mifflin.

Hochschild, Arlie. 1983. *The Managed Heart: Commercialization of Human Feeling.* Berkeley: University of California Press.

———. 1997. *The Time Bind: When Work Becomes Home and Home Becomes Work.* New York: Henry Holt.

Ho, Mae-Wan. 1997. "The Unholy Alliance." *The Ecologist* 27:152–158.

Hondagneu-Sotelo, Pierrette. 1994. "Regulating the Unregulated?: Domestic Workers Social Networks." *Social Problems* 41:50–64.

———. 2001. *Doméstica: Immigrant Women Cleaning and Caring in the Shadows of Affluence.* Berkeley: University of California Press.

Honig, Bonnie, ed. 1995. *Feminist Interpretations of Hannah Arendt.* University Park: Pennsylvania State University.

Honneth, Axel. 1992/1995. *The Struggle for Recognition: The Moral Grammar of Social Conflicts.* Translated by Joel Anderson. Cambridge: Polity.

———. 2001. "Invisibility: On the Epistemology of Recognition." *Aristotelian Society Supplementary Volume* 75:111–126.

Hochschild, Arlie Russell. 2002. "Love and Gold." In *Global Woman: Nannies, Maids and Sex Workers in the New Economy,* edited by Barbara Ehrenreich and Arlie Russell Hochschild. New York: Henry Holt.

Howard, Michael. 1978. *War and the Liberal Conscience.* New Brunswick, N.J.: Rutgers University Press.

Huddy, Leonie, Stanley Feldman, Charles Taber, and Gallya Lahav. 2005. "Threat, Anxiety, and Support of Antiterrorism Policies." *American Journal of Political Science* 49:593–608.

Hughes, Richard T. 2003. *Myths America Lives By.* Urbana, Ill.: University of Illinois Press.

Human Security Centre. 2006. *2005 Human Security Report: War and Peace in the 21st Century* [book in pdf] 2005 [cited 26 July 2006]. Available from http://www .humansecurityreport.info/.

Hume, David. 1978. *Treatise on Human Nature.* Edited, with an Analytical Index, by L.A. Selby-Bigge, Second Edition with text revised and notes by P.H. Nidditch. Oxford: Oxford University Press.

Hunter, James Davison. 1987. *Evangelicalism: The Coming Generation*. Chicago: University of Chicago Press.

Hyppolite, Jean. 1979. *Genesis and Structure of Hegel's "Phenomenology of Spirit."* Translated by Samuel Cherniak and John Heckman. Chicago: Northwestern University Press.

International Commission on Intervention and State Sovereignty. 2001a. *The Responsibility to Protect*. Ottawa: International Development Research Centre.

———. 2001b. *The Responsibility to Protect: Research, Bibliography, Background*. Ottawa: International Development Research Centre.

Jackson, Cecile. 1998. "Women and Poverty or Gender and Well-Being?" *Journal of International Affairs* 52:67–81.

Jacobs, Harriet. 1857/1987. "Incidents in the Life of a Slave Girl." In *The Classic Slave Narratives*, edited by Henry Louis Gates, Jr. New York: Mentor.

Jaggar, Alison M. 2000. "Ethics Naturalized: Feminism's Contribution to Moral Epistemology." *Metaphilosophy* 31:452–468.

———. 2005a. "Global Responsibility and Western Feminism." In *Feminist Interventions in Ethics and Politics*, edited by Barbara S. Andrew, Jean Keller, and Lisa H. Schwartzman. New York: Rowman and Littlefield.

———. 2005b. "'Saving Amina': Global Justice for Women and Intercultural Dialogue." *Ethics and International Affairs* 19:55–75.

———. 2006. "The Poorest of the Poor: Justice and the Feminization of Global Poverty." Presented at International Scholars Conference: Development, Globalization, and Global Ethics, held at Colorado State University (April).

James, Stanlie M., and Claire C. Robertson. 2005. "Introduction: Reimaging Transnational Sisterhood." In *Genital Cutting and Transnational Sisterhood: Disputing U.S. Polemics*, edited by Stanlie M. James and Claire C. Robertson. Urbana, Ill.: University of Illinois Press.

Jensen, Derrick. 2002. *The Culture of Make Believe*. New York: Context Books.

Jensen, Robert. 2004a. "Blow Bangs and Cluster Bombs: The Cruelty of Men and Americans." In *Not For Sale: Feminists Resisting Prostitution and Pornography*, edited by Rebecca Whisnant and Christine Stark. Melbourne, Australia: Spinifex Press.

———. 2004b. "A Cruel Edge: The Painful Truth About Today's Pornography—and What Men Can Do About It." Abridged version in Ms., Spring 2004, 54–58. Full text at http://uts.cc.utexas.edu/~rjensen/freelance/pornography&cruelty.htm.

———. 2004c. *Citizens of the Empire: The Struggle to Reclaim our Humanity*. San Francisco: City Lights.

———. 2007. *Getting Off: Pornography and the End of Masculinity*. Cambridge, Mass.: South End Press.

Johnson, Kenneth C., and Betty-Anne Davis. 2005. "Outcomes of Planned Home Births with Certified Professional Midwives: Large Prospective Study in North America." *British Medical Journal* 330:1416–1422.

Joint European Union–Latin American and the Caribbean Conference. 2002. Final Report: Conference on "Building Capacities for Peacekeeping and Women's Dimensions in Peace Processes," the Joint European Union–Latin American and the Caribbean Conference. Paper read at Building Capacities for Peacekeeping and Women's Dimensions in Peace Processes, 2–4 November, at Santiago, Chile.

Jovic, Aleksander, ed. 2003. *Lessons of Kosovo: The Dangers of Humanitarian Intervention.* Peterborough, Ontario: Broadview Press.

Joyce, Kathryn. 2006. "Arrows for the War." *The Nation,* 27 November. Available at http://www.thenation.com/doc/20061127/joyce.

Kahan, Dan M. 1999. "The Progressive Appropriation of Disgust." In *The Passions of Law,* edited by Susan A. Bandes. New York: New York University Press.

Kanbur, Ravi, and Lyn Squire. 2001. "The Evolution of Thinking About Poverty: Exploring the Interactions." Revised version in *Frontiers of Development Economics: The Future in Perspective,* edited by Gerald M. Meier and Joseph E. Stiglitz. Oxford: Oxford University Press.

Kant, Immanuel. 1795/2006. *Toward Perpetual Peace and Other Writings on Politics, Peace and History.* Edited by Pauline Kleingeld. New Haven, Conn.: Yale University Press.

Kaudjhis-Offoumou, Françoise. 1994. *Marriage en Côte d'Ivoire.* Abidjan: Éditions KOF. Translation by Claire C. Robertson in *Genital Cutting and Transnational Sisterhood: Disputing U.S. Polemics,* edited by Stanlie M. James and Claire C. Robertson. Urbana, Ill.: University of Illinois Press.

Kimmel, Michael. 2006. "Globalization and its Mal(e)contents: The Gendered Moral and Political Economy of the Extreme Right." Paper prepared for the "Gender Identity in a Globalized Society" conference organized by the Social Trends Institute and held in Barcelona, Spain, 13–14 October.

Kintz, Linda. 1997. *Between Jesus and the Market: The Emotions that Matter in Right-Wing America.* Durham, N.C.: Duke University Press.

Kittay, Eva Feder. 1999. *Love's Labor: Essays on Women, Equality and Dependency.* New York: Routledge.

Kleinberg, S.J. 2005. "How Did the Debate about Widows' Pensions Shape Relief Programs for Single Mothers, 1900–1940?" In *Women and Social Movements in the United States, 1600–2000,* edited by Kathryn Kish Sklar and Thomas Dublin. Alexander Street Press, L.L.C. 1997–2006. Available from http://www.alexanderstreet 6.com.

Knock, Thomas J. 1992. *To End All Wars: Woodrow Wilson and the Quest for a New World Order.* New York: Oxford University Press.

Kohn, Margaret. 2005. "Frederick Douglass's Master-Slave Dialectic." *Journal of Politics* 67:497–514.

Kojev, Alexander. 1969. *Introduction to the Reading of Hegel.* Translated by James H. Nichols Jr. New York: Basic Books.

Kramer, Michael. 1986. "Are You Running with Me, Jesus? Televangelist Pat Robertson Goes for the White House." *New York Magazine,* 18 August.

Kuhn, Thomas S. 1970. *The Structure of Scientific Revolutions.* 2nd ed. Chicago: University of Chicago Press.

Kukla, Rebecca. 2005. *Mass Hysteria: Medicine, Culture, and Mothers' Bodies.* Lanham, Md.: Rowman and Littlefield.

Kvinna, Kvinna till. 2006. *Women in the Peace Process: Questions and Answers About Resolution 1325* [internet], 8 May 2006 [cited 12 May 2006 2006]. Available from http://www.iktk.se/english/thematic_info/resolution_1325/1325faq.html.

LaHaye, Beverly. 1976. *The Spirit-Controlled Woman.* Eugene, Ore.: Harvest House Publishers.

———. 1980. *I Am a Woman by God's Design*. Old Tappan, N.J.: Fleming H. Revell Company.

———. 1984. *The Restless Woman*. Grand Rapids, Mich.: Zondervan Publishing House.

Laino, Charlene. 2006. "C-Section Rates: Obesity to Blame?" *WebMD*, 9 May. Available at http://www.webmd.com/content/Article/122/114508.htm. Accessed October 19, 2006.

Lan, Pei-Chia. 2003. "Maid or Madam? Filipina Migrant Workers and the Continuity of Domestic Labor." *Gender and Society* 17:187–208.

Lane, Sandra D., and Robert A. Rubinstein. 1996. "Judging the Other: Responding to Traditional Female Genital Surgeries." *Hastings Center Report* 26:31–40.

Larrabee, Mary Jeanne. 1993. "Gender and Moral Development: A Challenge for Feminist Theory." In *An Ethic of Care: Feminist and Interdisciplinary Perspectives*, edited by M.J. Larrabee. New York: Routledge.

Las Casas, Bartolemé. 1974. *The Devastation of the Indies: A Brief Account*. Translated by Herma Briffault. Baltimore: Johns Hopkins University Press.

Lazreg, Marnia. 1994. *The Eloquence of Silence: Algerian Women in Question*. New York: Routledge.

Leader, Nicholas. 2000. "The Politics of Principle: The Principles of Humanitarian Action in Practice." London: The Humanitarian Policy Group at the Overseas Development Institute.

Lienesch, Michael. 1993. *Redeeming America: Piety and Politics in the New Christian Right*. Chapel Hill: The University of North Carolina Press.

Linn, James W. 1935/2000. *Jane Addams: A Biography*. Urbana, Ill.: University of Illinois Press.

Locke, John. 1980. *Second Treatise of Government*. Indianapolis, Ind.: Hackett Publishing Company.

Longino, Helen E. 1990. *Science as Social Knowledge: Values and Objectivity in Scientific Inquiry*. Princeton, N.J.: Princeton University Press.

Lorraine, Tamsin. 1990. *Gender, Identity, and the Production of Meaning*. Boulder, Colo.: Westview Press.

Lugones, Maria. 2003. *Pilgrimages/Peregrinajes: Theorizing Coalition Against Multiple Oppressions*. Lanham, Md.: Rowman and Littlefield.

Lukacs, György. 1933/1975. *The Young Hegel: Studies in the Relations Between Dialectics and Economics*. London: Merlin.

Machiavelli, Niccoló. 1521/2003. *Art of War*. Translated by Christopher Lynch. Chicago: University of Chicago Press.

Mackenzie, Catriona, and Natalie Stoljar, eds. 2000. *Relational Autonomy: Feminist Perspectives on Autonomy, Agency, and the Social Self*. New York: Oxford University Press.

Maguire, Marjorie Reiley. 1989. "Symbiosis, Biology, and Personalization." In *Abortion Rights and Fetal "Personhood"*, edited by Edd Doerr and James W. Prescott. Long Beach, Calif.: Centerline Press.

Mahajan, Rahul. 2002. *The New Crusade: America's War on Terrorism*. New York: Monthly Review Press.

———. 2003. *Full Spectrum Dominance: U.S. Power in Iraq and Beyond*. New York: Seven Stories Press.

Mahowald, Mary Briody, ed. 1994. *Philosophy of Woman: An Anthology of Classic to Current Concepts*. 3rd ed. Indianapolis, Ind.: Hackett Publishing Company.

Marten, Kimberly Zisk. 2004. *Enforcing the Peace: Learning from the Imperial Past*. New York: Columbia University Press.

Martin, Andrew. 2006. "The Package May Say Healthy, But This Grocer Begs to Differ." *New York Times*, 6 November.

Martin, Theodora Penny. 1987. *The Sound of Our Own Voices: Women's Study Clubs, 1860–1910*. Boston: Beacon Press.

Marx, Karl and Frederick Engels. 1848/1998. *The Communist Manifesto*. London: Verso.

Mason, Gail. 2002. *The Spectacle of Violence: Homophobia, Gender, and Knowledge*. New York: Routledge.

Mason, Gail, Nancy C.M. Hartsock, and Karen Houle. 2006. "Symposium: *The Spectacle of Violence: Homophobia, Gender, and Knowledge*." *Hypatia* 21:174–206.

Mason, Otis Tufton. 1898. *Woman's Share in Primitive Culture*. New York: D. Appleton and Company.

McDaniel, Carl, and John Gowdy. 2000. *Paradise for Sale: A Parable of Nature*. Berkeley: University of California Press.

McGinley, Phyllis. 1963. "Help!" *Ladies Home Journal* 80:64.

McGirr, Lisa. 2001. *Suburban Warriors: The Origins of the New American Right*. Princeton, N.J.: Princeton University Press.

Mead, George Herbert. 1917. "Democracy's Issues in the World War." *Chicago Herald*, 4 August. http://spartan.ac.brocku.ca/~lward/Mead/pubs/Mead_1917i.html.

Meagher, Gabrielle. 2002. "Is it Wrong to Pay for Housework?" *Hypatia* 17:52–66.

Meyers, Diana Tietjens. 1987. "The Socialized Individual and Individual Autonomy: An Intersection Between Philosophy and Psychology." In *Women and Moral Theory*, edited by Eva Feder Kittay and Diana T. Meyers. Totowa, N.J.: Rowman and Littlefield.

———. 1989. *Self, Society, and Personal Choice*. New York: Columbia University Press.

———. 1994. *Subjection and Subjectivity: Psychoanalytic Feminism and Moral Philosophy*. New York: Routledge.

———. 2002. *Gender in the Mirror: Cultural Imagery and Women's Agency*. New York: Oxford University Press.

———. 2003. "Gendered Work and Individual Autonomy." In *Recognition, Responsibility, and Rights*, edited by Robin N. Fiore and Hilde Lindemann Nelson. Lanham, Md.: Rowman and Littlefield.

Miller, William Ian. 1997. *The Anatomy of Disgust*. Cambridge, Mass.: Harvard University Press.

Mills, Charles W. 1997. *The Racial Contract*. Ithaca, N.Y.: Cornell University Press.

Mills, Patricia Jagentowicz, ed. 1996. *Feminist Interpretations of G.W.F. Hegel*. University Park, Pa.: Pennsylvania State University.

Minow, Martha. 1998. *Between Vengeance and Forgiveness: Facing History after Genocide and Mass Violence*. Boston: Beacon Press.

———. 2002. *Breaking the Cycles of Hatred: Memory, Law and Repair*. Princeton, N.J.: Princeton University Press.

Mohanty, Satya. 1993. "The Epistemic Status of Cultural Identity: On *Beloved* and the Postcolonial Condition." *Cultural Critique* 24:41–80.

———. 2001. "Can Our Values Be Objective? On Ethics, Aesthetics, and Progressive Politics." *New Literary History* 32:803–833.

Money, John, and Anke Ehrhardt. 1972. *Man and Woman, Boy and Girl*. Baltimore: Johns Hopkins University Press.

Morgan, Lewis Henry. 1877/1963. *Ancient Society*. New York: The World Publishing Co.

Nakaya, Sumie. 2003. "Women and Gender Equality in Peace Processes: From Women at the Negotiating Table to Postwar Structural Reforms in Guatemala and Somalia." *Global Governance* 9:459–476.

Narayan, Deepa, Robert Chambers, Meera K. Shah and Patti Petesch. 2000. *Crying Out for Change: Voices of the Poor*. New York: World Bank Publications.

Narayan, Uma. 1995. "Colonialism and Its Others: Considerations on Rights and Care Discourses." *Hypatia* 10:133–40.

Nash, George H. 1996. *The Life of Herbert Hoover: Master of Emergencies, 1917–1918*. New York: W.W. Norton.

———. 2003. "Determined Humanitarians: Herbert and Lou Henry Hoover in Europe." In *Uncommon Americans: The Lives and Legacies of Herbert and Lou Henry Hoover*, edited by Timothy Walch. Westport, Conn.: Praeger.

Nasmyth, George. 1916/1973. *Social Progress and the Darwinian Theory: A Study of Force as a Factor in Human Relations*. New York: Garland Publishing, Inc.

National Center for Health Statistics. 2004. "Current Hospice Care Patients." http://www.cdc.gov/nchs/data/nhhcsd/curhospicecare00.pdf. Accessed November 3, 2006.

Nelson, Hilde Lindemann, and James Lindemann Nelson. 1996. "Justice in the Allocation of Health Care Resources: A Feminist Account." In *Feminism and Bioethics: Beyond Reproduction*, edited by Susan M. Wolf. New York: Oxford University Press.

Nelson, James Lindemann. 2001. "Knowledge, Authority and Identity: A Prolegomenon to an Epistemology of the Clinic." *Theoretical Medicine* 22:107–122.

Newton, Lisa H., and Catherine K. Dillingham. 2002. *Watersheds 3: Ten Cases in Environmental Ethics*. Belmont, Calif.: Wadsworth.

Nickel, James. 2006. "Are Human Rights Mainly Implemented by Intervention?" In *Rawls's Law of Peoples: A Realistic Utopia?*, edited by Rex Martin and David Reidy. Oxford: Blackwell Publishing.

Nicolai, G.F. 1918. *The Biology of War*. New York: Century.

Noddings, Nel. 1984. *Caring: A Feminine Approach to Ethics and Moral Education*. Berkeley: University of California Press.

Norberg-Hodge, Helena, Peter Goering, and John Page. 2001. "From Global to Local: Sowing the Seeds of Community." In *From the Ground Up: Rethinking Industrial Agriculture*, by Helen Norberg-Hodge, Peter Goering, and John Page. London: Zed Books.

Nussbaum, Martha. 1997. "Capabilities and Human Rights." *Fordham Law Review* 66:273–300.

———. 1999. "'Secret Sewers of Vice': Disgust, Bodies, and the Law." In *The Passions of Law*, edited by Susan A. Bandes. New York: New York University Press.

————. 2000. *Women and Human Development: The Capabilities Approach*. New York: Cambridge University Press.

————. 2001. *Upheavals of Thought: The Intelligence of Emotions*. Cambridge: Cambridge University Press.

————. 2003. "Capabilities as Fundamental Entitlements: Sen and Social Justice." *Feminist Economics* 9:33–59.

————. 2004a. "Beyond the Social Contract: Capabilities and Global Justice." *Oxford Development Studies* 32:3–18.

————. 2004b. *Hiding from Humanity: Disgust, Shame, and the Law*. Princeton, N.J.: Princeton University Press.

————. 2006. *Frontiers of Justice*. Cambridge, Mass.: Harvard University Press.

Olshansky, Barbara. 2005. "What Does It Mean to Be an 'Enemy Combatant'?" In *America's Disappeared: Secret Imprisonment, Detainees, and the "War on Terror,"* edited by Rachel Meeropol. New York: Seven Stories Press.

Ortner, Sherry, and Harriet Whitehead, eds. 1981. *Sexual Meanings: The Cultural Construction of Gender and Sexuality*. Cambridge: Cambridge University Press.

Pence, Gregory E. 2002a. *Designer Food: Mutant Harvest or Breadbasket of the World?* Lanham, Md.: Rowman and Littlefield.

————, ed. 2002b. *The Ethics of Food: A Reader for the 21st Century*. Lanham, Md.: Rowman and Littlefield.

Perry, Michael. 1998. *The Idea of Human Rights: Four Inquiries*. Oxford: Oxford University Press.

Peters, Julie and Andrea Wolper. 1995. "Introduction." In *Women's Rights, Human Rights: International Feminist Perspectives*, edited by Julie Peters and Andrea Wolper. New York: Routledge.

Peterson, V. Spike and Laura Parisi. 1998. "Are Women Human? It's Not an Academic Question." In *Human Rights Fifty Years On: A Reappraisal*, edited by Tony Evans. Manchester and New York: Manchester University Press.

Phillips, D.E. 1916. "The Psychology of War." *The Scientific Monthly* 3:569–578.

Philpott, Daniel. 2001. *Revolutions in Sovereignty: How Ideas Shaped Modern International Relations*. Princeton, N.J.: Princeton University Press.

Piercy, Marge, and Jane Freeman. 1972. "Getting Together: How to Start a Consciousness-Raising Group." Available at http://research.umbc.edu/~korenman/wmst/crguide2.html. Accessed October 2005.

Pieterse, Jan Nederveen. 2004. *Globalization and Culture: Global Mélange*. Lanham, Md.: Rowman and Littlefield.

Pinker, Robert. 1999. "Do Poverty Definitions Matter?" In *The International Glossary on Poverty*, edited by David Gordon and Paul Spicker. London: Zed Books.

Plumwood, Val. 1993. *Feminism and the Mastery of Nature*. New York: Routledge.

Pogge, Thomas, ed. 2001a. *Global Justice*. Malden, Mass.: Blackwell Publishing.

————. 2001b. "How Should Human Rights Be Conceived?" In *The Philosophy of Human Rights*, edited by Patrick Hayden. St. Paul, Minn.: Paragon Press.

————. 2003. *World Poverty and Human Rights*. Malden, Mass.: Blackwell Press.

Pogge, Thomas, and Sanjay Reddy. 2003. "Unknown: The Extent, Distribution, and Trend of Global Income Poverty," Version 3.4. The Institute of Social Analysis, 26 July.

Pollan, Michael. 2006. *The Omnivore's Dilemma: A Natural History of Four Meals*. New York: Penguin Press.

Prince, Mary. 1831/1987. "The History of Mary Prince." In *The Classic Slave Narratives*, edited by Henry Louis Gates, Jr. New York: Mentor.

Rao, Arati. 2001. "Right in the Home: Feminist Theoretical Perspectives on International Human Rights." In *The Philosophy of Human Rights*, edited by Patrick Hayden. St. Paul, Minn.: Paragon Press.

Rawls, John. 1971/1999. *A Theory of Justice*. Cambridge, Mass.: Harvard University Press.

———. 1993/1996. *Political Liberalism*. New York: Columbia University Press.

———. 1999. *The Law of Peoples*. Cambridge, Mass.: Harvard University Press.

———. 2001. *Justice as Fairness*. Cambridge, Mass.: Harvard University Press.

Razack, Sherene H. 2004. *Dark Threats and White Knights: The Somalia Affair, Peacekeeping, and the New Imperialism*. Toronto: University of Toronto Press.

Rees, Madeleine. 2002. "International Intervention in Bosnia-Herzegovina: The Cost of Ignoring Gender." In *The Postwar Moment: Militaries, Masculinities and International Peacekeeping, Bosnia and the Netherlands*, edited by Cynthia Cockburn and Dubravka Zarkov. London: Lawrence and Wishart.

Richmond, Oliver P. 2004. "UN Peace Operations and the Dilemmas of the Peacebuilding Consensus." *International Peacekeeping* 11:83–101.

Roberts, Dorothy. 1997. *Killing the Black Body: Race, Reproduction, and the Meaning of Liberty*. New York: Pantheon.

Robinson, Fiona. 1999. *Globalizing Care: Ethics, Feminist Theory, and International Relations*. Boulder, Colo.: Westview Press.

Rollins, Judith. 1985. *Between Women: Domestics and Their Employers*. Philadelphia: Temple University Press.

Romero, Mary. 1988. "Chicanas Modernize Domestic Service." *Qualitative Sociology* 11:4.

———. 1992. *Maid in the U.S.A.* New York: Routledge.

Ross, Ellen, and Rayna Rapp. 1997. "Sex and Society: A Research Note from Social History and Anthropology." Reprinted in *The Gender/Sexuality Reader: Culture, History, Political Economy*, edited by Roger N. Lancaster and Micaela di Leonardo. New York: Routledge.

Rozin, Paul, and April Fallon. 1987. "A Perspective on Disgust." *Psychological Review* 94:23–41.

Rubin, Gayle. 1975. "The Traffic in Women: Notes on the 'Political Economy' of Sex." In *Toward an Anthropology of Women*, edited by Rayna Reiter. New York: Monthly Review Press.

Ruddick, Sara. 1989. *Maternal Thinking: Toward a Politics of Peace*. Boston: Beacon Press.

Rudnick, P. and K. Andersen. 1989. "The Irony Epidemic: The Dark Dide of Fiestaware and the Flintstones." In *Utne Reader*, May/June.

Salleh, Ariel Kay. 1984. "Deeper Than Deep Ecology: The Ecofeminist Connection." *Environmental Ethics* 6:335–41.

Sarachild, Kathie. 1978. "Consciousness-Raising: A Radical Weapon." In *Feminist Revolution*. New York: Random House. Available at http://scriptorium.lib.duke.edu/wlm/fem/sarachild.html. Accessed October 2005.

Sartre, Jean Paul. 1943/1966. *Being and Nothingness*. Translated by Hazel B. Barnes. New York: Washington Square.

———. 1961. "Preface." In *The Wretched of the Earth* by Frantz Fanon. Translated by Constance Farrington. New York: Grove.

———. 1966. "Portrait of the Antisemite." In *Existentialism from Dostoevsky to Sartre*, edited by Walter Kaufmann. New York: The World Publishing Company.

Sassen, Saskia. 2002. "Global Cities and Survival Circuits." In *Global Woman: Nannies, Maids and Sex Workers in the New Economy*, edited by Barbara Ahrenreich and Arlie Russell Hochschild. New York: Henry Holt.

Schmitt, John, and Dean Baker. 2006. "Old Europe Goes to Work: Rising Employment Rates in the European Union." *Center for Economic and Policy Research Issue Brief* (September). http://www.cepr.net/publications/europe_2006_09_19.pdf. Accessed October 16, 2006.

Scott, Anne Firor. 1991. *Natural Allies: Women's Associations in American History*. Urbana, Ill.: University of Illinois Press.

Sen, Amartya. 1981. *Poverty and Famines*. Oxford: Clarendon Press.

———. 1983. "Poor, Relatively Speaking." *Oxford Economic Papers*, New Series, 35:153–169.

———. 1999. *Development as Freedom*. New York: Oxford University Press.

Sen, Amartya, and Jean Dreze. 1989. *Hunger and Public Action*. Oxford: Clarendon Press.

Sevenhuijsen, Selma L. 1996. *Oordelen met zorg: Feministische beschouwingen over recht, moraal en politiek*. Amsterdam: Boom.

———. 1998. *Citizenship and the Ethics of Care*. London: Routledge.

Sharpley-Whiting, T. Denean. 1997. *Frantz Fanon and Feminism*. Lanham, Md.: Rowman and Littlefield.

Shay, Jonathan. 1994. *Achilles in Vietnam: Combat Trauma and the Undoing of Character*. New York: Simon and Schuster.

Shepard, Ben. 2001. *A War of Nerves: Soldiers and Psychiatrists in the Twentieth Century*. Cambridge, Mass.: Harvard University Press.

SHIRBRIG. 2006. *SHIRBRIG: Standby High Readiness Brigade For United Nations Operations* [cited 7 August 2006]. Available from http://www.shirbrig.dk/index.htm.

Shiva, Vandana. 2000. *Stolen Harvest: The Hijacking of the Global Food Supply*. Cambridge, Mass.: South End Press.

Sinnerbrink, Robert. 2004. "Recognitive Freedom: Hegel and the Problem of Recognition." *Critical Horizons* 5:271–295.

Smith, Adam. 1981. *The Theory of Moral Sentiments*. Indianapolis: Liberty Press.

Smith, Andrea. 2005. *Conquest: Sexual Violence and American Indian Genocide*. Cambridge, Mass.: South End Press.

Smith, Richard Norton. 1984. *An Uncommon Man: The Triumph of Herbert Hoover*. New York: Simon and Schuster.

Spear, Joanna. 2002. "Disarmament and Demobilization." In *Ending Civil Wars: The Implementation of Peace Agreements*, edited by S.J. Stedman, D. Rothchild and E.M. Cousens. Boulder, Colo.: Lynne Rienner.

Spelman, Elizabeth V. 1997. *Fruits of Sorrow*. Boston: Beacon Press.

Spencer, Herbert. 1896. *The Principles of Sociology*. New York: D. Appleton and Co.

Spicker, Paul. 1999. "Definitions of Poverty: Eleven Clusters of Meaning." In *The International Glossary on Poverty*, edited by David Gordon and Paul Spicker. London: Zed Books.

Stange, Mary Zeiss. 2007. "A Dance for Chastity." Retrieved 28 March from the World Wide Web: www.blogs.usatoday.com/oped/2007/03/a_dance_for_cha .html.

Stedman, Stephen John, Donald Rothchild, and Elizabeth M. Cousens, eds. 2002. *Ending Civil Wars: The Implementation of Peace Agreements*. Boulder, Colo.: Lynne Rienner.

Stratton, George Malcolm. April 1916. "The Docility of the Fighter." *International Journal of Ethics* 26:368–376.

Strauss, David Levi. 2004. "Breakdown in the Gray Room: Recent Turns in the Image War." In *Abu Ghraib: The Politics of Torture*, sponsored by the Society for the Study of Native Arts and Sciences. Berkeley: North Atlantic Books.

Suskind, Ron. 2004. "Without a Doubt." *New York Times Magazine*, 17 October.

Swimme, Brian. 1990. "How to Cure a Frontal Lobotomy." In *Reweaving the World: The Emergence of Ecofeminism*, edited by Irene Diamond and Gloria Feman Orenstein. San Francisco: Sierra Club Books.

Tatum, James. 2004. *The Mourner's Song: War and Remembrance from the Iliad to Vietnam*. Chicago: University of Chicago Press.

Teitel, Martin, and Kimberly A. Wilson. 1999. *Genetically Engineered Food: Changing the Nature of Nature*. 2nd edition. Rochester, Vt.: Park Street Press.

Toubia, Nahid. 1995. "Female Genital Mutilation in the Perspective of Sexual and Reproductive Health." In *Report from the Seminar on Female Genital Mutilation, Copenhagen, May 29, 1995*. Copenhagen: Danida.

Tronto, Joan. 1987. "Beyond Gender Difference to a Theory of Care." *Signs* 12:644–663.

———. 1993. *Moral Boundaries: A Political Argument for an Ethic of Care*. New York: Routledge.

———. 1995. "Caring as the Basis for Radical Political Judgments." *Hypatia* 10:141–149.

———. 2002. "The Nanny Question in Feminism." *Hypatia* 17:34–51.

Tylor, Edward Burnett. 1871/1958. *Primitive Culture*. Repr. under the title, *The Origins of Culture*. New York: Harper and Row.

United Nations Population Fund. "Fast Facts on Maternal Mortality and Morbidity." Available at http://www.unfpa.org/mothers/facts.htm. Accessed September 2005.

Van Creveld, Martin. 1991. *The Transformation of War*. New York: Free Press.

———. 2002. *Men, Women, and War: Do Women Belong in the Front Line?* London: Orion.

Veblen, Thorstein. 1914. *The Instinct of Workmanship and the State of the Industrial Arts*. New York: Macmillan.

Waerness, Kari. 1990. "Informal and Formal Care in Old Age: What Is Wrong With the New Ideology in Scandinavia Today?" In *Gender and Caring: Work and Welfare in Britain and Scandinavia*, edited by Clare Ungerson. London: Harvester, Wheatsheaf.

Walker, Margaret Urban. 1998. *Moral Understandings: A Feminist Study in Ethics.* New York: Routledge.

———. 1999. "Getting Out of Line: Alternatives to Life as a Career." In *Mother Time: Women, Aging and Ethics,* edited by Margaret Urban Walker. Lanham, Md.: Rowman and Littlefield.

Walley, Christine J. 2005. "Getting Beyond the Ew! Factor: Rethinking U.S. Approaches to African Female Genital Cutting." In *Genital Cutting and Transnational Sisterhood: Disputing U.S. Polemics,* edited by Stanlie M. James and Claire C. Robertson. Urbana, Ill.: University of Illinois Press.

Walzer, Michael. 2000. *Just and Unjust Wars.* 3rd ed. New York: Basic Books.

Warren, Karen J. 1990. "The Power and Promise of Ecological Feminism." *Environmental Ethics* 12:125–146.

———. 1994. *Ecological Feminism.* London and New York: Routledge.

Weiss, Thomas G. 2004. "The Sunset of Humanitarian Intervention? The Responsibility to Protect in a Unipolar Era." *Security Dialogue* 35:135–154.

West, Cornel. 1999. "Black Strivings in a Twilight Civilization." In *The Cornel West Reader.* New York: Basic Civitas.

West, Robin. 1995. "The Harms of Consensual Sex." *The American Philosophical Association Newsletters* 94:52–55.

Whipps, Judy D. 2003a. "Introduction." to Jane Addams, Emily Balch, and Alice Hamilton. 1915. *Women at the Hague,* edited by Marilyn Fischer and Judy D. Whipps. Bristol, England: Thoemmes Press.

———. 2003b. "Introduction." to Jane Addams. 1922. *Peace and Bread in Time of War,* edited by Marilyn Fischer and Judy D. Whipps. Bristol, England: Thoemmes Press.

Whisnant, Rebecca. 2004. "Confronting Pornography: Some Conceptual Basics." In *Not For Sale: Feminists Resisting Prostitution and Pornography,* edited by Rebecca Whisnant and Christine Stark. Melbourne, Australia: Spinifex Press.

Whisnant, Rebecca, and Christine Stark. 2004. *Not For Sale: Feminists Resisting Prostitution and Pornography.* Melbourne, Australia: Spinifex Press.

White, Julie Anne. 2000. *Democracy, Justice and the Welfare State: Reconstructing Public Care.* University Park, Pa.: Pennsylvania State University Press.

White, Richard. 1991. *"It's Your Misfortune and None of My Own": A New History of the American West.* Norman, Okla.: University of Oklahoma Press.

Wilcox, Clyde. 1992. *God's Warriors: The Christian Right in Twentieth-Century America.* Baltimore, Md.: Johns Hopkins University Press.

Willett, Cynthia. 1995. *Maternal Ethics and Other Slave Moralities.* New York: Routledge.

Williams, Patricia J. 1991. *The Alchemy of Race and Rights: Diary of a Mad Law Professor.* Cambridge, Mass.: Harvard University Press.

Wolf, Susan M., ed. 1996. *Feminism and Bioethics: Beyond Reproduction.* New York: Oxford University Press.

Woodward, Susan L. 2002. "Economic Priorities for Successful Peace Implementation." In *Ending Civil Wars: The Implementation of Peace Agreements,* edited by S.J. Stedman, D. Rothchild and E.M. Cousens. Boulder, Colo.: Lynne Rienner.

Woolf, Virginia. 2006. *Three Guineas.* Annotated and with an introduction by Jane Marcus. Orlando, Fla.: Harcourt.

World Bank. 1990. *The World Development Report.* New York: Oxford University Press.

World Economic Forum. 2005. *Women's Empowerment: Measuring the Global Gender Gap.*

Wosnitzer, R., E. Scharrer, A. Bridges, C. Sun, and R. Liberman. 2007. "Aggression and Sexual Behavior in Best-Selling Pornography: A Content Analysis Update." Paper presented at the International Communication Association Annual Conference, San Francisco.

Yeomans, Matthew. 1999. "Chaos in Colombia." Salon.com, 19 March. Online at http://www.salon.com/news/1999/03/19newsb2.html.

Young, Iris Marion. 1980. "Throwing like a Girl." *Human Studies* 3:137–158.

———. 2003. "The Logic of Masculinist Protection: Reflections on the Current Security State." *Signs* 29:1–24.

———. 2006. "Responsiblity and Global Justice: A Social Connection Model." *Social Philosophy and Policy* 23:102–130.

Zablit, Jocelyne. 2007. "No Sex Please, We're Daddy's Little Girls." Retrieved 28 March from the World Wide Web: www.news.yahoo.com/s/afp/20070322/ts_alt_afp/afplifestyleussexchastity_070322082138.

Zarkov, Dubravka, and Cynthia Cockburn. 2002. "Introduction." In *The Postwar Moment: Militaries, Masculinities and International Peacekeeping, Bosnia and the Netherlands,* edited by Cynthia Cockburn and Dubravka Zarkov. London: Lawrence and Wishart.

Index

ontology, 145, 147, 213n1, 215n32; relational, 66

oppression, 84–85, 89, 94, 107, 112n6, 117, 166–68, 221, 229–30, 233–34, 238–39; of domestic workers, 23–24, 29, 39–40; in industrial meat production, 89; resistance to (*see* resistance); of women, x, xiii, 48, 75, 119, 141, 143–44, 161–62; of workers in public sphere, 30–32

outlaw states, 128

Overseas Development Institute, 193

pacifism, 64, 77

Palestine and Palestinians, 67, 201–202

palliative care, 18

paradigm shift; role of narratives in, 73; toward "responsibility to protect," 181–82, 184–87

parent(s), 55–56, 211–12, 237; *See also* mother(s); father(s)

Parisi, Laura, 142, 144

passions, 211, 222–24, 230–31

patents, 87

paternalism, xi, 34, 62, 194

patriarchy, x, xiii, 13, 35, 49, 156, 163–64, 167, 174n9, 220, 237; deprivation of women's bodily sovereignty in, 161–63

pay. *See* wages

peace, 70–72, 74, 78n3, 79n19, 158, 180–81, 187–89, 192–96, 198n11, 199n12, 199n13, 209

peacekeeping, 185, 197n2, 198n8, 198n12; definition of, 180; as feminist care practice, 186–95

Pence, Gregory, 82, 84, 87–93

peoples, 74, 161, 172, 211; law of (*see* Law of Peoples); meaning of in Rawls, 126–27; society of, 123–24, 128–30, 135n12, 136n31, 137n34

Perry, Michael, 150

persecution, 48, 151, 204

person(s), personhood

Petaluma Poultry, 91

Peters, Julie, 143

Peterson, V. Spike, 142, 144

Peterson, Laci, 232, 242n31

Philpott, Daniel, 158

physicians, x–xi, 4–9, 18, 19n2, 20n6, 56. *See also* obstetrics

Pieterse, Jan Nederveen, 10, 16, 20

Pinker, Robert, 102, 113

plants, 65, 70, 84, 86–88, 91, 134n9

play, 49, 50, 56, 134n9, 231

Plumwood, Val, 83–84

plurality, 55, 74–75, 235, 238–39

Pogge, Thomas, 79n17, 98, 113n12, 114n18, 153n9

police, 143, 200n20, 213

policy, 4, 12, 102, 129–30, 134n8, 221; health, 16, 18, 20n7; foreign, 125, 188

Pollan, Michael, 91

pollution. *See* contamination

population, 81, 83, 102, 130, 139, 159, 215n22, 220

pornography, xiii, 155, 163, 174n6, 175n12, 234; content of, 159–60, 164, 174n7, 175n14, 175n15, 176n24, 176n28; and taboo-violation, 167–68, 176n25

post-traumatic stress. *See* trauma

post-modernism, 47, 156

post-modernity, 204, 216n34, 222–23, 230–32

poverty, xii, 28, 36, 76, 87, 90, 93, 96, 113n10, 122, 129, 146, 221; as capabilities deprivation, xii, 96, 102–11, 113n13, 114n14, 114n15; causes of, 97, 113n9, 113n12; definitions of, xii, 95–98, 112n1, 112n2, 112n4, 112n5; as inequality, 101–102; as lack of income, 98–100, 114n17; as lack of resources, 100–101, 113n8; as social exclusion, 102; of women, x, xii, 3–4, 36, 44, 226

power, 16, 21n14, 39, 75, 104, 125–26, 131, 140, 143, 156, 158, 163, 169, 175n21, 181, 199, 208, 219, 234, 236; as capacity or capability, 120, 133, 183; in care relations, 194; to contaminate, 225–26, 232; of emo-

About the Editors and Contributors

Lynne S. Arnault is associate professor of philosophy at Le Moyne College, where she is a founding member of the Gender and Women's Studies Program and an affiliate of the Department of Physician Assistant Studies. Her teaching and research are focused in ethics, moral psychology, and social philosophy. She is currently working on the topic of HIV/AIDS in South Africa and on issues concerning cruelty.

Bat-Ami Bar On is professor of philosophy and women's studies at Binghamton University (SUNY). Her primary interests are in the theorization of violence, though she escapes them (often?) by pursuing other themes. She is the author of *The Subject of Violence: Arendtean Exercises in Understanding*, co-editor (with Lisa Tessman) of *Jewish Locations: Traversing Racialized Landscapes* and (with Ann Ferguson) *Daring to Be Good: Essays in Feminist Ethico-Politics*, and editor of *Women and Violence: A Special Issue of Hypatia, Engendering Origins: Critical Feminist Readings of Plato and Aristotle*, and *Modern Engenderings: Critical Feminist Readings in the History of Modern Western Philosophy*. She has published in feminist anthologies and in *Hypatia*. Her most recent work on terrorism and war appears in the British online resource *The Philosophers' Magazine* and the Swedish *ORD&BILD*, and in the journal *International Feminist Politics*.

Alyssa R. Bernstein is assistant professor of philosophy at Ohio University. She has a Ph.D. in philosophy from Harvard University, where she worked with John Rawls for a number of years as one of his research and teaching assistants as well as his dissertation advisee. Bernstein was a Fellow of the Carr Center for Human Rights Policy at Harvard University's Kennedy School of Government for two years prior to joining the faculty of Ohio

University. Her main areas of research and writing are human rights, global justice, social contract theory, and Kant's ethics and political philosophy.

Victoria Davion is head of the Department of Philosophy at the University of Georgia. She is founding and current editor of *Ethics & the Environment*. Her research areas include feminist philosophy, environmental ethics, ethics, and political philosophy.

Peggy DesAutels is associate professor of philosophy at the University of Dayton. Her research interests include moral psychology, feminist ethics, philosophy of mind, and medical ethics. She is co-editor (with Margaret Urban Walker) of *Moral Psychology: Feminist Ethics and Social Theory*, co-editor (with Joanne Waugh) of *Feminists Doing Ethics*, and co-author (with Larry May and Margaret Pabst Battin) of *Praying for a Cure: When Medical and Religious Practices Conflict*.

Marilyn Fischer is professor of philosophy at the University of Dayton. She is the author of *Ethical Decision-Making in Fund Raising* and *On Addams*, and co-editor of a four-volume set of *Jane Addams's Writings on Peace*. She is currently writing a book on Addams's internationalism.

Virginia Held is distinguished professor of philosophy at the City University of New York's graduate school and professor emerita at Hunter College. Her most recent book is *The Ethics of Care: Personal, Political, and Global*. Among her other books are *The Public Interest and Individual Interests*, *Rights and Goods: Justifying Social Action*, and *Feminist Morality: Transforming Culture, Society, and Politics*. She is currently working on a book about political violence.

Peter Higgins is a Ph.D. candidate at the University of Colorado, Boulder, specializing in contemporary political philosophy and feminist philosophy. He is currently writing a dissertation on how to determine what moral principles for regulating immigration are just.

Sabrina Hom is a doctoral candidate in philosophy at Stony Brook University and a lecturer at the McGill Centre for Research and Teaching on Women in Montreal. She is a co-founder of the Luce Irigaray Circle and is co-editing a volume based on its first annual conference, entitled *Thinking with Irigaray*. Her article "Disinterring the Divine Law" will appear in the forthcoming anthology *Luce Irigaray Teaches*. Her areas of interest include Hegel, Beauvoir, psychoanalysis, and feminist ethics and social theory, and her current research focuses on gendered relations to death.

Audra King is a Ph.D. student in the philosophy department at the University of Colorado, Boulder. Her areas of specialization include global justice, the ethics of international development, social and political philosophy, feminist theory, democratic theory, oppression, and nonideal theory. She is currently writing her dissertation, entitled "Making Development Just: From an Institutional Analysis of Development to an Instrumental Defense of Democracy," under the supervision of Professor Alison Jaggar.

James L. Nelson teaches about and writes on topics in bioethics and moral theory at Michigan State University. He is the author of *Hippocrates' Maze* and, with Hilde Lindemann, *The Patient in the Family*, among others. He is currently working on a book developing a feminist perspective on issues in moral psychology, with continual reference to Jane Austen.

Serena Parekh is assistant professor at the University of Connecticut, where she has a joint appointment in the Department of Philosophy and the Human Rights Institute. She writes and publishes in the areas of political philosophy, continental philosophy, the philosophy of human rights, and feminist philosophy.

April Shaw received a B.A. from the University of Arizona and is currently a graduate student at the University of Colorado, Boulder. Her areas of interest include social and political philosophy, with an emphasis on global justice theory.

Joan C. Tronto is professor of women's studies and political science at Hunter College and the City University of New York's graduate school. She is the author of *Moral Boundaries: A Political Argument for an Ethic of Care* and numerous articles about the nature of care. She is currently completing a book on democracy and care.

Rebecca Whisnant is assistant professor of philosophy at the University of Dayton and co-editor (with Christine Stark) of *Not for Sale: Feminists Resisting Prostitution and Pornography*. Her research interests include feminist theory, sexual ethics, nonviolence theory, and moral psychology.